PLAYS OF THE SIXTIES

Volume One

PLAYS OF THE SIXTIES

Volume One

Selected by

J. M. CHARLTON

A PAN ORIGINAL

PAN BOOKS LTD

LONDON AND SYDNEY

This collection first published 1966 by
Pan Books Ltd, Cavaye Place, London SW10 9PG

ISBN 0 330 33100 0

2nd Printing 1970
3rd Printing 1973
4th Printing 1974

PRINTED AND BOUND IN ENGLAND BY
HAZELL WATSON AND VINEY LTD
AYLESBURY, BUCKS

Contents

Acknowledgements

The Editor gratefully acknowledges the permission of the following authors, publishers and agents for the right to reproduce the plays in this collection:

Ross: Terence Rattigan, Hamish Hamilton Ltd, and A. D. Peters and Company.

THE ROYAL HUNT OF THE SUN: Peter Shaffer, Hamish Hamilton Ltd, A. M. Heath Ltd, and Christopher Mann Ltd.

BILLY LIAR: Keith Waterhouse and Willis Hall, Michael Joseph Ltd, Harvey Unna, and Evans Brothers Ltd.

PLAY WITH A TIGER: Doris Lessing, Michael Joseph Ltd, Curtis Brown Ltd, and Gregson & Wigan Ltd.

ROSS

By Terence Rattigan

Dedicated with gratitude to

ANATOLE DE GRUNWALD

Who brought Lawrence to me and me to Lawrence

© Terence Rattigan, 1960

NOTE

The author gratefully acknowledges his debt to Captain B. H.
Liddell Hart, both for the illumination afforded by his book
T. E. Lawrence in Arabia and After and for his help in
checking the script.

Ross was first produced at the Haymarket Theatre, London, on May 12th, 1960, with the following cast:

FLIGHT LIEUTENANT STOKER	Geoffrey Colvile
FLIGHT SERGEANT THOMPSON	Dervis Ward
AIRCRAFTMAN PARSONS	Peter Bayliss
AIRCRAFTMAN EVANS	John Southworth
AIRCRAFTMAN DICKINSON	Gerald Harper
AIRCRAFTMAN ROSS	Alec Guinness
FRANKS (*The lecturer*)	James Grout
GENERAL ALLENBY	Harry Andrews
RONALD STORRS	Anthony Nicholls
COLONEL BARRINGTON	Leon Sinden
AUDA ABU TAYI	Mark Dignam
THE TURKISH MILITARY GOVERNOR, DERAA DISTRICT	Geoffrey Keen
HAMED	Robert Arnold
RASHID	Charles Laurence
A TURKISH CAPTAIN	Basil Hoskins
A TURKISH SERGEANT	Raymond Adamson
A BRITISH CORPORAL	John Trenaman
ADC	Ian Clark
A PHOTOGRAPHER	Antony Kenway
AN AUSTRALIAN SOLDIER	William Feltham
FLIGHT LIEUTENANT HIGGINS	Peter Cellier
GROUP CAPTAIN WOOD	John Stuart

Directed by Glen Byam Shaw

Scenery and Costumes by Motley

CHARACTERS

(In order of appearance)

FLIGHT LIEUTENANT STOKER
FLIGHT SERGEANT THOMPSON
AIRCRAFTMAN PARSONS
AIRCRAFTMAN EVANS
AIRCRAFTMAN DICKINSON
LAWRENCE
FRANKS (*Lecturer*)
GENERAL ALLENBY
RONALD STORRS
COLONEL BARRINGTON
AUDA ABU TAYI
THE TURKISH MILITARY GOVERNOR, DERAA
 DISTRICT
HAMED
RASHID
A TURKISH CAPTAIN
A TURKISH SERGEANT
A BRITISH CORPORAL
ADC
A PHOTOGRAPHER
AN AUSTRALIAN SOLDIER
FLIGHT LIEUTENANT HIGGINS
GROUP CAPTAIN WOOD

The action of the play begins and ends at a Royal Air Force Depot, near London, on an afternoon, the same night and following morning of a day in Winter, 1922. The central passages cover the two years 1916–1918 and are set in the Middle East.

ACT I

Scene I

An Office. Behind a desk sits a Flight Lieutenant. He is an earnest, well-meaning young officer with a manner alternately avuncular and fierce.

A Flight Sergeant stands in front of him. He is an oldish man, with a harsh rasping voice, that inadequately conceals a soft heart for recruits and a contempt for all officers, including this one.

F/Lt: Next charge.

F/Sgt (*barking*): Sir.

>   (*He salutes with guardsmanlike punctiliousness, marches to the door, throws it open and shouts gabblingly and with a familiarity born of long usage.*)

Prisoner and escort, attention, quick march, left right, left right, halt, left turn. Aircraftman Parsons.

>   (Parsons *is a tough ex-sailor about thirty-five; of his two escorts,* Evans *is young and red-haired, and the other,* Dickinson, *is an ex-officer of the war-time Army, in the ranks of the RAF for economic reasons.*)

F/Lt (*inspecting a charge sheet*): 352179 A.C.2 Parsons?

Parsons: Sir.

F/Lt (*reading from the charge sheet*): Conduct to the prejudice of good order and Royal Air Force discipline in that on December 16th, 1922, at the 0830 hours colour-hoisting parade the accused broke ranks and swore aloud. (*Looking up*) What's all this, Parsons?

Parsons: Slammed my rifle butt on my toe, sir. Lifted my foot half an inch, sir. May have made a slight sound – but only to myself, of course, sir.

F/Lt (*to* Flight Sergeant): Witness present?

F/Sgt: I am the only witness, sir. I was drilling B Flight that morning.

F/Lt: Was the sound slight?

F/Sgt: Rang across the parade ground, sir.

F/Lt: And was it – identifiable?

F/Sgt: Very, sir.

F/Lt: I see. (*To* Parsons) You don't dispute the actual word you used?

Parsons: No, sir.

F/Lt: Merely its volume?

Parsons: Whisper, sir.

F/Lt: But it was heard clearly by the Flight Sergeant.

Parsons: Might have lip-read, sir.

F/Lt: It's still swearing on parade, isn't it?

Parsons: Yes, sir.

F/Lt: And that's a serious offence. (*Looking down at the paper on his desk*) However, I'm glad to see it's your first. Still, that's not saying much after only ten weeks in the Service. (*To* Flight Sergeant) How is he at drill, generally?

F/Sgt: He used to be in the Navy, sir.

F/Lt: Don't they order arms from the slope in the Navy?

Parsons: Yes, sir. But they do it proper time.

F/Lt: Careful, Parsons.

Parsons: Sorry, sir. I meant different time.

F/Lt: Well, you'll just have to get used to the timing we use here at the Depot – which is, anyway, exactly the same as the Guards. Also to learn to order arms properly without hitting your foot and swearing.

Parsons: Yes, sir.

F/Lt: Think yourself lucky I'm not putting this on your conduct sheet. All right. Accused admonished.

F/Sgt: Prisoner and escort right turn, quick march, left right, left right. Halt. A.C.2 Parsons. Dismiss.

    (Parsons *and his escort are marched out.*)

F/Lt: Next.

F/SGT (*barking*): Prisoner and escort, attention, quick march, left right, left right, halt, left turn. Aircraftman Ross.

> (*Another* AIRCRAFTMAN *has been marched in. The escorts are the same. The accused is a small man of thirty-five with a long face and a sad, shy expression. He speaks in a very gentle voice. His name is now Ross, and will, one day, be Shaw, but in the text he is designated by his first surname.*)

F/LT (*looking at the charge sheet*): 352087 A.C.2 Ross?

LAWRENCE: Yes, sir.

F/LT (*reading*): Conduct prejudicial to good order and Royal Air Force discipline in that the accused failed to report to the Guard Room by 2359 hours on December 16th, 1922, on expiry of his late pass issued on that date and did not in fact report until 0017 hours on December 17th, 1922. Period of unauthorized absence – eighteen minutes. (*He looks up at the* FLIGHT SERGEANT) Witness present?

F/SGT: Guard commander's report, sir.

F/LT (*looking at another document*): Oh yes. Well, Ross. Anything to say?

LAWRENCE: No, sir.

F/LT: You admit the charge?

LAWRENCE: Yes, sir.

F/LT (*looking at another document*): I see you've been on two charges already. Untidy turn-out, three days' confined to camp, dumb insolence to an officer, seven days' confined to camp. So this charge makes the third in the ten weeks you've been in the Air Force. That's bad, Ross. That's very bad indeed. (*Suddenly thumping the desk*) Ross, I'm speaking to you. I said that's very bad indeed.

LAWRENCE: I'm sorry, sir. I took it as an observation, not as a question. I agree, it's very bad indeed.

F/LT (*after a pause*): I've an idea you don't care for authority, Ross?

LAWRENCE: I care for discipline, sir.

F/LT: What's the distinction?

LAWRENCE: Very wide, I believe.

F/LT: Being late on pass is an offence against both authority and discipline, isn't it?

LAWRENCE: Yes, sir. The point was academic.

F/LT (*after a pause*): What made you join the RAF?

LAWRENCE: I think I had a mental breakdown, sir.

F/LT (*more hurt than angry*): That kind of insolence isn't called for, Ross. I'm here not only to judge you but to help you. Will you try and understand that?

LAWRENCE: Yes, sir.

F/LT: All right. Let's start again, Why did you join the R.A.F.?

LAWRENCE (*slowly*): Because I wanted to, because I was destitute, because I enjoy discipline, and because I had a mental breakdown.

> (*The* FLIGHT LIEUTENANT *stares at him, angrily.*)

If you prefer, sir, we can substitute for 'mental' – the word 'spiritual'. I don't happen to like it myself, but at least it avoids the imputation of insolence.

F/LT (*to* FLIGHT SERGEANT): Flight?

F/SGT: Sir.

F/LT: What is your report on this airman, in terms of general conduct?

F/SGT: Satisfactory, sir.

F/LT: No signs of being bolshie – or general bloody-mindedness?

F/SGT: No, sir.

F/LT: Drill?

F/SGT: Behind the others, sir, but then he's older and therefore slower. But he tries hard.

F/LT: P/T?

F/SGT: According to the sergeant instructor, sir, he has difficulty in keeping up with the squad, but then his age comes into that too, and his – physical handicaps.

F/LT: Physical handicaps? This is a recruit, Flight Sergeant, passed into the RAF as A.1. What physical handicaps are you talking about?

F/Sgt (*uneasily*): Well, sir. I only know that twice after P/T I've seen him being sick into a bucket, and he has some bad marks on his back, sir.

F/Lt (*to* Lawrence): What are these marks?

Lawrence: The scars of an accident, sir.

F/Lt: A serious accident?

Lawrence: At the time it seemed so.

F/Lt: And you were passed as A.1?

Lawrence: Yes, sir.

F/Lt (*to* Flight Sergeant): It seems very mysterious to me. (*To* Lawrence) Where did you go last night?

Lawrence: To a place in Buckinghamshire – near Taplow.

F/Lt: By bus or train?

Lawrence: Motor bicycle.

F/Lt: I see. Why were you late?

Lawrence: I fell off it.

F/Lt: Were you drunk?

Lawrence: No, sir. I only drink water, and I'm rather particular about that.

F/Lt: How did you fall off?

Lawrence: I was going through Denham rather fast, but with a good ten minutes in hand, when a dog ran out into the street and I swerved. A car coming the other way hit me, and I was left with very little bicycle. It became necessary to run, which, as the Flight Sergeant has just told you, I'm not as adept at as some.

F/Lt (*after a pause*): When I asked you just now if you had anything to say in answer to this charge, you said no.

Lawrence: Yes, sir.

F/Lt: You didn't think a motor cycle accident might be taken as a possible excuse?

Lawrence: No, sir. Only as a reason.

F/Lt: Another distinction?

Lawrence: Yes, sir. Another wide one.

    (*Pause.*)

F/Lt: Ross, I hope you realize that most officers trying your case would, by now, have given you the maximum sentence, or remanded you to the Station Commander with an additional charge of insubordination.

Lawrence: Yes, sir.

F/Lt: You think it's going to help your case if you impress me with the fact that you're an educated man. But that fact doesn't impress me at all – do you understand?

Lawrence: Yes, sir.

F/Lt: There are plenty of educated men in the ranks of the RAF nowadays.

(*He looks suddenly from* Lawrence *to one of his escorts* (Dickinson).)

You – escort – what's your name?

(Dickinson *very smartly steps a pace forward and stamps his foot in parade ground manner.*)

Dickinson: Dickinson, sir.

F/Lt: I know something about you. You were at a public school weren't you?

Dickinson: Yes, sir.

F/Lt: Weren't you also an officer in the Gunners'?

Dickinson: Yes, sir. Captain. War-time commission, of course.

F/Lt: At the front?

Dickinson: Yes, sir. Passchendaele and the big Hun push in March '18. I got a blighty there.

F/Lt: And why did you join the RAF?

Dickinson: I got a job when I was demobbed, selling motor cars, but found I preferred Service life, sir. I consider the RAF the Service of the future and, when they turned me down for a commission, I decided to join anyway and work my way up through the ranks.

(*His answer has plainly pleased the* Flight Lieutenant *who nods smilingly at him.*)

F/Lt: I hope you will. All right, Dickinson.

(Dickinson *steps back to his place beside* Lawrence *with supreme smartness.*)

16

You see, Ross, this airman is in your flight, and there are many others with similar records in other recruit squads. Where were you at school?

LAWRENCE: Oxford High School, sir.

F/LT: Were you in the war?

LAWRENCE: Yes, sir.

F/LT: In what capacity?

LAWRENCE: Oh – mostly – liaison work.

F/LT: Liaison work? Where?

LAWRENCE (*after a slight hesitation*): The Middle East.

F/LT: Where in the Middle East?

LAWRENCE: Oh, all kinds of places.

F/LT: You seem very vague about it.

LAWRENCE: It was rather a vague kind of job.

F/LT (*angrily*): For heaven's sake, man, you must have known what you were doing.

LAWRENCE: Not very often, sir.

F/LT: When you talk about mental breakdown you don't happen to mean just plain mad, do you?

LAWRENCE: Not certifiably so, sir.

F/LT: You're in trouble of some kind?

LAWRENCE (*quietly*): Yes, sir.

F/LT: Bad trouble?

LAWRENCE: It seems so, to me.

F/LT: You mean when you tell other people they don't find it so bad?

LAWRENCE: I don't tell other people, sir.

F/LT: No one at all?

LAWRENCE: No one at all.

F/LT: If I sent the Flight Sergeant and the escort out now – would you tell it to me?

LAWRENCE: No, sir.

F/LT (*after a pause*): Look here, Ross, I'm not just your Flight Commander. You've got to try and look on me as a sort of Dutch uncle. (*After another pause*) Well?

LAWRENCE: The untellable – even to a sort of Dutch uncle – can't be told.

(*There is a pause. The* FLIGHT LIEUTENANT, *frustrated, looks down at his desk.*)

F/LT: Why did you go to this place in Buckinghamshire?

LAWRENCE: To have a meal with some friends.

F/LT: Close friends?

LAWRENCE: Some of them.

F/LT: Give me their names.

LAWRENCE (*momentarily nonplussed*): Their names, sir?

F/LT (*barking*): Yes, their names. (*He has taken up a notebook and pencil.*)

LAWRENCE: But have you the right — ?

F/LT: Yes, I have the right. (*Shouting*) I want these people's names *now*. That's an order, Ross.

LAWRENCE (*with a faint sigh*): Very well, sir. Lord and Lady Astor, Mr and Mrs George Bernard Shaw, the Archbishop of Canterbury —

(*The* FLIGHT LIEUTENANT *has thrown his pencil down.*)

F/LT: All right. You now have two charges to answer — the present one and the one I'm putting you on tomorrow to be dealt with by the Group Captain — to wit — gross insubordination to your Flight Commander. On the present charge you get seven days' confined to camp. As for the second — well — I doubt if in future you're going to find much time to relax your troubled soul.

LAWRENCE: No, sir. I don't think it needs that kind of relaxation —

F/LT (*shouting*): That's enough, unless you want a court-martial. March him out, Flight.

F/SGT: Prisoner and escort right turn, quick march, left right, left right. Halt. Prisoner and escort, dismiss.

(LAWRENCE, DICKINSON *and* EVANS *march out. The* FLIGHT SERGEANT *turns at the door.*)

That is the last charge, sir.

F/LT (*wearily*): Thank God for that.

(*He collects the charge sheets from his desk and*

throws them into his 'Out' tray. Then he looks up at the FLIGHT SERGEANT.)

How's the Flight coming along generally?

F/SGT: About average, sir.

F/LT: Think you'll make airmen of them?

F/SGT: Of a sort, sir.

F/LT (*with a sigh*): I know what you mean. Shocking lot we're getting these days. (*With a change of tone*) But keep your eye on that chap Dickinson. I like the look of him. He ought to do well.

F/SGT: Yes, sir.

F/LT (*feelingly*): And give that cocky little bastard, Ross, hell.

F/SGT: Yes, sir.

(*He salutes magnificently, turns, stamping his feet as if to split his heelbones.*)

THE LIGHTS FADE

(*In the darkness we hear the sound of a mouth-organ playing, and men's voices singing, softly and sentimentally, a popular song of the period (The Sheik of Araby).*)

SCENE II

Part of a yard in the depot. PARSONS, EVANS *and* DICKINSON *are prominent among a small group of the other recruits, one of whom is playing a mouth-organ, while others, only intermittently visible, are singing or whistling gently to accompaniment.* EVANS *is talking to* PARSONS *while* DICKINSON *is sitting apart from the others, hands behind his head, eyes open, musing.*

EVANS (*excitedly*): But he did, Sailor. I promise you he did.

PARSONS (*incredulously*): Archbishop of Canterbury? Rossie say a thing like that? Our Rossie? Oh no —

EVANS: But I was there, Sailor. I was escort. I heard him,

clear as a bell. (*Indicating* DICKINSON) So did you, didn't you, Dickie-bird?

DICKINSON (*without moving*): What?

EVANS: When our officer – this morning said to Rossie 'Look here, my man, I want you to tell me who you went out with last night' – what a bloody nerve to ask such a thing, mind you – did Rossie say Mr and Mrs George Bernard Shaw and the Archbishop of Canterbury?

DICKINSON: Yes. Also – Lord and Lady Astor.

EVANS (*triumphantly to* PARSONS): You see. You couldn't have done better yourself, Sailor. (*To* DICKINSON) Weren't you proud of him, Dickie-bird?

DICKINSON: Not particularly.

PARSONS: Ex-ruddy-officer himself. Can't bear lip to one of his own kind.

DICKINSON (*quietly*): You know that's a bloody lie, Sailor.

PARSONS: Why weren't you proud of him, then?

DICKINSON (*without taking his eyes from the sky*): The Archbishop was enough. With the other names he overdid it.

> (LAWRENCE *comes in, staggering under the weight of a refuse bin.*)

PARSONS: And what do you think you're doing, Rossie, old bean?

LAWRENCE: There are still three left to fill in there.

PARSONS: Yes, Rossie-boy, and left by my own instructions for a very good purpose, which is in case some bloody officer sticks his nose out here and says: 'I see you bleeders have done your fatigue, so you can bleeding well do another'.

LAWRENCE (*contrite*): I'm sorry, Sailor. I should have thought.

PARSONS (*kindly*): Yes, you should, shouldn't you? (*To* EVANS) Ruddy marvel, isn't it? Reads Greek like it was the *Pink 'Un,* and don't know his bottom from Uxbridge Town Hall. (LAWRENCE *has turned to take the bin back again*) No, leave it there, for Gawd's sake. We don't want to have to fill it again – (*helplessly*) Cripes!

LAWRENCE (*flustered*): I'm sorry.

PARSONS: Never mind. Never mind. (*He suddenly thrusts out his hand*) Rossie-boy —

> (LAWRENCE *turns and looks at* PARSONS' *outstretched hand in bewilderment.*)

EVANS (*explanatorily*): The Archbishop.

LAWRENCE (*still bewildered*): The Archbishop?

PARSONS: And Mr and Mrs George Bernard Shaw, and in spite of what Dickie-bird says — Lord and Lady ruddy Astor — and though you might have added the Dolly Sisters and Gaby Deslys, no one can think of everything at once and I congratulate you, Rossie-boy. B Flight is proud of you.

LAWRENCE (*rather overwhelmed, and wincing at the force of* PARSONS' *famous handshake*): It wasn't much, really —

PARSONS (*to the others*): Salute our hero, boys.

> (*There is a mild and faintly ironic cheer, and a few bars, also ironic, of a triumphal march from the mouth-organist.*)

(*Putting his arm around* LAWRENCE's *shoulder*) Come and sing, Rossie. (*To the* MOUTH-ORGANIST) Give us the old Sheik again.

> (*The mouth-organ starts up.*)

LAWRENCE (*timidly*): I'm afraid I don't know the words.

PARSONS (*shocked*): Cor stuff me. You must be the only man in England who don't. (*To* MOUTH-ORGANIST) Know anything in Latin or Greek?

LAWRENCE: I know Tipperary.

PARSONS (*to the others, with irony*): He knows Tipperary. (*To* MOUTH-ORGANIST) Tipperary.

> (*The* MEN *begin to sing it,* PARSONS' *voice leading the others, but softly, because of fear of discovery.* LAWRENCE's *voice, rather quavering, can be heard, proving that at least he does know the words. They finish a chorus and* PARSONS *starts 'Pack up your Troubles.'* LAWRENCE *suddenly and brusquely breaks away from* PARSONS' *friendly embrace and moves quickly away from the group, his back to them.* PARSONS *looks after him,*

rather surprised, but says nothing, continuing to sing. The FLIGHT SERGEANT *comes in past* LAWRENCE *who turns quickly from him. The singing stops abruptly.*)

F/SGT: What's the idea of the concert?

PARSONS: We'd nearly finished fatigue, Flight.

F/SGT: Nearly isn't quite, is it? (*Pointing to bin*) What's that doing here? And how many more is there to fill?

PARSONS: Three, Flight.

F/SGT: Well, if you're smart and do 'em quickly I might find something else for you to do before supper. Jump to it now. Many hands make light work —

PARSONS: Oh. I wish I'd said that. How *do* you think of 'em, Flight?

F/SGT (*automatically*): None of your lip, Parsons, now — unless you want a dose of jankers.

(LAWRENCE *attempts to pick up the filled bin.*)

No. Not you, Ross. Evans — Dickinson, you take that. Rest of you inside, at the double. Ross, stay here.

(EVANS *and* DICKINSON *take the bin from* LAWRENCE, *and disappear, presumably towards the incinerator, in the opposite direction to the others.* LAWRENCE *and the* FLIGHT SERGEANT *are left alone. The* FLIGHT SERGEANT *stares at* LAWRENCE *curiously for a moment.*)

F/SGT: They been picking on you again, son?

LAWRENCE: No, Flight.

F/SGT: You don't ought to mind 'em so much.

LAWRENCE: I don't mind them, Flight.

F/SGT: Listen, I've got eyes in my head, haven't I?

(LAWRENCE *lowers his, in embarrassment.*)

LAWRENCE (*with a smile*): Flight, I'm sorry, but I'm afraid you've got it wrong. It was just that — suddenly — for the first time in five years I'd remembered what it was to feel life worth living.

(EVANS *and* DICKINSON *come in,* EVANS *with his hands in his pockets.*)

F/SGT (*barking*): Hands out of your pockets, you.

EVANS: Sorry, Flight. Can we go now, Flight?

F/Sgt: No. Get a broom and sweep up those leaves over there.

> (*He points off.* Dickinson *turns to make himself inconspicuous.*)

And you, Dickinson.

> (*The* Men *murmur 'Yes, Flight' and go off the way they came. The* Flight Sergeant *looks at* Lawrence, *frowning.*)

(*At length*) Yes. You've got it bad, all right, haven't you? Real bad. (*Smiling*) Don't worry, I'm not young 'greaser'. I'm not going to ask you what your trouble is.

Lawrence: Young 'greaser'?

F/Sgt: Flight Lieutenant Stoker to you. (*In 'officer' accent*) 'I'm not just here to judge you, you know, my man. I'm here to help you. Look on me as a sort of Dutch uncle, old fruit.' Makes you bloody vomit.

Lawrence: It does, rather.

F/Sgt: Mind you, I didn't say that and nor did you.

Lawrence: No, Flight.

F/Sgt: One day, if you want to tell me what's up with you, you can and I'll listen. If you don't, that's all right too. Meanwhile I've got to try and stop young greaser from having you hung, drawn and quartered —

> (*The* Men *have begun to come out of the building carrying the bins.*)

All right. At the double. And afterwards you can dismiss. But don't let anyone see you or I'll personally screw all your —

Parsons: Isn't our Flight Sergeant the best little Flight Sergeant in the world? Say yes, boys, or it'll seem rude.

F/Sgt (*shouting*): That's quite enough of that. (*To* Lawrence) All right. I'll do what I can. (*Suddenly roaring*) But don't ever let me hear you being insubordinate to your Flight Commander like that again, do you hear?

Lawrence: Yes, Flight.

F/Sgt (*to the corner, whither* Dickinson *and* Evans *have disappeared*) All right, you two. Fini. But keep out of sight of any bleeding officer, if you please.

(*He goes out. After a moment* DICKINSON *and* EVANS *come on.* DICKINSON *puts a broom against a wall and having done that turns and languidly looks at* LAWRENCE, *who has taken out a small notebook in which he is writing, squatting on the ground, with his legs tucked under his body.* EVANS *approaches* LAWRENCE.)

EVANS: Rossie?

LAWRENCE: Yes, Taff?

EVANS (*with acute embarrassment*): I wouldn't be asking this at all, but I thought perhaps – well – you're not the same as the rest of us and perhaps pay parade doesn't mean to you as much as it means to some of us, and —

LAWRENCE: I'm afraid it does, Taff. Quite as much.

EVANS (*overwhelmed with remorse*): Oh, but, then, please you must not on any account —

LAWRENCE: How much would it have been?

EVANS: Well, it was a ring you see – something I had to buy – you know – to make it up with my girl, you see, and she likes the best, always has – thirty-seven and six.

LAWRENCE: I wish I had it, Taff.

(EVANS *looks over at* DICKINSON, *who, almost imperceptibly, shakes his head.*)

EVANS (*with a sigh*): Oh well.

(*He goes sadly out.* LAWRENCE *continues to write in his notebook. Pause.* DICKINSON *walks slowly forward.*)

DICKINSON: Why do you sit like that?

LAWRENCE: I always do.

DICKINSON: It's the way the Arabs sit, isn't it?

LAWRENCE: I don't know.

DICKINSON (*squatting beside him*): But you should know – shouldn't you – after all that liaison work you did in the Middle East in the last war?

LAWRENCE: I'm sorry. I wasn't paying attention. Yes, it's the way the Arabs sit.

DICKINSON: Damned uncomfortable it looks. Why are you shivering?

LAWRENCE: I've got a touch of malaria.

DICKINSON: Middle East, I suppose? You're shaking quite badly. You'd better see the MO.

LAWRENCE: No. I'll have a temperature tonight and tomorrow it'll be gone.

DICKINSON: Yes, but you shouldn't take risks, old chap. After all, we don't want to lose you, do we?

LAWRENCE: I doubt if B Flight would notice.

DICKINSON: I wasn't talking about B Flight. I was talking about the nation.

(LAWRENCE *puts down the notebook at last, and stares steadily at* DICKINSON.)

Aren't you going to say what on earth do you mean? Aren't you going to try and act it out just a little longer?

(*Pause.* LAWRENCE, *staring at him steadily, says nothing.*)

I agree, old boy. Useless. At the same time I notice you're not falling into the trap of saying 'How on earth did you find out?' and so confirming what might, after all, be only a wild guess. Secret Agent training, no doubt. Well, it isn't a guess. It *was* until this morning, I grant. As a matter of fact I did see you once, in Paris, in 1919 – Peace Conference time – I was just a humble captain, walking down a street and suddenly I was shoved back against some railings by some brawny gendarmes and practically squashed to death by an hysterical crowd because *you* were leaving your hotel. I couldn't see you well, but *I* remember you walking shyly – oh so shyly – between two policemen – to your car, head well down under that Arab headdress and then – at the car – turning to talk to someone so that the crowd grew even more hysterical, and then, when you were in the car, modestly pulling down the blind. Still, I wouldn't necessarily have recognized you, old boy, from that – nor even from the lecture I went to at the Albert Hall which was supposed to be about the Palestine Campaign, but which had your picture on every other slide – very carefully posed, old boy, I hope you don't mind my saying.

(*He offers a cigarette to* LAWRENCE, *who shakes his head silently.* DICKINSON *lights one for himself.*)

Still think I'm guessing? Look, old chap, it isn't awfully hard – even for a humble airman like me – to find out the telephone number of Cliveden House, to ring up and ask if there'd been a raincoat left behind last night by Colonel Lawrence. 'Colonel Lawrence, sir?' Well-trained, this footman evidently. 'Yes, for heaven's sake – Colonel Lawrence – my dear man – Oh, very well, then, Aircraftman Ross, if you like.' Slight pause. Then 'No, sir. The Colonel left nothing behind last night. In fact I distinctly remember when he left that he had his raincoat strapped on to the back of his motor bicycle.' (*Pause*) Your hand really *is* shaking badly. I honestly think you'd better see the MO, old boy. After all, you can't do punishment drill with malaria.

LAWRENCE (*in a low voice*): What do you want from me?

DICKINSON (*genially*): Money.

LAWRENCE: I haven't any.

DICKINSON (*murmuring*): Oh yes. Destitute. I enjoyed that, this morning.

LAWRENCE: It was the truth.

DICKINSON (*hurt*): Don't treat me like a half-wit, old boy. I'm not like the others. *I* can use the old grey matter, you know. I can tell how much money a man with your name could make for himself if he tried. Your memoirs? God! They'd make you a bloody fortune, and don't tell me you're not writing them, old boy, because I've seen you scribbling away in that notebook when you think no one's looking.

LAWRENCE: What I'm writing is for my friends. It's not for money.

DICKINSON: Jolly noble. Well, a bit of it had better be for money, old boy, because to keep my trap shut about this little masquerade of yours, you're going to have to pay me a hundred quid. That's what I reckon I could get from Fleet Street —

(LAWRENCE *shakes his head.*)

Listen, I haven't an earthly what you're up to, old boy, and

I don't care either. Hiding? Spying? Having fun? Doesn't concern me. But it must be damned important to you that I don't give the story to the papers. So let's not haggle. Seventy-five, and I'll take a cheque.

(*Pause.*)

LAWRENCE (*at length*): No.

DICKINSON: You mean that?

LAWRENCE: Yes.

DICKINSON (*with a sigh*): Oh well, I thought you mightn't fork out. You were so damn careless this morning with young greaser, that I felt pretty sure you must have finished whatever it was you came into this thing to do —

LAWRENCE (*suddenly fierce*): I haven't finished. I haven't even started.

DICKINSON: What *did* you come into this thing to do?

LAWRENCE: To find peace.

(*Pause.* DICKINSON *laughs quietly.*)

DICKINSON: Oh yes – the mental and spiritual breakdown —

LAWRENCE: Go and telephone the papers —

DICKINSON: Oh, I'm not ringing them up. This transaction's got to be strictly cash.

LAWRENCE: You'll go and see them?

DICKINSON: Yes.

LAWRENCE: When?

DICKINSON: Tonight.

LAWRENCE: Have you got a late pass?

DICKINSON: No. Just ways of egress and ingress.

LAWRENCE (*bitterly*): I see. Well, have fun tomorrow with the headlines.

DICKINSON: Don't tell me you're frightened of headlines, old boy.

LAWRENCE: I am now. Oh yes, you spotted my enjoyment of that crowd in Paris and this morning too – showing off to the Flight Lieutenant, but forgetting all about the sharp-witted escort who was going to end my life —

DICKINSON: Suicide threat?

LAWRENCE: No. Statement of fact. I mean my life as Aircraftman Ross.

DICKINSON: What does that matter? Lawrence will still be alive.

LAWRENCE (*with anger*): Lawrence doesn't exist any more. If you kill Aircraftman Ross you kill me. Can I put it more simply than that?

(*Pause.*)

DICKINSON: I don't scare very easily, you know.

LAWRENCE: I'm sure you don't. I wish I didn't.

DICKINSON (*angrily*): Why the hell is all this so important to you?

LAWRENCE: Why is a monastery important to the man who takes refuge in it?

DICKINSON: A monastery is for someone who's lost his will to live. (*Angrily*) All right. The spiritual breakdown. I'll buy it. How did you lose your soul?

LAWRENCE: The way most people lose it, I suppose. By worshipping a false god.

DICKINSON: What god?

LAWRENCE: The will.

DICKINSON: The thing that's up in your head, you mean?

LAWRENCE: The thing that *was* up in my head.

DICKINSON: Isn't that what's made you what you are?

LAWRENCE: Yes.

DICKINSON: I meant Lawrence of Arabia.

LAWRENCE: I meant Ross of Uxbridge.

DICKINSON (*hotly*): Self-pity – that's all it is. There's nothing in the world worse than self-pity –

LAWRENCE: Oh yes there is. Self-knowledge. Why shouldn't a man pity himself if to him he is pitiable? But to know yourself – or rather to be shown yourself – as you really are – (*he breaks off*). Yes. How stupid those ancient Greeks were. With your public school education I'm sure you'd understand what I mean. Can I borrow a couple of pounds?

(DICKINSON *takes out his wallet and extracts two*

pound notes from it. Then he walks over to LAWRENCE *and hands them to him*.)

Thank you. That proves it. You're going to do it.

DICKINSON: Good psychology. Yes, I'm going to do it, all right — because I'm damn well not going to be cheated out of money I need by a bit of fake play-acting —

LAWRENCE: Aren't you confusing Ross with Lawrence? Or is Ross a fake too? Perhaps you're right. It doesn't matter much anyway. Fake or not he's been a dreadful failure. Lets the Flight down at drill and P/T, can't tell a dirty joke to save his life and never sees the point of one either, talks la-de-da and spoils any party by trying too hard. Still, just now, with Sailor and Tipperary I thought it was just possible — (*he breaks off*). No. That was sloppy thinking. Ross dies tomorrow and he'll be better dead. (*He looks dispassionately at his shaking hand, then up at* DICKINSON, *with a quick smile*) Do you really think the papers will pay you a hundred?

DICKINSON: More, perhaps.

LAWRENCE: Really? You will tell me how much they *do* pay, won't you?

(*He turns and goes out.*)

THE LIGHTS FADE

(*In the darkness we hear the distant sound of the 'Last Post'.*)

SCENE III

A hut. Four beds are visible. PARSONS *lies on one, in his underclothes. He is working out racing results from an evening paper.* EVANS *lies on another, in pyjamas. He is writing a letter.*

PARSONS: Taff — what's six to four on, doubled with a hundred to eight against?

EVANS: Sorry, Sailor, I'm not a racing man. (*Bent over his letter*) You tell me something.

PARSONS (*bent over his calculations*): What?

EVANS: Another word for love.

(PARSONS *looks at him morosely without replying.*) (*Explosively*) Love, love, love. Man, you get sick of it. I tell you. (*Waving letter*) Don't you know another word?

PARSONS: Who's it to?

EVANS: My girl. The one I'm marrying.

PARSONS: That Minister's daughter? (EVANS *nods*) I don't know another word.

EVANS: But she's different, you know, Sailor. Not at all what you'd imagine. Free-thinking, that's what she is —

PARSONS (*muttering*): Free-doing, too, I hope.

EVANS: You'd be surprised.

(DICKINSON *comes in and goes to one of the unoccupied beds.*)

PARSONS: Dickie-bird — you'd know. Six to four on doubled with a hundred to eight against in half crowns?

DICKINSON: Let's see. Two thirds of twelve and a half — roughly eight and a third. Two over three plus twelve and a half — thirteen and a bit. Twenty-one and a half to one double — two pounds thirteen and threepence.

PARSONS (*admiringly*): Now that's the sort of brainwork I appreciate — not — (*he nods his head disparagingly towards the fourth bed*). I'll bet *you* don't read Greek poetry in the lats, Dickie-bird.

DICKINSON: You're damn right, I don't, old boy. The *Police Gazette*'s about my level.

(LAWRENCE *comes in and goes to the fourth bed, passing* DICKINSON *as he does so.* DICKINSON *is lying on his bed, fully dressed, and does not look at* LAWRENCE, *who begins to take his jacket off with evidently rather uncertain fingers.* LAWRENCE *suddenly seems to remember something. He walks across to* EVANS, *takes two pounds out of his trouser pocket and hands them to him.*)

LAWRENCE: Have you got half-a-crown?

EVANS: But you said you didn't have it.

LAWRENCE (*not looking at* DICKINSON): I managed to raise it.

EVANS: Oh Ross, you shouldn't have. Will he wait — your man?

LAWRENCE: I'm sure he will.

EVANS: For how long?

LAWRENCE: I should think — for eternity.

EVANS (*handing him half-a-crown*): Pay day after next you shall have it back. It's a promise. And one day —

LAWRENCE: That's all right.

EVANS (*back to his letter*): Rossie — you'd know. Aren't there any other words for love, except love, in the English? Think of something to surprise her —

LAWRENCE: I'm not an expert.

EVANS: Try.

LAWRENCE: Tenderness, devotion, the communion of two spirits —

EVANS (*doubtfully*): A bit tame.

LAWRENCE: I'm sorry —

PARSONS (*who has been staring at* LAWRENCE, *frowning*): Hey. What's the matter with you?

LAWRENCE: Nothing.

(*He goes to his bed.* PARSONS *follows him.*)

PARSONS: You're shaking like a ruddy shimmy dancer. The sweats, too. Got a dose of something?

(LAWRENCE *does not answer.* DICKINSON *answers for him, quietly.*)

DICKINSON: Malaria.

PARSONS: Malaria?

LAWRENCE: It's all right, Sailor. It's not catching.

PARSONS: I don't care if it is or it isn't. I'm the senior here and I'm not taking no chances. (*Peremptorily, as* LAWRENCE *continues silently to undress*) Put your things on again and go and report sick. Don't play 'silly bleeders' now —

(*He thrusts* LAWRENCE'S *tunic towards him roughly trying to manoeuvre his arm into the sleeve.*)

LAWRENCE (*quietly, but in a voice of sudden, unmistakeable authority*): Take your hands off me.

PARSONS (*bewildered*): What you say?

LAWRENCE: I dislike being touched.

(*He takes his jacket from* PARSONS, *and hangs it up*.)

PARSONS: Listen, Ross. I'm telling you to report sick.

LAWRENCE (*still quietly, but with the same authority*): I'm not going to report sick. I'm going to sleep it off here.

(*He lies down on the bed, half-undressed, shivering, and pulls the blanket over him*.)

PARSONS: I'm warning you, my lad, if you're not reporting sick tonight, you're doing your bleeding P/T tomorrow morning – malaria or no malaria. Compris?

LAWRENCE (*half-asleep*): Compris.

PARSONS: Enjoy torturing yourself by any chance?

LAWRENCE: It's a fair comment, I suppose. Goodnight, Sailor. If I make too much noise in the night, wake me up.

PARSONS: I'll keep a boot handy.

(*Defeated, he turns to* DICKINSON *who is still lying, fully dressed, on his bed*.)

And what do you think you're doing? Going to sleep like that?

(DICKINSON *gives him a lazy wink*.)

What again? (DICKINSON *nods*) Who is she tonight?

DICKINSON: No she tonight. Business.

PARSONS: Funny time for business.

DICKINSON: It's funny business.

PARSONS: Well, for God's sake don't get caught.

DICKINSON: I won't.

PARSONS (*lowering his voice*): I'll expect the usual half-nicker.

DICKINSON: You might get a whole nicker if things go right.

PARSONS: I'll believe that when I see it.

(*The lights go out suddenly*.)

EVANS (*with a wail*): Oh no. Just when I'd got sort of inspired. I won't remember it tomorrow.

PARSONS: What?

EVANS: A time we were together one night on a beach near Rhyl.

PARSONS: You'll remember it tomorrow.

EVANS: Not the words I was using —

PARSONS: You'll be remembering some other words if you don't put a sock in it.

EVANS: But the words were good, Sailor —

PARSONS: Pipe down, you sex-mad Celt. 'Night, all.

EVANS
DICKINSON } 'Night, Sailor.

*(After a moment of silence and near darkness, DICK-
INSON quietly gets up from his bed and moves on tiptoe towards the door. He stops a second by LAWRENCE's
bed and looks down. Then he goes on. LAWRENCE suddenly flings out his arm in a pleading gesture.)*

LAWRENCE *(murmuring)*: No. No —

(DICKINSON stops and turns back.)

DICKINSON *(in a whisper)*: Speaking to me, old boy?

*(There is no answer, save a faint moan. It is plain that
LAWRENCE was talking in his sleep.)*

Happy dreams — Colonel —

*(He tip-toes cautiously to the door, opens it a fraction,
peeps out furtively, and then quickly slips from sight,
closing the door behind him.)*

THE LIGHTS DIE TO A COMPLETE BLACK-OUT IN THE HUT

*(After a pause we hear a muffled roll of drums and
then the opening bars of 'Land Of Hope and Glory'
played by an organ, but coming apparently from a distance. As the lights gradually come on we find that
a large magic lantern screen has been lowered, on which
is a photograph of LAWRENCE in spotlessly white Arab
dress, with a large, curved, ornamental dagger around
his waist. He is lying on the ground, a rifle by his side,
gazing thoughtfully into space. A camel squats sleepily
behind him. The desert background looks decidedly
unreal and the whole effect is phony and posed. In front
of the screen is a lecturer (FRANKS) in dinner jacket.)*

FRANKS: This is the man. The Colonel himself – perhaps the most legendary figure of modern times – the scholar-soldier – the uncrowned King of the Desert – wearing, as yoyu see (*he points to* LAWRENCE's *dagger*), the insignia of a Prince of Mecca – an honour awarded him by Prince Abdullah —

> (*He breaks off and speaks testily to the unseen RAF hut.*)

FRANKS: Surely this is what you always wanted —?

LAWRENCE'S VOICE (*actual, not recorded*): Not now. Now I only want you to tell them the truth.

FRANKS: But what is the truth? Does anyone know? Ah – Field-Marshal.

> (*A man whom we are later to meet as* ALLENBY *appears from the darkness beside* FRANKS.)

What was your view of Lawrence?

ALLENBY: Well, I was never too sure how much of a charlatan he was. Quite a bit, I should think. Still, there's no disputing the greatness of what he did.

> (FRANKS *turns to the other side of the stage where another figure, a civilian in tropical clothes, has become visible.*)

FRANKS: And you, Mr Storrs?

STORRS: I think the importance of what he did has perhaps been exaggerated – by the press, by people like you and – to be fair – by himself. It's in what he *was* that he was great – in my view, probably the greatest Englishman of his time.

> (*A British Brigadier-General* (BARRINGTON) *in tropical uniform appears on the opposite side of the stage.*)

FRANKS: Ah. General. You knew Lawrence, didn't you?

BARRINGTON: Oh, very well. Couldn't bear him. Awful little show-off – quite a bit of a sadist, too. Cold-blooded. No feelings. Doubt if his private life would bear much looking into, either. As for what he did – well, a lot of chaps did just as well, but didn't get the publicity.

> (*The splendidly dressed figure of* AUDA ABU TAYI

stalks on to the stage, shouldering BARRINGTON *contemptuously out of the way.*)

AUDA (*thunderously*): Tell them in England what I – Auda Abu Tayi – say of el Aurans. Of Manhood – the man. Of Freedom – free. A spirit without equal. I see no flaw in him.

LAWRENCE (*from the darkness, agonizedly*): No flaw?

AUDA: I see no flaw in him.

(*He stalks away into the darkness. A man in the uniform of a Turkish General approaches the screen, but remains silent, looking towards the hut.*)

FRANKS: You see how difficult it is. Where *is* the truth? They can't all be right, can they? I really think it's safe to stick to the simple story – that boy scout epic of yours. You're a legend, you see – and I mustn't spoil it for the public. They want Lawrence – not Ross. They want a world-hero, not a fever-stricken recruit, sick of life, sick of himself, on the threshold of self-ending. (*To the* TURKISH GENERAL) Who are you? Are you part of the great Lawrence story?

GENERAL: Not of the legend. But I'm part of the truth. (*Behind* LAWRENCE'S *bed, looking down*) But don't worry, my friend. I won't tell. I never have and I never will.

LAWRENCE (*off*): One day I will.

GENERAL (*politely*): Will you indeed? I never denied your bravery. But that would really be *very* brave —

(*The* GENERAL *goes into the darkness.*)

FRANKS (*relieved*): That's enough of that unsavoury nonsense. Next slide, please.

(*A large map of the Middle East (pre-1914 war) is flashed on to the screen.*)

In 1916 the whole of this vast area (*he points*) was under the domination of the Turkish Empire, with which the Allies were at war. (*He points again*) The Turks were menacing the Suez Canal, and the British were too weak to attempt a counter-offensive. The great battle of the Somme had just cost them nearly half a million casualties, with no result. The whole vast war had bogged down in a morass of blood

– and there seemed no way for either side to win. However, on June the fifth, 1916, an event occurred down here (*he points to Mecca*) on which the newspapers barely deigned to comment, although it was later to change the world's history. The Sherif of Mecca revolted against the Turks, captured their garrisons at Mecca and Jeddah, and with his sons the Princes Feisal and Abdullah challenged the might of the vast Turkish Empire with his tiny force of Bedouin tribesmen. Disaster, of course, would have followed, but on October the sixteenth, 1916, there landed at Jeddah (*he points*) two Englishmen – one a mature, clever and farseeing diplomat – Ronald Storrs – and the other – next slide, please —

  (*A photograph of* LAWRENCE *is flashed on to the screen. He is in Army uniform* (CAPTAIN) *looking sternly and soulfully straight into the camera lens.*)

A young man – filled with an implacable devotion to the cause of Arab unity, and a stern sense of duty to his own country —

  (*From the darkness there is a gentle laugh.*)

What's the matter?

  LAWRENCE (*off*): You make it all sound so dull.

  FRANKS: Dull?

  LAWRENCE (*off*): Yes. It wasn't like that at all. Not in the beginning. It was fun.

  FRANKS (*sternly*): Fun, Aircraftman Ross?

  LAWRENCE (*off*): Yes. In the beginning —

      THE LIGHTS FADE

  (*There is the sound of Arab martial music, jaunty and barbaric, but not at all stern and military. Interposed are the sounds of shouting and laughter.*)

SCENE IV

The interior of an Arab tent. As the lights come on LAWRENCE *is being helped into an imposing-looking*

white Arab gown by a ferocious-looking, plainly dis-
approving Arab servant (HAMED). *Another servant*
(RASHID), *younger and gentler-seeming than the first,*
holds a mirror for LAWRENCE *to look into. One of the*
men we have seen with FRANKS (STORRS) *sits on a stool,*
smoking a cigar. The Arab music continues.

LAWRENCE (*surveying himself*): Storrs, how do I look?

STORRS: The most Anglo-Saxon Arab I ever saw.

LAWRENCE: That's all right. In Syria, before the war –
when on archeological jaunts – I used to pass as a Circassian.

STORRS: May I remind you we're about a thousand miles
south of Damascus. Have you ever heard of a Circassian
in the Hejaz?

LAWRENCE (*still distracted by his appearance*): No. I can't
say I have. Still, *one* might have wandered —

(*The noise of martial music subsides.*)

The parade must be over. I told Abdullah his men were
shooting off far too many bullets that should be kept for
the Turks. If I can't say Circassian, what *shall* I say?

STORRS: If I were you I'd say you were an English Intelligence Captain on leave from Cairo, going on an un-
authorised visit to Prince Feisal's headquarters, through
country that no Christian has ever crossed before. They
can't possibly believe you and so all they may do is to make
a small incision in your skull to let the devil of madness
out. It hurts quite a lot, I believe – but at least there's a
chance of survival —

LAWRENCE: Don't you think I need something round the
waist?

STORRS: What sort of something?

LAWRENCE: I don't know. Some sort of ornament. A
dagger for instance. I'm supposed to be dressed as a great
lord of the desert, you see. Abdullah thinks that the more
conspicuous I look, the less attention I'll cause, which is
rather sensible – don't you think? (*To* HAMED) Go to the
Lord Abdullah and beg him in the name of Allah to lend

to his servant Captain Lawrence a dagger that would befit a Prince of Mecca.

>   (HAMED *stares angrily at him for a moment, then turns and goes*.)

He seems to do what I tell him, which is a comfort. I hope the others do —

STORRS: What others?

LAWRENCE: Abdullah also wants me to take some of his own men to reinforce his brother —

STORRS: Now I put your chance of survival at zero. The minute they're out of sight of Abdullah's camp they'll slit your infidel throat.

LAWRENCE: That's what Abdullah thinks too.

>   (*He begins to walk up and down*.)

A sheik walks differently from ordinary mortals.

STORRS (*unhappily*): I ought to stop you from going.

LAWRENCE: You can't, and well you know it. I don't come under you.

STORRS: Seriously, TE, the risks are out of all proportion to any good you think you can do. Oh yes — I know it'll be fun for you if you get back to Cairo to infuriate the senior officers by telling them that they've got their facts all wrong — that you've inspected the situation at first hand and *know*. But I honestly don't think you will get back to Cairo —

LAWRENCE: When I was an undergraduate I wanted to write a thesis on Crusader Castles. So I went to Syria alone, without money, in the height of summer, and walked twelve hundred miles in three months. I was completely dependent on the Arab laws of hospitality. People said then they didn't think I'd get back to Oxford —

STORRS (*impatiently*): This isn't Syria. This is their Holy Land. Down here the Arab laws of hospitality don't extend to Christians. It's their religious duty to kill you —

LAWRENCE: Ah — but I have a bodyguard — don't forget.

STORRS: A bodyguard? You mean that thug over there — and his murderous-looking friend —

LAWRENCE: Oh, I don't think Rashid is a thug. I even got him to speak to me. He spat afterwards, of course, to clean his mouth, but in quite a polite way. I admit I haven't yet had the same success with Hamed, but I won't give up trying.

(STORRS *gets up suddenly and goes up to* LAWRENCE.)

STORRS (*touching his arm*): TE. (LAWRENCE *withdraws his arm quickly*) You might easily get killed.

LAWRENCE: I might easily get run over by a staff motor in Cairo.

STORRS: Why are you really doing this? (*As* LAWRENCE *opens his mouth*) Don't tell me any more about that mysterious kinship you feel with the Arab race. I don't believe it. You don't love the Arabs. You happen to speak their language and get on with them, but you're not a mystic like Burton or Doughty. You're doing this for some very personal reason. What is it?

LAWRENCE (*after a pause and speaking with far more weight than his words*): I need air.

(*Before* STORRS *can reply* HAMED *comes in with an ornamental belt and dagger which he brusquely hands to* LAWRENCE.)

(*With a winning smile*) May Allah bless you, Hamed, friend of my heart and guardian of my life —

(HAMED *turns his back and walks away with great dignity to stand beside* RASHID.)

(*Shrugging*) Oh well. Everything takes time. (*Showing* STORRS *the dagger*) I say, Storrs — look at this. Isn't this splendid? (*He begins to put it on, with apparent glee*) Rashid, hold the mirror up again. (RASHID *does so*) By jove, yes. With this I shall really be one of the lords of the desert —

(*Another man we have seen with* FRANKS (BARRINGTON) *comes into the tent, dressed in tropical uniform. He looks hot and bad-tempered.*)

BARRINGTON: Storrs?

(STORRS *has got up with alacrity.* LAWRENCE *has*

39

glanced quickly over his shoulder at the new arrival, and then reverts to his image in the mirror.)

STORRS: Ah, Colonel. It's good to see you again.

BARRINGTON: I'm sorry I wasn't on the quay to meet you. The message from HQ about your arrival came late. How did you find your way to Abdullah's camp?

STORRS: Captain Lawrence found some man to guide us —

BARRINGTON: But that's very dangerous, you know, out here — strictly against regulations, too. And who's Captain Lawrence?

STORRS (*helplessly*): He's over there.

LAWRENCE (*turning, affably*): How do you do. You're Colonel Barrington, aren't you, our representative in Jeddah.

BARRINGTON: Yes. I am.

LAWRENCE: Tell me, what do you think of Abdullah?

BARRINGTON (*bewildered*): What do I think of His Highness? Well, I think he's an exceptionally able and gifted person —

LAWRENCE: Exactly. He's too able and gifted to see anything except defeat. I don't blame him for that, but I don't think he's really our man — do you? I'm putting my money on Feisal.

BARRINGTON: Are you?

LAWRENCE: Ah. You probably see Feisal as a fool because he thinks he can win, and, of course, if he merely *thinks* that, then, I agree, he is a fool. But if — just by some strange chance — he happened to believe it, then — well, he'd be our man, wouldn't he? It seems to me worth a trip, anyway. Excuse me, but I really must make use of as much daylight as possible. Hamed, Rashid, tell the men to make ready and mount.

(HAMED *and* RASHID *disappear silently.* LAWRENCE *turns to* STORRS.)

Well, goodbye, Storrs. I'll see you in about a month.

BARRINGTON: Are you intending to ride to Feisal? Is that the meaning of this rig-out?

LAWRENCE: It is a bit peculiar, isn't it? At first Abdullah wanted to disguise me as a woman, with a yashmak, but I thought that was going a bit too far. Also — sort of cheating too, don't you think?

BARRINGTON: Do you happen to realize the risks involved?

LAWRENCE: Oh yes. We've been into all that.

BARRINGTON: But do you know anything about the sort of country between here and the Wadi Safru?

LAWRENCE: A bit rough, I'm told.

BARRINGTON: Are you? Well, this is what *I'm* told. Bare desert without any shelter at all, for three days. Then four days climbing a virtually impassable range of mountains, another two days climbing down it, and then another three days across an even worse desert. Then — (*he breaks off.* LAWRENCE *is counting up on his fingers*) What are you doing?

LAWRENCE: You've already made it twelve days. Quite frankly, Colonel, I'll be disappointed if we don't do it in six —

(*He goes out.*)

BARRINGTON: Who on earth *is* that awful little pip-squeak?

STORRS: Lawrence? My super-cerebral little companion? He's from the Arab Bureau in Cairo —

BARRINGTON: Ah, he's one of *that* menagerie, is he? Why was he sent out here?

STORRS: He wasn't. He just came.

BARRINGTON: Good Lord. Unauthorized?

(STORRS *nods.*)

What's his job in the Arab Bureau?

STORRS: Making maps.

BARRINGTON: Fine lot of use that's going to be to him.

STORRS: I don't know. His maps are very good.

BARRINGTON: Very artistic, I've no doubt — with the desert a tasteful yellow, and the mountains a pretty shade of mauve. (*Angrily*) Listen, Storrs — I don't want to have

41

anything to do with this business. I know nothing about it whatever – do you understand?

STORRS: Yes. Very clearly.

BARRINGTON: From now on Captain precious Lawrence of the Arab Bureau is entirely on his own —

STORRS: Yes, I think he'd prefer it that way.

THE LIGHTS FADE

(*We hear the sound of a man singing an Arab song, quietly, from a distance.*)

SCENE V

A desert place. There is no feature except a rock against which LAWRENCE *reclines, writing in a notebook. The rest is sky and a burning sun.*

(*Beside* LAWRENCE *lies* RASHID, *flat on his back.* HAMED *is asleep, some distance away*).

LAWRENCE: What music is that, Rashid?

RASHID: It is the music of an Howeitat song, el Aurans, in praise of Auda Abu Tayi.

(*He spits surreptitiously.*)

LAWRENCE: A noble man. They do well to honour him.

RASHID (*surprised*): Even in Cairo they know of Auda?

(*He spits again.*)

LAWRENCE: Even in Cairo *I* know of Auda. Seventy-five blood enemies killed by his own hand, and all his tribesmen wounded in his service at least once. Assuredly the greatest warrior in all Arabia. (*Wistfully*) What an ally he would make to Feisal!

RASHID: The Turks pay him too much money. He is a great man but he loves money. How is it you know so much about our country and our people, el Aurans?

(*He spits again.*)

LAWRENCE (*mildly*): Rashid, for the last five days I have wondered much whether Allah might not forgive you if, in conversation with me, you saved everything up for just one great spit at the end?

RASHID: Don't tell Hamed or he will beat me. He is angry that I speak to you at all.

LAWRENCE: Your guilty secret will be safe, I swear.

RASHID: Answer my question, then, el Aurans.

LAWRENCE: How do I know so much about your country and your people? Because I have made it my business to learn.

RASHID: Why do you, an Englishman and a Christian, seek to serve our cause?

LAWRENCE: Because in serving your country I also serve my own. Because in serving your cause I serve the cause of freedom. And in serving you I serve myself.

RASHID: The last I don't understand.

LAWRENCE: I don't quite understand it myself. (*He gets to his feet*) The hour is nearly finished. In ten minutes you must rouse the others.

RASHID (*groaning*): Oh no, el Aurans. The sun is still too high —

LAWRENCE: We must reach Prince Feisal's camp tonight.

RASHID: You will kill us all. For five days we have had no rest. Look at Hamed there. (*He points to the sleeping bodyguard*) Never have I known him so weary. And I, I am a dying man, el Aurans.

LAWRENCE: Resurrect yourself, then, corpse.

(*He playfully prods him with his rifle.* RASHID, *smiling, staggers to his feet, overplaying his weariness.*) Are you, Bedouins of the desert, to be put to shame by a man who, until a week ago, had spent two years of his life astride an office stool in Cairo. I am ashamed to lead so weak and effeminate a band —

RASHID (*with a giggle*): Who was it who yesterday had to hold you on your camel – to save you from falling down that ravine through weariness?

LAWRENCE: It was you, Rashid, and I thank you. But I would not have fallen.

RASHID: Allah would not have saved you.

LAWRENCE: No.

RASHID: Who then?

LAWRENCE: The only god I worship. (*He taps his head*) It lives up here in this malformed temple and it is called — the will. (*Looking at* HAMED) Surely Hamed will kill me for bringing him from such a happy dream.

RASHID: Let him dream on, el Aurans. And let me join him.

(*He sinks to the ground in pretended exhaustion.*)

LAWRENCE (*gently*): You are with him in everything else, Rashid. I think at least you should allow him the solitude of his own dream. And it can only last another seven minutes.

RASHID (*pleadingly*): El Aurans, why not wait until the evening? What do five hours matter?

LAWRENCE: They can make the difference between winning and losing a war.

RASHID: A war? (*Pityingly*) Forgive me, el Aurans, but I am an Arab and you are an Englishman and you do not understand. For five days I have heard you talk of an Arab war, but there *is* no war. We fight the Turks because we hate them, and we kill them when we can and where we can, and then when we have killed we go home. You speak of the Arab nation — but there *is* no Arab nation. My tribe is the Harif, and our neighbours are the Masruh. We are blood enemies. If I kill a Turk when I might have killed a man of the Masruh, I commit a crime against my tribe and my blood. And are the Harif and the Masruh the only blood enemies in Arabia? How then can we be a nation, and have an army? And without an army, how can we fight a war against the Turks? When you speak of the Arab war you dream foolish dreams, el Aurans —

LAWRENCE: Very well. I dream foolish dreams. (*Looking at his watch*) Five minutes and we leave.

RASHID (*disgusted*): To give Prince Feisal these few men when with a thousand times their number he could not

44

storm the Turkish guns that face him at Medina. Is that the only purpose of this mad gallop that is killing us all?

LAWRENCE: No. Not to give Feisal a few men to help him storm Medina, but to give him one who will stop him from trying to storm it at all.

RASHID: Yourself?

(LAWRENCE *nods*.)

You will not persuade him. He believes in his madness he can drive the Turkish armies from all of the Hejaz.

LAWRENCE: And so do I, Rashid, and I am not mad.

RASHID: By Allah I think you are madder. How can he drive the Turks from the Hejaz and not attack their fortresses?

LAWRENCE: Precisely by not attacking their fortresses, Rashid.

RASHID: And so he will win his battles by not fighting them?

LAWRENCE: Yes. And his war too – by not waging it.

RASHID: It is a splendid riddle, el Aurans.

LAWRENCE: The answer is easy, Rashid. It lies all around you. You have only to look. (*He points to the horizon*) What do you see?

RASHID: Empty space.

LAWRENCE (*pointing again*): And there – what do you see?

RASHID (*shrugging*): Our camels.

LAWRENCE: Desert and camels. Two weapons that are mightier than the mightiest guns in all the Turkish armies. The two weapons that can win Feisal his war – if only we are in time to stop him destroying his army and his own faith and courage against the guns of Medina.

(*He breaks off at the sound of a shot, followed by confused shouting, coming from close at hand.*)

See what that is. Tell the men to save their energies for the ride, and their ammunition for the Turks. Get them mounted.

(RASHID *runs off in the direction of the sound of angry voices which still continues.*)

45

(*Pushing* HAMED *with his foot*) Leave your dreams, Hamed.
It is time to go.

> (HAMED *looks up at* LAWRENCE *bewildered, and then
> quickly jumps to his feet. He picks up* LAWRENCE's
> *pistol.* LAWRENCE *takes the pistol from him and inspects
> it.*)

LAWRENCE: If this pistol could speak it would surely
say: 'See how my guardian reveres me. He keeps me spot-
less and gleaming, and ready for my master's use'.

> (*Pause.*)

Is that not so, Hamed?

> (HAMED *makes no reply.*)

(*Sighing*) May Allah give us a short war and not a long
one, or your lack of conversation may grow oppressive by
the end.

> (HAMED *looks quickly at him.*)

(*Cheerfully*) Yes, Hamed. By the end. I mean to ask Prince
Feisal to appoint you and Rashid permanently as my personal
bodyguards. So the only way you will ever gain your freedom from my service will be to ask me for it, and without
a spit to follow it.

> (HAMED *appears to pay no attention to news that is
> plainly unwelcome. He picks up a cartridge belt that*
> RASHID *had left behind.*)

He is safe, Hamed. I sent him on an errand —

> (*The sound of voices off grows loud again.* RASHID
> *runs on quickly. He looks startled.*)

Well?

RASHID (*breathlessly*): Mahmoud the Moroccan has killed
Salem of the Ageyli. Salem had insulted Mahmoud's tribe,
and Mahmoud took his rifle and shot him when he lay
asleep. Now the men of the Ageyli have bound Mahmoud
and will leave him here for the vultures when we go.

LAWRENCE (*quickly*): And the other Moroccans? Where
are they?

RASHID: Guarded by the Ageyli, each with a rifle to his
back. They can do nothing, el Aurans. There are two Ageyli

to each one of them.

LAWRENCE: And the others?

RASHID: They say it is no concern of theirs. Perhaps they will listen to *you*, el Aurans, but they would not hear me.

> (*There is a pause.* LAWRENCE *looks at the ground in thought.*)

LAWRENCE (*at length, quietly*): Yes, Rashid. They must listen to me. I am their leader.

> (HAMED *smiles.* LAWRENCE'S *eyes meet his.*)

(*Raising his voice slightly and speaking to* HAMED) They are soldiers in the field, and I lead them. If Mahmoud has committed murder then he must be killed. But — (*after evident difficulty in forcing the thought into speech*) by me — and not by them.

RASHID: They will not allow that, el Aurans. The Ageyli must kill him themselves, or their honour will not be avenged.

LAWRENCE: And the honour of the other Moroccans who fight for Feisal? How will that be avenged when they no longer have Ageyli rifles in their backs? You know well enough, Rashid, and so do I. And then another Moroccan will die. And another Ageyli. No. *One* life for *one* life.

> (*He looks at his pistol and abstractedly fingers it.*)

If they wish the Moroccans can avenge *their* honour by killing me. Then it is only a Christian who dies and there will be no blood feud. (*Looking at his pistol*) Once with this I could hit a matchbox at twenty yards. I wonder now if I can kill a man at one.

> (*He turns to go.* RASHID *and* HAMED *make to follow him.*)

No. Stay here. I'll face them without a bodyguard. At least I must try to make them think I am not afraid.

> (*He goes out.*)

THE LIGHTS FADE

> (*In the darkness we hear first the sound of confused shouts and cries and, at a moment, growing much louder. Then there is a quick silence, broken by a voice*

47

crying suddenly, in agonized fear:'Have pity, el Aurans.
Give me mercy. Let me live!' Then comes a pistol shot
followed at uncertain intervals by two more.)

Scene VI

The lights come on to illuminate a large wall map of the
Hejaz railway. It is being studied by two men, one the
Turkish General *whom we have previously seen in*
front of the lecturer's screen, and the other a Turkish
Captain.

General (*pointing at the map*): The latest report then
puts him about here.

Captain: Further east. Here. Nearer to Wadi Sirhan.

General: But that's over a hundred miles from the railway. Are you sure that's correct?

Captain: It was confirmed by our agents.

General: When was his last raid on the railway?

Captain: Ten days ago at kilometre 1121. (*He points to a*
place on the railway which is marked in kilometres) He
blew up the line in three places.

General: And nothing since then?

Captain: No. Perhaps our railway patrols are getting too
hot for him.

General: The history of the last few months would hardly support that rather optimistic hypothesis. But why has
he gone north-east away from Feisal? (*He turns away from*
the map. Peremptorily) Take this down.

(*The* Captain *picks up a pencil and notebook.*)
(*Dictating*) Proclamation. To all loyal inhabitants of Southern Arabia. For some time past the criminal activities of a
British spy, saboteur and train-wrecker, named Lawrence,
sometimes known as el Aurans, Laurens Bey or the Emir
Dynamite, has been causing severe damage to Arabian property, notably the Holy Railway route from Damascus to

Medina. In addition his acts of wanton destruction pose a severe threat to the supplies of our garrison at Medina. A reward, therefore, of ten thousand pounds will be paid —

CAPTAIN (*looking up, surprised*): For a figure like that we'll need authorization from Damascus.

GENERAL: I'll write to them. (*continuing*) – will be paid to any person giving information leading to his capture. By order of the Military Governor, District of Deraa.

CAPTAIN: Isn't that rather expensive for a terrorist?

GENERAL: For a terrorist. But not, I think, for Lawrence.

CAPTAIN: What's the difference?

GENERAL: The difference between a nuisance and a menace.

CAPTAIN: Menace? (*Scornfully*) The Emir Dynamite?

GENERAL (*turning to the map*): The Emir Dynamite seems to be skilled in other things than high explosives. Strategy for instance. I don't think ten thousand is too much for a man who, in a few months, has transformed a local disturbance into a major campaign – who has isolated Medina (*he points to the map*) and who has drawn down (*he points to the area of the Hejaz and Southern Arabia*) into Southern Arabia, reinforcements from all over the Turkish Empire which are needed elsewhere. (*Abstractedly*) Oh no. For this man I think ten thousand's rather cheap. (*With sudden excitement*) Nearer to the *Wadi Sirhan*? Isn't that what you said?

CAPTAIN (*at the map*): Yes. (*He points*) Here.

GENERAL: But, of course. Auda!

> (THE LIGHTS FADE *as the sound of Auda's Battle Song can be heard being sung to Arab musical accompaniment.*)

SCENE VII

Outside an Arab tent. The sound of a song is coming from somewhere in the distance. LAWRENCE, *in Arab*

clothes, is squatting on the ground with eyelids lowered.
RASHID *comes in quickly and speaks in a low voice.*
RASHID: El Aurans, there is danger.

> (LAWRENCE *raises his head slowly, as if interrupted in some process of thought.*)

Hamed has just heard that the Turks have lately been to this camp and were received with great friendliness.

> (LAWRENCE *looks at him vaguely, his thoughts evidently elsewhere.*)

(*Desperately*) El Aurans, all Arabia knows this man loves money and takes it from the Turks. Hamed says we should leave at once.

LAWRENCE: Then he should come and tell me so himself.

RASHID: You know well he cannot. (*Giggling*) And now he has made it even harder to break his silence to you. He has bound himself by the holiest vow he knows.

LAWRENCE: Well – at least that shows he feels temptation.

RASHID: Oh yes. He is tempted.

LAWRENCE: Hamed's must surely be the most prolonged religious sulk in world history.

RASHID (*urgently*): We have the camels ready, el Aurans. We can leave now.

LAWRENCE (*quietly*): No, Rashid. Not yet. I will tell you when.

> (*The* SHEIK AUDA ABU TAYI *appears in the tent opening, studying a map with intense concentration. We have seen him already from the lecturer's screen, but we now see him more clearly as an old man, of great vigour, with a booming voice, a handsome, hawklike face and a natural, unassumed majesty of presence. The latter quality is enhanced by the splendour of his clothes. At a nod from* LAWRENCE, RASHID *has disappeared.*
>
> AUDA *lowers the map and glares at* LAWRENCE.)

LAWRENCE: Well?

AUDA (*at length*): No. It is impossible.

LAWRENCE: Since when has Auda Abu Tayi been turned

back from any venture by the dull bonds of possibility?

AUDA: El Aurans, it is only a few hours that I have known you, but I understand you better than you think I do. You have said to yourself, Auda is an old man who feeds on flattery. All I need to do to bend him to my will is to remind him of the great feats of his youth. (*Suddenly shouting*) Of course there was a time when I ignored the word impossible. There was a time, forty years ago, when I led a hundred men across the Southern Desert against ten times that number to avenge an insult to my tribe – and by the great God, avenged it too. That day I killed seven men by my own hand.

LAWRENCE: Seven? In the Ballad of Auda it says ten.

AUDA (*carelessly*): No doubt some others died of their wounds. Yes, by heaven. That feat was impossible. And there were others too — (*He changes tone*) But I am no longer twenty and what you suggest is — (*shouting, off, angrily at someone offstage*). Kerim! Order that man, on pain of instant decapitation, to stop singing his foolish song. The words are exaggerated and his voice disturbs our thought. (*He turns back to* LAWRENCE) There is a boundary between the possible and the impossible that certain exceptional beings such as myself may leap. But there is a boundary between the impossible and a madman's dream — (*The song stops abruptly*) Thank Allah! There are fifty-six verses to that song – each in praise of either one of my battles or one of my wives. By the dispensation of God the numbers are exactly equal.

LAWRENCE: Wouldn't it be supremely fitting to the memory of a great warrior if his wives were outnumbered by just one battle – and that one the greatest of all?

AUDA (*passionately*): El Aurans, I have no great love for the Turks. Feisal is my friend and I would be his ally. But what are you asking? A march in the worst month of the year across the worst desert in Arabia – el Houl – the desolate – that even the jackals and vultures fear – where the sun can beat a man to madness and where day or night a wind of such scorching dryness can blow that a man's skin is stripped from his body. It is a terrible desert — el Houl — and terrible is not a word that comes lightly to the lips of Auda Abu Tayi.

LAWRENCE (*mildly*): I had believed it a word unknown to him.

AUDA: My friend, your flattery will not make wells. And it will not stop the few wells there *are* on the fringe of that desert from being poisoned by the Turks the moment they learn of our objective — as they must —

LAWRENCE: Why must they?

AUDA: Do you think I am unknown in Arabia? Do you think that when Auda rides out at the head of five hundred men the Turks will not ask questions?

LAWRENCE: Indeed they will, but will they get the right answer?

AUDA: They are not fools.

LAWRENCE: No. And that is why the last thing they will look for is an attack across el Houl on the port of Akaba. If such a project seems mad even to Auda, how will it seem to the Turks?

AUDA (*chuckling*): By heaven — there is some wisdom there, el Aurans. They would not even guess at it. No sane man ever could —

LAWRENCE (*taking the map*): But just in case they do, the direction of our march should be north-west at first, to make them believe we are aiming at a raid on the railway.

AUDA (*abstractedly interrupting*): Has Feisal much gold?

LAWRENCE: Alas — he is rich only in promises — and so am I on his behalf.

AUDA: And what would you have promised me if I had consented to this madness?

LAWRENCE: A higher price than the Turks could pay.

AUDA: Then it must be high indeed. What is it?

LAWRENCE: The praise of the whole world for the most brilliant feat of arms in Arabian history.

(*Pause.*)

AUDA (*gazing at the map*): Akaba! Even your own all-powerful Navy has not dared attack it.

LAWRENCE: Oh yes.

AUDA: And were defeated?

LAWRENCE: Oh no. Our Navy is never defeated.

AUDA: Well?

LAWRENCE: After a successful bombardment they withdrew.

AUDA: Beaten off by the Turkish guns.

LAWRENCE: They are very powerful guns.

AUDA: Have *I* powerful guns?

LAWRENCE: You have no need of guns.

AUDA: How? No need?

LAWRENCE: There is no gun – however powerful – that can fire backwards.

(*Pause.*)

AUDA: They all point out to sea?

LAWRENCE: All out to sea.

AUDA: Fixed?

LAWRENCE: Fixed.

(*Pause.*)

AUDA: How strong are the Turks?

LAWRENCE: About two thousand in the area.

AUDA: Against five hundred?

LAWRENCE: Four to one. Auda's odds.

AUDA (*chuckling*): Auda's odds. Have they made no preparations against an attack from the land?

LAWRENCE: None.

AUDA: They believe it impossible?

LAWRENCE: A madman's dream.

AUDA (*chuckling*): The fools. No fortifications facing the land at all?

LAWRENCE: A few – a very few – but they will be easy to surprise.

AUDA: A camel charge, at night. My battle cry, to panic the idiots from their beds, and then amongst them.

LAWRENCE: They may well surrender at the very sound.

AUDA (*genuinely alarmed*): May Allah forbid! My friend, do you think I am marching across el Houl in the deadliest month of the year, to be rewarded at the end with a tame surrender —?

LAWRENCE: Well – then – perhaps no battle cry —

AUDA: That, too, is unthinkable. Even Turks must know who it is that kills them. A charge in daylight, then – after due warning —

LAWRENCE: Not too long a warning.

AUDA: Not too long and not too short. Akaba! What a gift to make to Feisal —

TURKISH CAPTAIN (*off*): Keep the men mounted —

(*The* TURKISH CAPTAIN *walks in, past* LAWRENCE *without glancing at him, and up to* AUDA *who has turned at his tent opening. He salutes.*)

CAPTAIN: God be with you, Auda Abu Tayi!

AUDA: And with you, Captain.

(LAWRENCE *moves unobtrusively to go, but finds his escape barred by a* TURKISH SOLDIER, *whose back can be seen as he lounges at the entrance.* LAWRENCE *slips to the ground adopting the same squatting attitude in which we first saw him in this scene. He keeps his head lowered.*)

CAPTAIN: I bring the greetings and love of my master, the Governor, and the precious gift for which you asked —

(*He holds out a small package.* AUDA *snatches it eagerly.*)

AUDA: By God, but this has been fast work —

CAPTAIN: His Excellency telegraphed to Damascus and had it sent down by the railway.

AUDA: Ah – this is a noble sight —

(*He reveals the contents of the package with a delighted flourish. They are a set of false teeth.*)

By Allah, these are surely the false teeth of which all other false teeth are but vile and blaspheming copies. Your master's generous answer to his servant's dire need is a great and splendid thing, and will not be forgotten —

CAPTAIN: I shall tell him of your pleasure – it will add to his own.

AUDA: See how well they are made, and how they gleam in the sun. By the prophet, with these in my mouth, I shall be young again. You must eat with me tonight, Captain – and you shall see them in action —

CAPTAIN: I am afraid that will not be possible. I must start back at once.

AUDA (*still admiring the teeth*): A pity. You must ask your master what gift he would like from me in return —

CAPTAIN: You know the gift.

AUDA: Ah yes, I remember —

(*He puts the teeth back in the package a trifle abstractedly.*)

Why are you so sure he will come to me?

CAPTAIN: The Governor believes that he'll try to win you to the rebel cause.

AUDA: That would be very foolish.

CAPTAIN: Let us hope he is so foolish, Auda. I know my master would rather you earned the reward than anyone.

AUDA (*interested*): Reward? You said nothing before of a reward.

CAPTAIN: It had not then been authorised.

AUDA (*abstractedly*): How much?

CAPTAIN: Ten thousand pounds.

AUDA (*with a gasp*): Ten thousand! By Allah – is this Englishman worth so much?

CAPTAIN: The Governor believes him to be.

AUDA: Ten thousand. (*Suddenly speaking to* LAWRENCE'S *lowered head*) Do you hear that, my friend?

(*Pause.* LAWRENCE *slowly raises his head.*)

LAWRENCE (*looking up at him*): Yes, Auda. I hear it.

AUDA: What do you say?

LAWRENCE: That it is indeed a high price for so low a scoundrel.

AUDA: It is indeed a high price. A very high price. Would you like to see me win it?

LAWRENCE: I would rather win it, myself. But if not I, then let it be you. For surely no reward is too great for Auda Abu Tayi.

> (*Pause. The* CAPTAIN *has glanced at* LAWRENCE *with only mild interest.* AUDA *turns back to him.*)

AUDA: He speaks loyally and well.

CAPTAIN: He does. (*Reassuringly*) We have no fears, Auda. We know that you and all the men about you are loyal. But *you* must fear this Englishman. He has a glib and flattering tongue and by it has lured good men into treachery.

AUDA: Below medium height?

CAPTAIN: Yes.

AUDA: And dresses usually in white?

CAPTAIN: So it is said.

AUDA: Looking more English than Arab?

CAPTAIN: Yes. But you won't need to recognize him, Auda. He will surely announce himself to you. And then —

AUDA: And then?

CAPTAIN: You know what to do to gain ten thousand pounds.

AUDA: Yes. I know what to do.

CAPTAIN: I shall give your messages to the Governor.

AUDA (*to* LAWRENCE, *abruptly*): Escort the captain —

> (LAWRENCE *gets to his feet.*)

CAPTAIN: Thank you, but there is no need —

AUDA: Do you think we have no manners here?

CAPTAIN (*smiling*): God be with you, Auda.

AUDA: And with you, captain.

CAPTAIN (*to* LAWRENCE, *who has stationed himself behind him*): Oh, thank you —

> (*He goes out.* AUDA *moves quickly to look after him, looking tense and anxious. We hear the sound of a barked word of command, and of horses' hooves moving away.* AUDA *relaxes and shrugs his shoulders.* LAWRENCE *comes back.*)

AUDA: By heaven, el Aurans, what a joke that was!

What a joke to remember —

LAWRENCE (*in a low, uncertain voice*): It won't be easy to forget.

AUDA (*touching his arm*): My friend, you are trembling.

LAWRENCE: Yes. I am.

AUDA: You were afraid?

LAWRENCE: Yes.

AUDA: Of what? Of a degenerate Turk and his few followers? There are five hundred men in this camp. They could have accounted for them in twenty seconds.

LAWRENCE: Yes. They could. The question is whether they would.

AUDA: By Allah, they would if I had ordered them.

LAWRENCE: Yes. But would you have ordered them?

AUDA: Can you doubt it?

LAWRENCE: With some ease.

AUDA: But, my friend, if I had wanted the reward —

LAWRENCE: Auda, do you believe your thoughts are so hard to read? To betray a guest is a great sin, but ten thousand pounds is ten thousand pounds, and surely worth a spin of the wheel of fate. If the Turk recognizes the foreigner, then the foreigner is not betrayed. But, to be recognized, he must first be made to raise his head and show the Turk his English features and then to stand up to show the Turk his white clothes and his meagre height —

AUDA (*chuckling*): What a fool he was, that Turk! (*To* LAWRENCE) Of course I knew he was a fool or I would never have taken that risk.

(LAWRENCE *looks at him, without replying*.)

(*Moving to the tent*) Come, my friend. We have plans to make.

(LAWRENCE *makes no move to follow him*.)

Very well. I admit that I was tempted. You offered me honour and they, money. Both I love exceedingly and not the one much more than the other. But I spun the wheel and honour won. There is no going back now.

LAWRENCE: And if they raised my price?

AUDA: Ah. But they will not raise your price until after we have taken Akaba.

(LAWRENCE *smiles, shrugs his shoulders and goes slowly towards the tent opening.* AUDA *has picked up the package and is looking at his precious false teeth. Suddenly he hurls them to the ground, picks up a rifle and smashes the butt on them, again and again. After a moment he stops, stoops and picks up the shattered fragments, looking at them with eyes of tragic longing. Then he throws them carelessly away.*)

The path of honour.

(*He puts his arm round* LAWRENCE *and escorts him into the tent.*)

THE LIGHTS FADE

(*In the darkness we hear the sound of 'Tipperary' played on a rather scratchy record.*)

SCENE VIII

A small hut in a British Army camp near Suez.
As the lights come on they focus first on an ancient (to our eyes) gramophone, complete with horn. A man is humming the song to this accompaniment and, as the lights come up more strongly, we see he is a BRITISH CORPORAL *and is using a disinfectant spray in time to the music. The camp has been abandoned through an outbreak of plague, and the hut bears a dilapidated appearance. A door is open at the back, showing the night sky.* HAMED, *looking ragged and desert-stained, comes into the hut and looks round.*

CORPORAL (*gesticulating*): Yellah! Yellah! Shoo!

(HAMED *pays no attention, but walks over to a desk where he has seen a telephone.*)

Get out of here, woggie. Go on. Hop it, now —

(HAMED *picks up the receiver gingerly – rather as if*

58

he expected from it some kind of electric shock.)
Get out, woggie, or I'll have to shoot you, and you wouldn't like that, now, would you? This is British Army property and I'm in charge – see. Shoo! Yellah! Shoo!

(HAMED, *still paying no attention to the* CORPORAL, *lifts the receiver rather fearfully to his ear, still evidently expecting to be electrocuted. Reassured by his immunity he listens for a moment, until a voice can be heard asking for a number.*)

(*Meanwhile*) Shoo, shoo, shoo, shoo! Out, woggie, out!

(HAMED, *still paying no attention to the* CORPORAL, *but satisfied, apparently, with what he has heard on the telephone, replaces the receiver and walks out.*

The CORPORAL, *after a shrug, continues his fumigating. The record comes to an end. He is bending over the gramophone as* LAWRENCE *comes in. He looks as travel-stained and dirty as* HAMED.)

CORPORAL: Cripes! Another one. (*Shouting*) Yellah! Yellah! Yellah! Shoo! (*He uses his spray on* LAWRENCE) Get to hell out of here, woggie! I nearly shot your chum and I'll shoot you, I swear, if you don't buzz off!

LAWRENCE (*at telephone*): Does this telephone work, Corporal?

CORPORAL (*at length*): Did you speak?

LAWRENCE: Yes, I asked if this telephone works. I want to ring up Suez —

CORPORAL (*beyond his depth*): I am in charge of this camp, which is Government property, and which has been closed down on account of plague – and no unauthorized person may —

LAWRENCE (*into telephone*): Naval Headquarters. It's urgent. (*To* CORPORAL) Ah. Plague. So that explains it. For the last half hour I've been wondering if the British troops on the Suez Canal had got bored with the war and gone home.

CORPORAL (*pointing to telephone*): Listen – I said no unauthorized person —

LAWRENCE (*into receiver*): Hullo, Naval Headquarters? I want your senior chap, whoever he is . . . Admiral Makepeace? Right. Put me through . . . No. I don't want any duty officer. I want the man in charge. . . . Then get him away from dinner. . . . Then you'll have to forget your orders, won't you? . . . My name will mean nothing to you and my rank is unimportant, but I can only tell you that if you fail to get your Admiral to the telephone this instant you will probably face a court-martial for having delayed the ending of the war by roughly three months . . . I see. Just hold on a moment.

> (*He puts his hand over the receiver and turns to the* CORPORAL.)

Get me some water from that tap outside, would you, old chap?

CORPORAL: It's not for drinking. Strict orders are to boil all water —

LAWRENCE: The last well I drank from — yesterday morning – had a dead goat in it.

CORPORAL: Yes – er – sir. As you say.

> (*He goes.*)

LAWRENCE (*into the telephone, mildly*): Now, in answer to your question I am not off my bleeding chump. I am speaking the simple truth. At your switchboard you hold in your hands the lives of five hundred Allied soldiers and the possession of the most valuable port in Southern Arabia, in which at the moment those soldiers are victoriously sitting, with nothing whatever to eat except their camels or their prisoners, and if I know them, they'll start on the prisoners. . . . Thank you.

> (*The* CORPORAL *has come back with a mug of water.* LAWRENCE *takes it from him.*)

By jove, Corporal, it's worked. I think he still thinks I'm off my rocker, though —

CORPORAL (*politely*): Does he, sir? Fancy.

> (LAWRENCE *splutters into the mug from which he is avidly drinking. After a moment he puts it down.*)

LAWRENCE: I've got some men outside who need food and drink. Would you look after them?

CORPORAL: Yes, sir. I don't speak their lingo, sir.

LAWRENCE: If you smile at them and treat them as if they were human, you'll find them quite easy to handle —

CORPORAL: Yes, sir. I'll do my best.

(*He goes out.*)

LAWRENCE (*into telephone*): Oh, hullo, Admiral. Sorry to disturb you . . . My name's Lawrence, Captain Lawrence . . . Oh, no. Just Army. Look. I want you to send a destroyer to Akaba . . . Destroyer, that's right, but it doesn't *have* to be a destroyer. As a matter of fact a bigger thing – might be better. It's got to take a lot of stuff, you see – food for five hundred men, about six howitzers, thirty machine guns, as many grenades and rifles as the Army will let you have – oh – and some armoured cars would come in very handy. Also – most important of all really – about fifty thousand pounds in cash . . . Fifty thousand . . . Oh, I'm sorry. Didn't I tell you. . . . Yes, we took it. . . . From the land. Rather a long way round, but it seemed to work all right. . . . No. They didn't appear to expect us . . . Oh, about five hundred killed and seven hundred prisoners. . . . Ours? Two. Unhappily we lost five more on the march, including one of my body-guard. You see conditions in the desert were a bit – rough. We had three bad sandstorms, and I'm afraid my compass work wasn't all that good, and we missed a well – . . . No, Admiral, I promise you this isn't a joke. Akaba is ours . . . . A rather picturesque fellow called Auda Abu Tayi is holding it, but don't let him sell it to you, because he'll certainly try. Now you will get that boat there tonight, won't you? You see, the Turks are bound to react violently, and mount a counter-offensive in the next few days. Will you please inform Cairo for me? I'm a bit tired . . . No. I won't be available tomorrow. I shall be asleep tomorrow and probably the next day. If they want to talk to me after that they'll find me in my old office in Cairo . . . Making maps . . . Yes. The C-in-C does know of me. In fact General Murray and I

have often exchanged words . . . Gone? Gone for good?
(*Plainly delighted*) Oh dear! Who, then . . . Allenby?
No, I've not heard of him. Thank you, sir. Goodnight.

> (*He rings off and rests his head on the desk.* HAMED
> *stalks angrily into the office, holding a sausage on a
> fork, keeping it as far away from him as possible.* LAW-
> RENCE *looks up.*)

Yes, Hamed?

> (HAMED *thrusts the fork angrily at him.* LAWRENCE
> *takes it.*)

Ah, I see. The infidel corporal has not understood the laws
of Allah. You must forgive him.

> (*He pulls the sausage from the fork and begins to eat
> it.*)

Avert your pious eyes from your master's vile gluttony,
Hamed, and remember that he has not eaten since yesterday's dawn. Remember too that it was to the Faithful that
he gave up his rations.

> (HAMED *lowers his eyes.* LAWRENCE *looks up at him,
> wearily, without getting up.*)

(*Smiling*) Since Rashid died I have not seen you smile,
Hamed. Not once. But before you had begun to learn the
trick. (*Quietly*) Tell me. Is it that you blame me?

> (HAMED *signifies dissent.*)

You can tell me if it is true. I shall understand.

> (HAMED *again signifies dissent.*)

You smile, then, at no one? At nothing ?

> (HAMED *signifies agreement.*)

Because of your grief, and only because of that?

> (HAMED *signifies assent.*)

I am sorry, Hamed. If there was anything that I could have
found to say to you that might have helped you, I would
have found it. But I will not insult you by trying to tell you
that one day you will forget. I know as well as you that you
will not. But, at least, in time you will not remember as
fiercely as you do now — and I pray that that time may be
soon. I shall see that the corporal gives you food more fit-

ting to Moslem warriors. I want anyway to say goodbye
to you all —

> (*He gets up showing his utter exhaustion. His back
> is turned to us as* HAMED *speaks.*)

HAMED (*with certainty*): You will come back to us, el
Aurans.

> (LAWRENCE *turns slowly to look at him. There is a
> long pause.*)

LAWRENCE: Others will come, Hamed. Many others of
my countrymen. That is certain.

HAMED: There are no others we need, but you.

> (*There is a pause. The telephone rings.* LAWRENCE
> *makes no move to pick up the receiver.*)

You must come back to us, el Aurans. It is you that we
need.

LAWRENCE (*finally picking up receiver*): Yes . . . Yes,
this is Lawrence . . . Who? Flag Lieutenant? Hold on a
moment.

> (*He lowers the receiver.*)

LAWRENCE: Go to the men, Hamed. I'll join you there.
(HAMED *turns to go*) And Hamed. (HAMED *turns*) Thank
you for your words. Any words from you would have
been welcome, but those words more welcome than all.

> (HAMED *goes.*)

(*Into receiver*) I'm sorry . . . To get across the Canal? Well,
I thought I'd get some fellow to row me . . . The Admiral's
barge? I say, how splendid. Thank you. (*He rings off. Sitting at the desk he suddenly raises his head in fierce and
glowing pride. Softly*) Ross, can you hear me?

> (*Pause.*)

I've done it. Done it. I've captured Akaba. I've done what
none of the professional soldiers could have done. I've captured the key to Southern Arabia with five hundred ineffi-
cient, untrustworthy Arab bandits. Why don't you enjoy
the memory? What makes you so unhappy? Is it that Moroccan I shot in the desert and couldn't kill cleanly because my
hand was shaking so much? The mangled Turkish bodies

in the dynamited trains? Those men that died in the desert? ... Rashid? ... Is it Rashid?

(*Pause.*)

War is war, after all. The enemy has to be killed and our own men have to die. And surely, at least I've been more sparing of them than any red-tabbed superman?

(*Pause.*)

(*Angrily*) What is wrong in trying to write my name in history? Lawrence of Akaba – perhaps – who knows?

(*Pause.*)

Oh Ross – how did I become you?

(*He gets up and goes wearily out of the hut.*)

CURTAIN

ACT II

Scene I

A room in GHQ, Cairo. There is an imposing desk, a large wall map, and comfortable armchairs: behind the desk sits ALLENBY, *a large, heavy man, his appearance rather belying his character.*

A very decorative ADC *steps smartly into the room and comes to parade-ground attention.*

ALLENBY: Are they here?

ADC: Yes, sir.

ALLENBY: Show them in.

    (*The* ADC *turns and goes out. After a moment* STORRS *and* BARRINGTON *come in.*)

Good morning, Colonel. Ah, Storrs — good of you to come.

STORRS: Not at all, sir. Even in my lax office a request from the Commander-in-Chief is usually counted as an order.

ALLENBY (*not smiling*): Sit down, gentlemen, please.

    (*They do so.*)

I've called you here because I understand you both know this fellow Lawrence.

    (*They signify assent.*)

I don't want to hear too much of what you think of him as a man. I'm prepared to form my own judgement on that. I'm seeing him later on. I want you to tell me what you think of him as a potential leader. Storrs?

STORRS: Lawrence as a leader? (*Thoughtfully*) He's pure intellectual, and not by nature a man of action at all. He's strongly introverted, withdrawn and selfconscious, and will never allow anyone to see his true nature. He hides everything behind a manner that's either over-meek, over-arrogant, or over-flippant, whichever is going to disconcert the most. He thinks far too much for the good of his soul and feels far too much for the good of his mind. Consequently he's a highly unstable personality. Finally, he has a sublime contempt for authority – in any form, but chiefly military.

ALLENBY: I see. Not very promising —

STORRS: On the contrary, sir. I think he'd make a military leader of the highest class.

ALLENBY (*snapping*): Why?

STORRS: Because I find to my surprise that I've just given a description of most great commanders from Julius Caesar to Napoleon.

ALLENBY (*nodding after a moment*): Barrington?

BARRINGTON: I disagree, sir, I'm afraid. I don't deny his success in Akaba – though how much luck there was in that, we'll never know. (*Angrily*) But give him all credit for Akaba – it still makes no difference. He's irresponsible – a useful man, no doubt, to have charging around behind the enemy lines, with his Bedouins blowing up trains. But in a position of responsibility – no. Definitely, no. May I ask, sir, what appointment you had in mind?

ALLENBY: In a report to me he has recommended a plan for general revolt of all the Arab peoples in the north – to be timed to coincide with my offensive through the Gaza Gap in November. (*To* BARRINGTON) By the way, security must be dangerously bad here for him to have known both the time and the place of my offensive.

BARRINGTON: On the contrary, sir, security here is very good. I didn't know either time or place and I'm sure Storrs didn't – did you?

STORRS: No.

ALLENBY: Well, then, how on earth did *he*?

(*Pause.*)

STORRS (*mildly*): A point to me, I think.

BARRINGTON: Guesswork.

STORRS: One of the qualities of a leader, isn't it?

ALLENBY: Possibly. Still, I wish he'd confine his attention to the enemy's plans, and not to mine. However, he
suggests that, to support my offensive, four separate Arab
forces should be organized to operate east of the Hejaz railway, between Maan and Damascus here – (*he points*) along
the Turks' main line of communication —

(*Pause.*)

BARRINGTON (*ironically, at length*): A rather ambitious
plan, isn't it?

ALLENBY (*shortly*): Highly, but I'm accepting it. In fact,
I'm accepting all his recommendations, except one – that a
high-ranking officer be appointed to direct these operations.
I'm thinking of appointing Lawrence himself.

BARRINGTON (*pained*): A captain?

ALLENBY: He was gazetted major this morning. And I've
recommended him for an award.

BARRINGTON: I'm afraid my opinion must remain that it
would be a very dangerous appointment. Forgive my frank-
ness, sir.

ALLENBY (*drily*): It does you credit. Storrs?

STORRS: I'll stick to my opinion too.

(ALLENBY *presses a bell on his desk.*)
I'm grateful to you both.

(*The* ADC *appears.*)
Is Major Lawrence here?

ADC: He's just arrived, sir.

ALLENBY: Send him in.

(*The ADC goes.*)

ALLENBY (*to* STORRS): I'm a bit scared of this meeting.
Do you think he'll try to floor me with Baudelaire or something?

STORRS: Very likely, sir.

ALLENBY: I wonder if I could floor him with my pet
subject.

BARRINGTON: What's that, sir?

ALLENBY: Flowers.

(BARRINGTON *looks startled. A door is opened and*
67

LAWRENCE *comes in. He is dressed in a uniform that was never from Savile Row, but now — after loss of weight in the desert — hardly fits him at all. He sees* STORRS *first.*)

LAWRENCE: Oh, hullo, Storrs. I was coming to see you this aft —

(*A firm sign from* STORRS *indicates the* COMMANDER-IN-CHIEF.)

Oh, I'm sorry.

(*He delivers a rather informal-looking salute. Even* ALLENBY, *determined to be surprised at nothing, has to comment.*)

ALLENBY: Good gracious!

LAWRENCE: What's the matter?

ALLENBY: Do you always salute like that?

LAWRENCE: Why, sir? Is it wrong?

ALLENBY: It's a little — individual.

LAWRENCE: I was never taught.

ALLENBY: But you must have done some drill training, surely?

LAWRENCE: Well, no. I was a civilian in the Map Section of the War Office in 1914 and one of my jobs was to take maps along to some old general — and he always used to roar at me that he hated civilians in his office and why the dickens wasn't I in uniform? So, one day, I went out to the Army and Navy Stores and bought a uniform.

ALLENBY (*unsmiling*): You mean that you've never been properly commissioned in the Army?

LAWRENCE: I don't think so, sir. No. I'm sure I'd remember it if I had.

ALLENBY: I see. Well, I'm happy to inform you that you've now been gazetted a major.

LAWRENCE (*mildly*): Oh? Good.

ALLENBY: And I've put in a recommendation for you for the CB.

LAWRENCE (*startled*): CB?

ALLENBY: Companion of the Bath.

LAWRENCE: Oh. Thank you.

ALLENBY (*to the other two*): Very well, gentlemen. Thank you very much.

> (*They turn to go.*)

LAWRENCE: Oh, Storrs. (*To* ALLENBY) Excuse me.

> (ALLENBY *nods.*)

Freddie Strong has dug up something at Luxor which I know you'll go absolutely mad about.

> (STORRS, *detained by the door, is looking acutely embarrassed.* BARRINGTON *flashes* ALLENBY *his parade-ground salute and goes, his face meaningful.*)

(*Apparently oblivious*) It's a small alabaster perfume jar, exquisite shape, twentieth dynasty I should think, with what seems like a strong Minoan influence —

ALLENBY (*quietly*): Minoan influence in the twentieth dynasty?

> (LAWRENCE *turns to look at him, apparently seeing him for the first time.*)

LAWRENCE (*at length*): I suppose it couldn't be, could it? I must have got the dynasty wrong.

ALLENBY: Or the influence.

LAWRENCE (*slowly*): Yes. Or the influence.

ALLENBY (*with authority*): Goodbye, Storrs, and thank you.

STORRS: Goodbye, sir.

> (*He goes with evident relief.*)

ALLENBY: Sit down, Lawrence.

> (LAWRENCE *sits. There is a pause.*)

(*Smiling suddenly*) Tell me — did Freddie Strong really dig up a twentieth dynasty perfume jar?

> (*There is a pause while* LAWRENCE *and* ALLENBY *look at each other appraisingly across the large desk.*)

LAWRENCE (*at length — with a good-humoured shrug*): Well, he does dig things up all the time, you know.

ALLENBY (*nodding appreciatively*): Good. I'm glad we understand each other so soon.

LAWRENCE (*without rancour*): Yes. So am I.

ALLENBY: I was lucky with the Minoan influence. I've

just been reading Arthur Evans' book, *The Palace of Minos in Crete*.

LAWRENCE (*politely*): It's pleasant to meet a general who's read anything except Clausewitz.

ALLENBY: Yes. You won't catch me on Clausewitz, although I confess I'm a bit rusty. But please don't try me on the campaigns of Belisarius. I gather that *is* one of your pet subjects?

LAWRENCE: Yes. How did you know?

ALLENBY: I've made it my business to find out. No doubt you've done the same about me.

LAWRENCE: Flowers?

ALLENBY: Correct.

LAWRENCE: Shakespeare, Chippendale, mobile warfare, Chopin and children. Not, of course, necessarily, in that order.

ALLENBY: Your spies have done even better than mine.

LAWRENCE: I expect yours had less to find out.

ALLENBY: More, I think – but your talent for self-conceal-ment is greater.

LAWRENCE: Perhaps it needs to be.

ALLENBY: Perhaps.

LAWRENCE (*smiling*): A lesser man would have said: 'Oh no – I'm sure not'.

ALLENBY: I'm not interested in the secrets of your soul, Lawrence. I'm interested in only one thing. Are you the right man for the job?

LAWRENCE (*genuinely puzzled*): What job?

ALLENBY (*impatiently holding up Lawrence's report and tapping it*) This, of course.

LAWRENCE (*still puzzled*): My report?

(*He gets up, evidently really disturbed.*)

Oh no, Great heavens, no. Not me. That would be disastrous.

(*He is plainly agitated.* ALLENBY *looks at him enquiringly, evidently wondering whether this is not just another trick.*)

70

ALLENBY: You echo Colonel Barrington.

LAWRENCE: Even Colonel Barrington can be right once in a war's duration. He is now.

ALLENBY: You surprise me.

LAWRENCE: Why?

ALLENBY: I thought you were an ambitious man.

LAWRENCE: So I am.

ALLENBY: Well, here might be your chance.

LAWRENCE (*shaking his head*): I've had my chance. Akaba and being made a major, and the – what's the thing – CB – that's enough, isn't it?

ALLENBY (*thoughtfully*): I wouldn't have thought so – for you. When you were writing this report, did it never occur to you I might consider *you* for the job?

LAWRENCE: Of course it did. That's why I was so determined to make it plain exactly what qualities your man would need. He must be a man of authority, with the patience to remain cheerful in the face of incompetence, cowardice, greed and treachery. He must have a deep practical knowledge of strategy, and of the principles of irregular warfare. Above all he must know how to lie and flatter and cheat in a cause that is not his own, but in which he must appear to believe. And he must forget that he's ever heard of the Sykes-Picot Agreement.

ALLENBY: What agreement?

LAWRENCE (*impatiently*): The secret treaty partitioning post-war Arabia between the French and us.

ALLENBY: I've never heard of it.

LAWRENCE: No? Nor, for the moment, has Feisal, but if he finds out there'll be hell to pay. So it's vital that he and his people should continually be fed, from now on, the right kind of lies by the right kind of liar. Therefore this man of yours has to be a very senior officer. Then his lies will have real weight.

ALLENBY: I thought you didn't approve of senior officers.

LAWRENCE: I don't approve of the man I've just described. And nor, I suspect, do you. But it's the man you want for the job. Not me, General.

ALLENBY: Possibly. The difficulty is that another man hasn't already operated successfully for months behind the Turkish lines, hasn't already won the trust of the Arab rebels, and hasn't taken Akaba.

LAWRENCE: What does Akaba prove?

ALLENBY: Enough.

LAWRENCE: Do you know why I took Akaba? Do you know why I went off alone into the desert in the first place?

ALLENBY: Escape from an office?

LAWRENCE: A little true.

ALLENBY: Escape from yourself?

LAWRENCE: I'm a Greek scholar. I have a profound belief in the virtues of self-knowledge.

ALLENBY: A man can have a belief without practising it.

LAWRENCE (*appreciatively*): I grant you the point. Escape from myself then. What else?

ALLENBY: Escape from too much thinking?

LAWRENCE: No. You can't escape from that, even in the desert.

ALLENBY: But the desert is a cleaner place to think in than an office.

LAWRENCE: There's nothing clean or dirty but thinking makes it so. And death is dirty, even in the desert. Still, I grant you the point.

ALLENBY: Finally, a burning desire to show off to my predecessor, General Murray?

LAWRENCE: Also true. (*Admiringly*) I must say you've done pretty well, so far.

ALLENBY: Thank you. (*Politely*) Well, now, shall we get back to the business on hand?

LAWRENCE (*sadly*): This *is* the business on hand, I'm afraid. You've diagnosed my motives for Akaba and the rest of it quite accurately – although you left out the most important one of all – a cold-blooded experiment with will-power – but at least you must admit that all these motives have one thing in common. They're all flagrantly selfish.

ALLENBY: Possibly. Does that matter?

LAWRENCE: This job is for a Messiah. For a visionary with real faith – not for an intellectual misfit.

ALLENBY (*off-handedly*): But you like the Arabs, don't you?

LAWRENCE: It's not enough to like them. Your man must believe in them and their destiny.

ALLENBY: What about your own country and *its* destiny?

LAWRENCE (*quietly*): Oh yes. I believe in that. And I grant you that in war my country has a perfect right to demand my life. I doubt if it has the right to demand more.

ALLENBY: Aren't you exaggerating the demands of this job a bit?

LAWRENCE (*simply*): No. You're a trained commander, you see. When you send men out to die, you don't question whether it's *right* – only whether it's *wise*. If it's unwise, it's wrong, and only then your conscience pricks. My conscience isn't Sandhurst trained. It's as undrilled as my salute, and so soft it must have the armour-plating of a cause to believe in. (*After a pause*) How on earth can one *think* oneself into a belief?

(*Pause.*)

ALLENBY (*again off-handedly*): I suppose one can't. But mightn't it be possible to *will* oneself into it?

(*Pause.*)

LAWRENCE (*laughing*): You're a bit of a Mephisto, aren't you?

ALLENBY: I'm flattered to be thought so.

LAWRENCE: Do you know, General – I think you and I might get along very well.

ALLENBY: I'm sure I hope so, Major.

(*Pause.*)

LAWRENCE: Well, the first thing will be money.

ALLENBY: How much?

LAWRENCE: The Turks are lavish spenders and we shall

have to outbid them. Say two hundred thousand.

ALLENBY (*doubtfully*): Hm.

LAWRENCE (*cheerfully*): Thinking of the Treasury? Put it under the head of propaganda. They'll like that. It's fashionable. I shall want it all in gold, of course. The Arabs distrust bits of paper. (*Turning to the map*) Akaba must be made the main Arab base, instead of Jeddah; and I suggest you put Colonel Joyce in charge of it.

ALLENBY: What about Colonel Barrington?

LAWRENCE: Oh, put him on somebody's staff. Make him a general, I'm sure he's overdue. Now the most important thing of all, and this you *must* do—

ALLENBY (*mildly*): One moment, Major Lawrence. I think I must remind you that I have not yet offered you this appointment.

LAWRENCE: No. Nor you have. And I haven't accepted it, yet, either. Still, I might as well give you my views – don't you think – as I'm here. So – proceeding – Feisal must be detached from the forces of the Sherif of Mecca and made Commander-in-Chief of all Arab forces in the field, under the orders of yourself. And – for reasons purely of prestige – a small regular Arab force must be formed and trained to operate frontally at the decisive moment – but, of course, our main and vital effort will continue to lie in irregular operations behind the enemy lines. (*After a moment*) I think that's all.

ALLENBY: Good.

LAWRENCE: Well. I'd better not take up any more of your time, General. I'm sure you've got a host of important things to do. So I'll be off now, if that's all right.

ALLENBY: That's all right.

LAWRENCE: I've got a few things to turn over in my mind, too. By the way, some time you must convert me about Chippendale. I've always thought he was over-rated. But I'm rather a Philistine about furniture. I don't use it much, you see. (*At the door*) Well, goodbye, sir.

ALLENBY: Goodbye.

LAWRENCE: And I suppose I shall hear from you?

ALLENBY: Yes. You'll hear from me.

(LAWRENCE flashes a smile of farewell, turns to the door, and then turns back, having evidently forgotten something. He produces his eccentric salute.)

One of these days I really must show you how to do that.

LAWRENCE: Yes, sir, when we both have the time.

(He goes out.)

THE LIGHTS FADE

SCENE II

A spotlight comes on gradually to illuminate the face of the TURKISH GENERAL. *He is speaking into the mouthpiece of a dictaphone.*

GENERAL: Circular telegram to all centres of Turkish Military Intelligence, Central Arabia. Most secret. Begins. Despite all our endeavours and the raising of the reward for Lawrence's capture to the unprecedented sum of twenty thousand pounds, he remains at large, operating behind our lines.

(The lights have come on to show the room in which the GENERAL *sits, or rather reclines, for he is on a divan, leaning against pillows. It is a small sitting room with two doors, one leading to his bedroom, the other to the stairs. The* TURKISH CAPTAIN *sits in an armchair in a carelessly informal attitude, looking at an illustrated magazine.)*

The elimination of this terrorist has now become of vital concern, not only to the success of our military operations, but to the very continuance of our dominion in Arabia.

CAPTAIN: You're making him sound too important. You don't want to start a panic, do you?

GENERAL *(mildly)*: Don't interrupt. Read your magazine. *(Into mouthpiece)* Since his return to Arabia six months

75

ago Lawrence has been known to have contacted secret revolutionary groups in places as far apart as Jerusalem, Damascus and Beirut. At present he is reported to be operating in the district of Deraa itself. His aim is, probably, to start a general uprising against us, timed to coincide with a British offensive in Palestine. Meanwhile he continues his guerilla activities against our lines of communication. All this poses a threat that must on no account be taken lightly.

CAPTAIN (*angrily*): Can you see them taking it lightly? They already think he has supernatural powers.

GENERAL (*into mouthpiece*): Paragraph Two. Certain additional facts on Lawrence have now come to light. One. Despite rumours to the contrary he does not wear female disguise. The recent practice of forcible unveiling of women will therefore cease, as injurious to civilian goodwill. Two. The description of Lawrence as already circulated is accurate and has been vouched for (*with a look at the* CAPTAIN) by an officer of my staff, who once came into close contact with him.

(*The* CAPTAIN *has jumped up.*)

CAPTAIN: Delete that.

GENERAL (*mildly*): I wasn't going to say which member of my staff.

CAPTAIN: You would if Constantinople asked.

GENERAL: I will, if you don't sit down and keep quiet. (*Into mouthpiece*) Three. In view of information recently come to hand regarding Lawrence's sexual proclivities, the watch at present being maintained on brothels and similar places may be discontinued —

CAPTAIN (*eagerly*): That's interesting. What information?

GENERAL: I'm sorry to disappoint you. The information was decisively negative.

CAPTAIN: In every way? (*The* GENERAL *nods*) That doesn't seem likely to me.

GENERAL (*genially*): I'm sure it doesn't, but ascetics do exist, you know.

CAPTAIN: But no one is born an ascetic. Is Lawrence very religious?

GENERAL: His self-denial is self-imposed. It has also a very revealing aspect.

CAPTAIN: What?

GENERAL: He avoids physical contact of any kind. Even shaking hands requires an effort.

CAPTAIN: I can't see what's so revealing about that —

GENERAL: Can't you? (*Into mouthpiece*) Paragraph Four —

CAPTAIN (*sulkily*): What does it reveal?

GENERAL (*patiently*): A rebellious body, a strong will and a troubled spirit. May I go on?

CAPTAIN: You mean he'd like to, but won't admit he'd like to, and so he doesn't?

GENERAL: You put it very subtly. (*Into mouthpiece*) Paragraph Four. Most important. It must be brought to the attention of all personnel that the capture of Lawrence alive should now be their primary objective. When captured the criminal will not be interrogated locally, but will be handed over forthwith to the requisite high authority. By Order Military Governor, District of Deraa. Message ends.

> (*He puts down the mouthpiece and goes over to the table where he pours himself out a glass of wine. The* CAPTAIN *watches him disapprovingly.*)

A real French burgundy. Have some?

> (*The* CAPTAIN *shakes his head.*)

You're such a good boy. (*Examining the glass*) I'm so glad I'm not a Christian. In their religion this isn't a sin —

CAPTAIN: If I capture Lawrence, I shall shoot the swine.

GENERAL (*mildly*): You really are very foolish, aren't you. Your bullet might well lose us Arabia. Can't you see that the man's death, by itself, would solve nothing? The Arabs would go on believing in this myyth that he's taught them, Arabia for the Arabs — one race, one land, one nation. For a thousand years out here before he came, that idea was only the harmless dream of a few religious fanatics. But he's shown them the way to turn it into fact. Only half a fact as

77

yet, Allah be praised, but even that half is a grave danger to our Empire. The whole fact? Well, then the world is in danger.

CAPTAIN (*carelessly*): The world can sleep easily, I think.

GENERAL (*gravely*): Feisal has chosen Damascus as his capital.

(*The* CAPTAIN *laughs.*)

I'd laugh too if I didn't know that the brain that planted that fantasy is as brilliant, ice-cold and ruthless as any revolutionary's in history. Do you really think that a bullet in that brain will turn the Arabs back now?

CAPTAIN (*shrugging*): What will?

(*Pause. The* GENERAL *sips his wine.*)

GENERAL: Well, I suppose that what a brain can create, the same brain can destroy.

CAPTAIN: Get him to recant, you mean?

GENERAL: It's the traditional method of dealing with heresy.

CAPTAIN: But how do you do it?

GENERAL (*shrugging*): By persuasion, I suppose. (*Looking at him*) What a pity about this climate. It ruins a fair complexion. It shouldn't have affected yours, though, with your Circassian blood.

CAPTAIN: I have no Circassian blood.

GENERAL: I thought you told me that you had.

CAPTAIN: It was you who told me that I had.

GENERAL: Some time ago, I imagine.

CAPTAIN: I don't think you'll get Lawrence to recant by torture.

GENERAL: Who said anything about torture? Persuasion was the word I used.

CAPTAIN (*incredulously*): You'd argue him into it?

GENERAL: Isn't that the best way of getting someone to admit he's wrong? After all, he is wrong. The Arabs' readiness of statehood is a lie and he knows it. That should give his interrogator a considerable advantage. To get him to admit that it's a lie? Difficult. With a man of faith, a real fanatic — like Feisal — impossible. But with an intellectual Englishman who believes only in his own will — and his own destiny — well, such faiths might be shaken. And another faith too — even more vulnerable — what I hear he calls his bodily integrity. One would probably have to start by teaching him a few of the facts of life.

CAPTAIN: Surely if he's an intellectual he must know the facts of life.

(*The* GENERAL *laughs.*)

Have I said something stupid?

GENERAL: Don't let it concern you. (*He finishes his glass*) Yes, it's a strange relationship I have with Lawrence. He doesn't even know of my existence, while I probably already know more about him than he knows about himself. I wish all relationships were so pleasant and uncomplicated.

(*He looks at the* CAPTAIN, *who turns away.*)

There's one thing I don't know about him. I wonder if he really believes that all the sacrifice is worth it.

(*The* GENERAL *has poured himself another glass of wine.*)

CAPTAIN: Sacrifice? Sacrifice of what?

GENERAL (*taking a sip of his wine and ruffling the* CAPTAIN'S *hair*): Oh, of everything that makes life worth living.

THE LIGHTS FADE

SCENE III

A railway embankment. Reclining against a telegraph pole is LAWRENCE, *dressed in inconspicuously ragged Arab clothes. As the lights come on he is working on a pencil sketch of the railway.* HAMED *comes on, and drops down beside him. There is a silence as* LAWRENCE *continues to sketch.* HAMED *feels in his clothes for a chicken bone, which he proceeds to gnaw.*

HAMED (*at length*): Bad news.

LAWRENCE: Your face told me.

HAMED: They refused the money, and promised nothing.

LAWRENCE (*still sketching*): Why?

HAMED (*between bites*): Frightened. With good cause. Of the three men you visited in this town last month, two have been arrested and the other is in hiding. But they have his family and the families of the other two.

LAWRENCE (*after a pause*): Who talked?

HAMED: One of Dakhil's children. It seems you gave him a present — an English half-penny. He showed it in the market and tried to sell it. The great el Aurans had given it to him, he said. A policeman heard him.

(*Pause.*)

LAWRENCE: Is Dakhil arrested?

HAMED: Yes, and Ali. It was Suleiman who escaped.

LAWRENCE (*still sketching*): But they have his family?

HAMED: Yes. Even the old grandmother. Or so they say.

(*Pause.*)

LAWRENCE: An English half-penny. It was there with the gold. I don't know why. Because it was bigger and brighter the child wanted it and I let him play with it. I meant to get it back from him when I left — but — I forgot. (*With sudden tension in his voice*) I forgot. (*He resumes his sketching. In a level voice*) Have they killed Dakhil and Ali?

HAMED (*shrugging*): Let us hope so.

LAWRENCE: Yes.

HAMED: What are you doing?

LAWRENCE: Drawing a plan of the Deraa airfield. Also that road, down there in the valley, along which our men will march — when the day comes.

HAMED: Will the day come?

LAWRENCE (*gently*): You only ask that to anger me, Hamed. It pleases you sometimes to anger me. You know the day will come.

HAMED: But when?

LAWRENCE (*after a pause*): In Allah and Allenby's good time.

HAMED (*stretching himself out*): Sometimes I think both have deserted us.

LAWRENCE: They haven't – but if you talk like that, they may. And so may I.

HAMED (*laughing*): You?

> (*The thought is plainly only laughable to* HAMED. *He stretches himself out, and belches happily.*)

What will happen after we win the war? Will you make Prince Feisal King of all Arabia?

LAWRENCE: It won't be for me to make anybody king of anything, Hamed. Prince Feisal will choose for himself. Who am I to make kings?

HAMED (*after a pause*): There was a story in our camp at Azrak last night that the English King and the French President have made an agreement after the war to divide Arabia between them. The English will take all the lands beyond the Jordan and the French will take Syria and the North.

> (*Pause.*)

LAWRENCE (*with bland unconcern*): You have a fine ear for a story, Hamed.

HAMED: The Headman of Russia – a great and noble rebel – whose name I don't remember —

LAWRENCE: Lenin.

HAMED: Yes, Lenin. He has told it to the world. It was an agreement made two years ago – before you came to us, el Aurans —

LAWRENCE (*interrupting*): The great and noble rebel lies in his teeth. There is no such agreement. Could there be, and I not know?

HAMED (*after a pause*): You could be lying to us. You could have lied to us from the beginning.

> (*He has said it for fun, hoping to get an irritated response from* LAWRENCE. LAWRENCE, *however, does not answer nor meet his glance.*)

(*Rather pathetically, after a pause*) That was a joke, el Aurans.

LAWRENCE: Yes, Hamed, I know. (*He continues his sketch*) Whenever you hear this story again, will you remember that you are my friend, and beat the man who tells it?

HAMED: Yes. (*Without moving*) There is a Turkish soldier walking towards us.

LAWRENCE (*also not moving*): Did he see me sketching?

HAMED: I don't know.

LAWRENCE: Have you anything on you, if you are searched?

HAMED: The gold and the list.

LAWRENCE: Be asleep. We don't know each other. Whatever happens, have nothing to do with me.

> (HAMED *obediently closes his eyes.* LAWRENCE *placidly continues to sketch as a* TURKISH SERGEANT *comes on. He walks past the two* MEN, *apparently not noticing them. Then he stops and walks back to* LAWRENCE.)

SERGEANT: An artist?

LAWRENCE: I get pleasure in this, but I am no artist.

SERGEANT: Let me see.

LAWRENCE: I would not affront your Excellency's eyes.

> (*He drops the sketch on to his lap.*)

SERGEANT: You have a white skin for these parts. What is your race?

LAWRENCE: Circassian.

SERGEANT: Circassian? They are rare here.

LAWRENCE: Yes. We are rare.

SERGEANT: What are you doing in Deraa?

LAWRENCE: My business is lawful.

SERGEANT: What is it?

LAWRENCE: Travelling.

SERGEANT (*looking at* HAMED): Alone?

LAWRENCE: Alone.

SERGEANT: Where to?

LAWRENCE: Damascus.

SERGEANT: On your feet, Circassian.

(LAWRENCE *gets up quietly, apparently not alarmed.*)
You're lying, aren't you?

LAWRENCE: Why should I lie to your Excellency?

SERGEANT: I think you're a deserter.

LAWRENCE: With respect, we Circassians are exempt from
military service —

SERGEANT: Don't argue. You're of military age, and therefore a deserter.

LAWRENCE: The argument has force, but hardly logic. By
a special decree —

SERGEANT (*smiling*): You want logic, do you?

(*He draws his revolver.*)
Well, here it is. (*Quite mildly*) Now come with me.

LAWRENCE: Where to?

SERGEANT: Why should I tell you?

(*He digs him in the ribs with his revolver.* LAWRENCE
*drops the sketch, then stoops to pick it up. He glances at
it. Then carelessly crumples it up and throws it away. It
lands close to* HAMED.)

LAWRENCE (*going*): Why indeed, your Excellency?

(*He goes off with the* SERGEANT. HAMED, *as if in sleep,
puts an arm out and picks up the drawing.*)

THE LIGHTS FADE

SCENE IV

The lights come on slowly to reveal the TURKISH
GENERAL *sitting in his room in an attitude and with an
expression that denotes considerable nervous tension.
He seems too to be straining to hear something, but it is
not apparent what; although, at one moment, we hear
a shout of harsh laughter, cut off abruptly by the evident
closing of a door. After a pause the* CAPTAIN *comes in.*

The GENERAL *does not look at him. The* CAPTAIN *sits in his favourite chair, and picks up a magazine.*

CAPTAIN: What in the name of God is going on in the guard room?

(*Pause.*)

GENERAL: They're beating a deserter.

CAPTAIN: Your orders?

GENERAL: Yes.

CAPTAIN: Why?

GENERAL (*after a pause*): He was insolent.

CAPTAIN: I didn't see much. I don't like those sights. But I did see a white skin. At least it *was* white, I suppose?

GENERAL: Yes.

CAPTAIN: A Circassian?

GENERAL: Yes.

CAPTAIN: Do I guess accurately at the form his insolence took?

GENERAL: I expect so.

(*Pause.*)

CAPTAIN: If it's reported there could be trouble.

GENERAL: I don't think so.

CAPTAIN: You should stop it.

GENERAL: Why?

CAPTAIN: They look as if they might kill him.

GENERAL: He can stop it himself. He can stop it at any second. He has only to say yes.

(*Pause.*)

CAPTAIN: By the look I caught of him he's not paying you much of a compliment.

GENERAL: No.

(*The* CAPTAIN, *after staring at the* GENERAL, *gets up suddenly.*)

CAPTAIN: I'm going to stop it.

GENERAL: No.

CAPTAIN: I'm going to. For your sake, as much as his.

(*He goes to the door. The* GENERAL *bars his way.*)

GENERAL (*quietly*): Now, listen carefully. It will be better for you if you don't go down there.

(*The* CAPTAIN, *after staring at him, walks past him and out. The* GENERAL *turns back into the room, and pours himself a glass of wine. He is pouring himself another when the* CAPTAIN *comes back, and stares at him with unbelieving eyes.*)

CAPTAIN (*violently*): Do you know who it is?

(*He reads his answer in the* GENERAL'S *face.*)

So that's why you tried to stop me from going down there —

GENERAL: I told you it would be better for you if you didn't.

CAPTAIN: Is that a threat?

GENERAL: Yes. Did you say anything to the men?

CAPTAIN: No.

GENERAL (*strength returning to his voice*): You will say nothing to anyone, now or at any time. If you do, I'll have you shot. He's a Circassian deserter, called Mohammed Ibn Dheilan. He comes from Kuneitra. He is being punished for insolence.

CAPTAIN (*with disgust*): Punished? Do you know what they're doing to him now?

GENERAL: They've stopped beating him?

CAPTAIN: Yes.

GENERAL: I see.

CAPTAIN (*hysterically*): What they're doing to him now — are those your orders too?

(*There is no reply from the* GENERAL.)

I thought you couldn't have known — not even you, I thought, could have ordered that —

GENERAL: You misjudged me.

CAPTAIN: I hate the man, but this is vile and horrible.

GENERAL: It's vile and horrible to be mangled in a wrecked troop train.

CAPTAIN: So it's revenge —

GENERAL: No. If it were I might enjoy it.

CAPTAIN: What about your talk that you'd persuade him to admit he's been wrong?

GENERAL: What about it?

CAPTAIN: Is that what you meant?

GENERAL: I said, if you remember, that his interrogator might have to start by teaching him a few of the facts of life.

CAPTAIN (*sitting suddenly*): And this is only the beginning?

GENERAL: It may be the ending too.

CAPTAIN (*muttering*): You mean he may die under it?

GENERAL: No. They have my orders not to kill him. I mean that if my plan succeeds tonight it will be the end for him. Bodily violated, will broken, enemy destroyed. (*Sharply*) There's someone on the stairs.

CAPTAIN (*at the door*): They're bringing him up. (*Hysterically*) I don't want to see it.

GENERAL: Control yourself.

> (*The* TURKISH SERGEANT *and another* MAN *appear on the threshold. They are supporting* LAWRENCE *between them. He is half-conscious and his head has fallen on to his chest.*)

(*Quietly*) Very well, Captain. Report to me in the morning.

> (*The* CAPTAIN *comes automatically to attention. Then he goes out, averting his eyes from the sight of* LAWRENCE *as he passes him.*)

(*To* SERGEANT) Well?

> (*The* SERGEANT, *with a broad grin, nods slowly.*)

He said yes?

> (*The* SERGEANT *shakes his head, still grinning. The* GENERAL *looks at him questioningly.*)

SERGEANT (*at length*): He didn't need to say it.

> (*The* GENERAL, *after a pause, nods quietly.*)

He's a strange one, this, General, I'm telling you.

GENERAL (*sharply*): All right. Let him go.

> (*The two* MEN *release* LAWRENCE *whose knees buckle under him. He slips face downwards and motionless on to the floor.*)

86

GENERAL: Get out.

(*The two* MEN *go. The* GENERAL *goes slowly over to*
LAWRENCE. *He kneels down and, quite gently, pulls his*
head back and looks at him.)

(*Quietly*) You must understand that I know.

(*He replaces* LAWRENCE'S *head gently on the floor.*)
You can hear me, I think. (*Slowly repeating*) You must
understand that I know.

(*There is no sign from* LAWRENCE *that he has heard.*
Throughout the ensuing scene he remains completely
motionless.

The GENERAL *pours a glass of wine and takes it over*
to LAWRENCE. *He thrusts it in front of his face, but*
LAWRENCE *makes no movement. The* GENERAL *puts the*
glass on the floor beside LAWRENCE *and then stands near*
him, looking down.)

I do pity you, you know. You won't ever believe it, but
it's true. I know what was revealed to you tonight, and I
know what that revelation will have done to you. You can
think I mean just a broken will, if you like. That might have
destroyed you by itself. But I mean more than that. Far
more. (*Angrily*) But why did you leave yourself so vulnerable? What's the use of learning if it doesn't teach you to
know yourself as you really are?

(*Pause.*)

It's a pity your desert adventure couldn't have ended
cleanly, in front of a firing squad. But that's for lesser
enemies – not for you.

(*He kneels down.*)

For you, killing wasn't enough.

(*He lifts* LAWRENCE'S *head again.*)

You had to be – destroyed.

(*He lowers* LAWRENCE'S *head, and stands up.*)

The door at the bottom of the stairs through there is un-
locked. It leads into the street.

(*He walks into his bedroom.* LAWRENCE, *at length,*
waveringly thrusts out a hand towards the glass of wine.

He draws it to him and drains it. Then, painfully and slowly, he begins to drag himself across the floor towards the other door.)

THE LIGHTS FADE

Scene V

Before the lights come on we hear the sound of a military band playing a jaunty march, and the sound of voices and laughter.

Voice (*from darkness*): Hold it, General.

    (*There is a flash from the darkness, and the sound of general laughter.*

    The lights go on to show a room in Allenby's *field headquarters.* Allenby, Storrs, Barrington, *the* ADC, *a war correspondent* (Franks, *recognized as the lecturer*) *and a* Photographer *are all present. Everyone seems very jovial. A band is playing outside.*

    It is Allenby *who has just had his photograph taken.*)

Franks: I think, if you don't mind, General, just one more. And this time can we, perhaps, have a slightly more triumphant expression?

Allenby: What? More triumphant? I thought I'd made myself odiously so in that one.

Franks: Forgive me, sir, but you really didn't look as if you'd just won a great battle.

Allenby: How does one look as if one had just won a great battle? What do you suggest, Storrs?

Storrs: A rather bored and impassive expression, sir, as if taking Jerusalem was something that happened to you every day.

Franks: No, no. Not bored. Impassive, if you like, but stern and unyielding and – well – victorious. Now shall we try again, sir? (*To* Photographer) Ready?

    (*The* Photographer *nods.*)

Right, sir, if you don't mind.

    (ALLENBY *does as bidden.*)

Just a little to the left. That's right. Now – can we try that expression?

    ALLENBY (*muttering*): Oh God, this is agony.

    FRANKS: It won't last very long, sir.

    (ALLENBY *tries an unyielding expression.*)

No. That isn't quite right.

    STORRS: Of course a backcloth of Jerusalem would help. And what about some Turkish prisoners, lying on the floor in chains.

    ALLENBY: Careful, Storrs. That appointment isn't official yet.

    FRANKS: What appointment is that?

    ALLENBY: Military Governor of Jerusalem.

    FRANKS: Oh. Good. (*To* STORRS) We must take a photograph of you.

    STORRS (*cowering*): Oh no.

    ALLENBY (*laughing*): Oh yes. And get him to look gubernatorial.

    FRANKS (*patiently*): Now, sir. Can we try again?

    (ALLENBY *poses.*)

Now think of Jerusalem.

    ALLENBY (*through his teeth*): Jerusalem I've got. I'm thinking of Damascus.

    BARRINGTON (*admiring his expression*): Very good, sir. That has the real Wellington look.

    ALLENBY: Quiet, Brigadier – unless you want to be a colonel again.

    BARRINGTON (*aggrieved*): I meant it seriously, sir.

    FRANKS: Hold it, General.

    (*The flashlight is released again and the photograph taken.* ALLENBY *relaxes with relief.*)

Perhaps just one more —

    ALLENBY: No, certainly not. (*Pointing to a tray of drinks*) Have a drink, gentlemen, and then leave me to fight my war.

(BARRINGTON, STORRS, *and the* ADC *go towards the tray, where the* ADC *pours them drinks. The* PHOTO-GRAPHER *begins to pack up his apparatus.*)

FRANKS (*to* ALLENBY, *with notebook now handy*): There's not very much more of your war left to fight, is there, General?

ALLENBY (*sharply*): There certainly is, and please don't give people at home any other impression. The Turkish Army is by no means beaten. It's suffered a defeat, but it's retiring in good order. There are many more battles to come and they'll become increasingly harder as the Turks shorten their lines of communication.

PHOTOGRAPHER (*at door*): Will that be all, Mr Franks?

FRANKS: Yes. Thank you.

(*As* PHOTOGRAPHER *prepares to leave.*)

Just a moment. (*To* ALLENBY) We've rigged up a makeshift studio next door. Is there any hope of enticing you there tomorrow?

ALLENBY: I'm afraid I'm far too busy.

FRANKS: Pity. (*To* PHOTOGRAPHER) All right.

PHOTOGRAPHER: Goodnight, gentlemen.

(*He goes.*)

FRANKS: I've just one last request, sir.

ALLENBY: Come and have a whisky and soda while you make it.

(*They join* BARRINGTON *and* STORRS.)

FRANKS: My editor is very anxious for me to get an interview with Major Lawrence.

ALLENBY: I've no doubt he is.

FRANKS: Could I have your authority?

ALLENBY: My authority over Lawrence is sketchy, at the best of times. As regards an interview — even with you — I should say it was non-existent. Do you agree, Storrs?

STORRS: I would imagine that it might be rather easier for Mr Franks to get an interview with the Dalai Lama —

ALLENBY: Besides, when last heard from he was at Deraa, some hundred and fifty miles behind the enemy lines —

BARRINGTON: No, sir. He's here. Didn't you know?

ALLENBY (*bewildered*): Here?

BARRINGTON: Yes, sir. I saw him an hour ago. He was waiting to see you, he said. I'm sorry, sir, I thought you must have been told.

ALLENBY (*To* ADC): Did you know?

ADC: No, sir.

ALLENBY: Well, go and get him at once.

ADC: Yes, sir.

   (*He goes out.*)

ALLENBY: Lawrence waiting? Usually he doesn't even knock. I look up and he's standing facing me. (*To* STORRS) I'd have thought he'd have let you know, at least.

STORRS (*shrugging*): I've ceased to speculate. It's unfruitful.

ALLENBY: Anyway he's here, which is the main thing, and he couldn't have come at a better time. I suppose he knew exactly when I'd take Jerusalem, although, God knows, I didn't. The man's prescience is satanic.

FRANKS: May I stay, sir, for a moment?

ALLENBY: Yes, if you like. I doubt if it'll be much use to you. Storrs, get me a whisky and soda —

ADC (*opening door*): Major Lawrence.

   (LAWRENCE *comes in, walking with a limp that he is evidently at pains to conceal. He is in Arab clothes.*)

ALLENBY: Why didn't you let me know you were here?

LAWRENCE: I understood you were busy with the press.

ALLENBY (*with a glance at* FRANKS): Ah. I see. This gentleman is the culprit. Mr Franks, Major Lawrence.

LAWRENCE (*politely*): How do you do.

ALLENBY (*taking his whisky from* STORRS): Oh, thank you.

STORRS: Hullo, TE.

LAWRENCE: Hullo.

BARRINGTON: Hullo, Lawrence. Have you hurt yourself? You're limping a bit.

LAWRENCE: An accident with a camel. I got dragged

through some barbed wire.

ALLENBY (*mischievously*): I think Mr Franks has a request to make of you, Lawrence.

LAWRENCE (*turning politely to* FRANKS): Oh really?

FRANKS (*nervously*): Well – Major – we war correspondents have our duty to perform like everyone else – so don't be too harsh with me. But you realize that the public interest about you at home has become pretty intense lately and colourful figures are rare enough in this war, and —

> (*Glancing nervously at* ALLENBY *and* STORRS, *who are plainly enjoying their anticipation of* LAWRENCE's *response.*)

Well, I suppose I'd just better come straight out with it. Can I have an interview?

LAWRENCE: When?

FRANKS: Well – tomorrow.

LAWRENCE: What time?

FRANKS: Any time that would suit you. Ten o'clock?

LAWRENCE: Yes. Where?

FRANKS: Well, anywhere, but of course, what would be far the best would be if you would come along to the studio I've rigged up – and then we could get some really beautiful photographs.

LAWRENCE: Where is your studio?

FRANKS (*hardly able to believe his luck*): Next door to here.

ALLENBY (*approaching* LAWRENCE *with a slightly worried frown*): He has backcloths at his studio.

FRANKS (*writing feverishly*): Oh, General, you go on far too much about those backcloths. A photographic cloth can be quite plain, you know. Would you allow yourself to be photographed in front of a backcloth?

LAWRENCE: Whatever you think best.

FRANKS: Good. Oh, good. Ten o'clock, then?

> (LAWRENCE *nods.*)

You're not going to let me down, are you?

LAWRENCE: No, I'll see you tomorrow.

FRANKS: Thank you, Major. (*To* ALLENBY) Goodnight, sir. (*To the others*) Goodnight.

> (*He goes.* STORRS, *conscious of an atmosphere, hastily finishes his whisky.*)

STORRS: We'd better leave you too, sir.

ALLENBY (*looking at* LAWRENCE): If you would.

STORRS (*casually to* LAWRENCE): I hope I shall see something of you while you're here.

LAWRENCE: I won't be here long.

STORRS (*to* ALLENBY): Well, goodbye, sir.

> (*He goes.*)

BARRINGTON: Could I have just two words with Lawrence, sir? Rather important.

> (ALLENBY *nods.* BARRINGTON *turns to* LAWRENCE.)

I've had a rather sharp inquiry from the Foreign Office regarding the question of so-called atrocities on your front —

LAWRENCE: I have no front.

BARRINGTON: Well, during your raids and ambushes and things. It's been alleged through a neutral embassy that you don't take prisoners.

> (*He awaits a response from* LAWRENCE. *He remains silent.*)

An official denial from you would help enormously.

LAWRENCE (*politely*): Then you shall have it.

BARRINGTON: Good. Would you let me have it tomorrow, in writing?

LAWRENCE: In writing?

> (BARRINGTON *nods.*)

All right.

BARRINGTON: Thank you. (*He turns to go.*)

LAWRENCE: The Arabs have been less demanding. My denials to them on more important issues are confined to the verbal.

BARRINGTON (*stopping short*): You mean the denial would be untrue?

LAWRENCE: Not entirely untrue. Misleading is a better word. We do take prisoners — when we are not being chased, and can spare the men to escort them to Feisal, and I've managed to keep some control of the situation. A combination of those contingencies is unhappily rare.

BARRINGTON: But this admission is very serious.

LAWRENCE (*raising his voice slightly*): I agree. Did the neutral embassy have anything to say about the Turkish treatment of Arab prisoners?

BARRINGTON: No, but if there have been reprisals —

LAWRENCE (*with a sharp laugh*): Reprisals? The old game of who started it? Who's to say? And does it matter? I can only tell you that for a long time now no wounded Arab soldier has been left on the field for the Turks to take. If we can't move him we shoot him.

BARRINGTON (*hotly*): Listen, Lawrence — the Turk's a clean fighter.

LAWRENCE: I've no doubt, General, but ours isn't a clean war. It's an Asiatic revolution, and a European who tries to direct the course of such a thing is apt to find himself rather out of his depth.

BARRINGTON: But —

ALLENBY (*interposing*): That's enough, Barrington. You can see Lawrence tomorrow.

BARRINGTON: Yes, sir.

(*He salutes punctiliously, turns on his heels and goes.*)

ALLENBY: Don't worry about that.

LAWRENCE: No, sir. I won't.

ALLENBY: You made it sound pretty grim, I must say.

LAWRENCE: I could have made it sound grimmer.

ALLENBY: Well, you've come at a good time.

LAWRENCE: Yes, sir. Congratulations.

ALLENBY: Thank you. Tell me, how did you get the news?

LAWRENCE: I didn't, until I reached here.

ALLENBY: What did you come for, then?

LAWRENCE: To ask you to find me another job.

(*Pause.*)

ALLENBY: What other job?

94

LAWRENCE: Any one at all, providing that it has nothing whatever to do with the Arab Revolt. At a pinch I suppose I could still draw you some quite useful maps.

ALLENBY (*nodding, at length*): I see. Go on.

LAWRENCE: Is my request granted?

ALLENBY: It may be. Go on. Tell me why you wish to relinquish your present post.

LAWRENCE: You're going to make it hard for me, are you?

ALLENBY (*quietly*): I see no reason to make it easy.

LAWRENCE: Yes. I admire you for that. You want my excuses for desertion?

ALLENBY: Your reasons.

LAWRENCE (*nodding appreciatively*): Very well. (*Quietly matter of fact*) I have come to believe that the Arab Revolt is a fake, founded on deceit and sustained by lies, and I want no further part in it.

ALLENBY (*making notes*): Go on.

LAWRENCE: On the military side I have only failure to report. The bridge at Yarmuk has not been blown and Arab forces have at no time successfully intervened in your campaign to date.

ALLENBY (*quietly, continuing writing*): Yes?

LAWRENCE: To sum up, the whole venture is morally, militarily and financially unjustifiable – a total washout, and should be abandoned. (*After a pause*) Anyway, I can't go on.

> (*He looks at* ALLENBY *who makes an impassive final note, laying down his pen.*)

However, if you don't agree with what I've said about the Arab Revolt and want me to suggest someone to take my place —

ALLENBY (*quietly*): There is no one to take your place. Now, dealing with your points in reverse order and leaving out the last. (*Looking at his notes*) Your military failure is untrue, even after taking into account your tendency for histrionic exaggeration. I haven't required Arab intervention yet in my campaign, and I don't expect you to succeed in blowing up every damn bridge I ask you to destroy. The Arab Revolt a fake? That's for you to say, but you told me once that you could will yourself into believing it wasn't.

LAWRENCE: I think it was you who told me. Anyway, my will has proved less trustworthy than I thought.

ALLENBY: What's happened, Lawrence?

LAWRENCE (*suddenly tired*): Can't we say battle weariness?

ALLENBY: No. Not for you.

LAWRENCE: Disillusionment, cowardice —?

ALLENBY: No. Something extraordinary happened. What?

LAWRENCE: I had a vision. It happens to people in the desert.

ALLENBY: A vision of what?

LAWRENCE: Of the truth.

ALLENBY: About the Arab Revolt?

LAWRENCE: No. About myself.

ALLENBY: And the truth is (*tapping his notes*), 'I can't go on'?

LAWRENCE: That's part of the truth.

ALLENBY: The most important part, isn't it?

LAWRENCE: No. Only the most relevant.

(*Pause.*)

ALLENBY (*suddenly*): What a pity! What an awful pity.

(LAWRENCE *looks at the floor saying nothing.* ALLENBY *gets up brusquely.*)

All right. I'll send you back to England.

LAWRENCE: I haven't asked for that.

ALLENBY: The War Office should be glad to have you. You're due for promotion, so I'll appoint you Lieutenant Colonel. I've also recommended you — some weeks ago — for the DSO so with that and your CB and your wound stripes you should make quite a show there.

(*The* SENTRY *appears.*)

Yes?

SENTRY: Mr Storrs has an urgent telegram.

ALLENBY: Send him in.

SENTRY: Yes, sir.

(LAWRENCE *gets up to go*.)

ALLENBY: No, stay. I want a word with you about your successor.

(STORRS *comes in*.)

STORRS (*handing* ALLENBY *a telegram*): Downing Street, sir. They want you to make a triumphal entry into Jerusalem on Wednesday.

ALLENBY: What do they think I am? A Roman Emperor?

STORRS: Brass bands, victory marches, beautiful girls hurling flowers at us. I'm looking forward to it. (*To* LAWRENCE) Your man Hamed is outside. Wants to see you.

LAWRENCE: He should have gone. I ordered him back to Prince Feisal's camp two hours ago.

STORRS: Well, he's determined to talk to you. Seems very agitated. When are you going back, TE?

ALLENBY (*with sudden harshness*): He's not going back.

STORRS: What?

ALLENBY: He feels he can't go on any more. He's had all that flesh and blood will stand. I see his point. I'm sending him to the War Office.

LAWRENCE (*looking at the ground*): May I go, sir? I'm feeling tired. We can talk about my – successor some other time.

ALLENBY (*carelessly*): Very well. (*As* LAWRENCE *reaches the door*) Just one moment. I shall want you to take part in this entry on Wednesday.

LAWRENCE: In what capacity?

ALLENBY: Chief British Liaison Officer to Arab Forces in the field, of course.

LAWRENCE (*murmuring*): No, sir.

ALLENBY (*coldly*): It's an order. You will march directly behind me, and attend all the various ceremonies at my side.

LAWRENCE (*with a sudden hard laugh*): Oh yes. Good textbook stuff. (*Indicating the telegram*) A general should be ready at one instant to exploit any opportunity suddenly laid open to him —

ALLENBY (*coldly*): You seem to think my order is a punishment. It isn't. The honour that is being done to you on Wednesday is an award for your past. If it gives you uncomfortable thoughts about your present that's your affair, and not mine.

LAWRENCE (*now suddenly weary*): And that's from the same textbook, isn't it? How to deal with deserters. I've learnt how to deal with them too – but not from Sandhurst training. From experience. Sad, scared, broken-willed little creatures – you can't persuade them or threaten them or even joke them back into battle. But sometimes you can shame them back. It's surprising how often – if you use the right technique. (*In a voice drained of emotion*) You know, I think that I admire you more than any man on earth, and I've never admired you more than I do at this moment. On my way here I had worked out for myself every stratagem you might use to get me to go back, and had planned all my moves to counter them. But, I'm beaten in five minutes. Can I see my bodyguard? Storrs says he's outside.

ALLENBY (*calling*): Sentry!

SENTRY (*appearing*): Sir?

ALLENBY: Get Major Lawrence's Arab servant.

SENTRY: Yes, sir.

    (*He goes out.*)

LAWRENCE: I suppose what I left out of account is the splendid core of cruelty that all great generals should have.

    (*HAMED comes in.*)

LAWRENCE: Hamed, why are you still in Gaza? You had my strict orders to return to Prince Feisal's Camp. Is that not so?

HAMED (*murmuring*): It is so, el Aurans.

LAWRENCE: Why then have you disobeyed me?

HAMED: My camel has died.

LAWRENCE (*gently*): Has it? She seemed all right this morning.

HAMED: A sudden illness must have struck her, el Aurans.

LAWRENCE: Yes. Very sudden. There was my camel —

HAMED (*looking at the ground*): She has died too.

LAWRENCE: Of the same illness?

HAMED: Assuredly. (*Looking up at* LAWRENCE) So now I must stay with you, here, el Aurans. There is now no means of leaving, is there?

LAWRENCE: Until you find another camel.

HAMED: In Gaza they are hard to find.

LAWRENCE: By Thursday morning, you must have found two new camels —

HAMED: *Two* —?

LAWRENCE (*continuing*): Two fine, fast camels every bit as good as those you have just got rid of.

HAMED (*his face lighting up with joy*): In an hour—

LAWRENCE: Listen. Thursday at the first light of dawn. (*With a look at* ALLENBY) I have a duty to perform in Jerusalem on Wednesday.

HAMED: This is not a joke?

LAWRENCE: No.

HAMED: But you said —

LAWRENCE: You should not always confuse what I say with what I do.

> (HAMED *bows suddenly to* LAWRENCE, *takes his hand, kisses it, and then places it on his head, Arab fashion. Then he turns and goes out quickly.*)

LAWRENCE (*shrugging his shoulders, facing* ALLENBY): Well, sir, I told you my will isn't what it was.

ALLENBY: I think it'll mend.

LAWRENCE: No. I'll have to try and find a substitute. (*Turning away*) But there are just two things I wish you knew.

ALLENBY: What?

LAWRENCE: The kind of deserter you're sending back. And the kind of battle you're sending him back to —

> (LAWRENCE *goes. There is a pause.*)

STORRS: You'd have made as good a diplomat as a soldier.

ALLENBY: I deserve the insult.

STORRS: No insult. But were you right to get him to go back?

ALLENBY (*angrily*): Am I supposed to care about what's right? It was necessary. That's all that concerns me. (*Unhappily*) All that ought to concern me.

(*He gets up and goes to pour himself a drink.*)
(*With a sigh*) Oh God, Storrs, won't it be wonderful when this damned war's over.

THE LIGHTS FADE

SCENE VI

(*In the darkness we hear the distant rumble of heavy gunfire.*)
Outside LAWRENCE'S *tent.* LAWRENCE *himself is shaving, using a canvas basin and a mirror hung up on a pole. A young RAF officer* (HIGGINS) *comes out of the tent with some typescript in his hand. The gunfire continues throughout the scene.*

HIGGINS: I've done it, Sir. I hope I've got it all right. Would you check it as soon as possible?

LAWRENCE: Does your pilot want to take off?

HIGGINS: Well – it's getting a bit late, sir, and the C-in-C is waiting for this. Highest priority.

LAWRENCE: Read it to me.

HIGGINS (*reading*): Operations of 25th and 26th September, 1918. I decided to place the main Arab force in the direct path of the Turkish Fourth Army's line of retreat. My staff considered this a hazardous enterprise, in view of the fact that the Fourth Army was retreating intact to cover Damascus. They thought that our untried force, outnumbered by roughly four to one, might prove no match for disciplined troops. I, on the other hand, reckoned that the element of surprise would outweigh this disadvantage. I am glad to report that events have justified my unweary optimism.

LAWRENCE: Unweary? This report has enough hubris in it without your adding to it. I said unwary.

HIGGINS (*brightly*): Oh. Sorry, sir. Unwary. (*He makes a correction*) And what was the other word you used? Hu – something?

LAWRENCE: Hubris. It's the Greek for showing-off.

HIGGINS: Oh but, sir – I mean – surely you've got something (*indicating report*) to show off about, I'd say.

LAWRENCE: You think so?

HIGGINS: The Turks caught in a trap between our chaps in the south and your chaps up here. I mean it's bloody marvellous, sir.

(*There is again no reply.*)

Bloody marvellous. (*Continuing to read*) I am happy to report that the Fourth Turkish Army has, since eleven hundred hours this morning, ceased to exist. A detailed report of the operation follows —

LAWRENCE (*interrupting*): Very well. As I have your sanction for hubris, you might as well add this to the main report. After 'ceased to exist' —

(HIGGINS *has his pencil and pad.*)

In view of this situation it is my intention to enter the City of Damascus at first light tomorrow, and to hold it in the name and authority of Prince Feisal. I assume this action will meet with your approval – an assumption forced on me by the fact that should it not it will anyway be too late for you to inform me.

HIGGINS: My gosh I'll be able to write my memoirs after the war. *Lawrence of Arabia and I* by S. R. Higgins.

LAWRENCE (*interrupting*): Did you invent that name?

HIGGINS: What? Higgins?

LAWRENCE: No. The other one.

HIGGINS: Lawrence of Arabia? Good heavens, no, sir. That's what the press have been calling you for months.

LAWRENCE: Have they? I didn't know.

(*He sits down on the ground, Arab fashion, his face expressionless, but lost in thought.*)

HIGGINS: Shall I read the detailed stuff, sir?

LAWRENCE: No. You'd better take off. Was there anything that seemed wrong to you in it?

HIGGINS (*doubtfully*): No. Well – there was just one thing –

(*He stops, looking rather scared.*)

LAWRENCE: What's that?

HIGGINS: The night raid on that station.

LAWRENCE: What about it?

HIGGINS: There's something in it, I wonder if it's wise to – I mean it is an official report.

LAWRENCE: Read it.

HIGGINS (*reading*): Operations of September 18th. (*Murmuring*) In order to complete the encirclement of Deraa – a night assault on the railway – surprise not wholly achieved – ah. Here we are, sir. Ordering the Zaali to give covering fire I went down the embankment with my personal bodyguard and laid charges. These were successfully detonated, and the bridge destroyed, but the enemy now directed his fire at the bridge, my companion being badly hit at the first burst. I attempted to drag him up the embankment but without success and, as the Turks were beginning to issue from their blockhouse, I had no recourse but to leave him, after carrying out the usual practice in such cases. I rejoined the troop, and the retirement was completed without further loss.

(*He stops.* LAWRENCE *is still looking at the ground.*)

LAWRENCE (*at length*): What part specifically do you object to?

HIGGINS: Well, sir, the implication.

LAWRENCE: That I killed the man that was wounded?

HIGGINS: Yes, sir.

LAWRENCE: But I did kill him.

HIGGINS (*shocked*): Oh. Well — (*Defiantly*) But it's not the kind of thing you say in an official report.

LAWRENCE: Isn't it? I describe later on how we killed four thousand Turks.

HIGGINS (*horrified*): Yes – but they're the enemy and this is one of your own men.

LAWRENCE: Yes.

HIGGINS: Of course, I know he was only an Arab, but still it does sound – do forgive me, sir – a bit – callous.

LAWRENCE: I see. And you'd like me to make it sound less callous?

HIGGINS: I really think you should take it out altogether, sir. I mean, there might be trouble with his wife or something—

LAWRENCE: He didn't have a wife. He once had a friend, but he's dead too.

HIGGINS (*a little cross at* LAWRENCE's *lack of imagination*): Well, I'm sure he must have had someone who'll care about his death —

LAWRENCE: Yes, he did. But I doubt if that person will give much trouble.

HIGGINS: Well, you never know. Anyway, sir – have I your permission to edit the passage a little? I could just say the burst of machine-gun fire missed you but killed him instantly.

LAWRENCE (*politely*): A very happy invention.

HIGGINS: I'll do it when I get to HQ. Goodbye, sir.

LAWRENCE (*getting up*): Goodbye.

(AUDA ABU TAYI *strides on. He looks angry, hot and weary. His clothes are torn and bloodstained.*)

AUDA: Who would have thought the day would come when Auda would grow tired of killing Turks? (*He throws down his rifle*) Old age is a terrible thing.

HIGGINS (*to* LAWRENCE): Well, sir, I'll be off.

AUDA (*squinting at him venomously*): By Allah – a Turk.
(*He picks up his rifle.*)

LAWRENCE: No. No – British.

AUDA (*accusingly*): I know the British uniform. That is a Turk.

LAWRENCE: No. An officer in King George's Air Force. (*To* HIGGINS) You'd better clear off. He thinks you're the enemy.

HIGGINS: Oh Lord! — I say — what a scruffy-looking old wog, or is he one of your generals?

LAWRENCE: Yes. That's exactly what he is.

HIGGINS: Gosh! Poor old Higgins. Always putting his foot in it. Well — goodbye, sir.

> (*He salutes again, turns and meets* AUDA's *darkly suspicious gaze. Rather nervously he salutes him too, and then goes.*)

AUDA (*wearily*): Well, my friend, is it over?

LAWRENCE: Yes.

AUDA: Tomorrow — Damascus?

LAWRENCE: Yes.

AUDA: Our enemy destroyed and the dream of two years fulfilled. Damascus! Allah indeed is good.

LAWRENCE: Allah is good.

> (*Pause.* AUDA *looks at* LAWRENCE *with thoughtful and sympathetic eyes.*)

AUDA: They have told me about Hamed.

LAWRENCE: I would not have told you.

AUDA: I am the one you should have told.

LAWRENCE: It's not a tale that should be told to a friend.

AUDA: Who else but a friend?

LAWRENCE: An enemy — or a stranger. To anyone but a friend.

AUDA (*gently*): Let's speak of other things. Let's speak of yesterday's great battle.

> (*Pause.*)

LAWRENCE: He opened his eyes for a moment when I lifted my revolver. He had them tightly closed until that moment. He was in great pain. But it was the will of fate that he should open his eyes and see me pointing the revolver at his head. He said 'Rashid will be angry with you, el Aurans.'

AUDA: I remember Rashid. He died on our march in the desert.

LAWRENCE: Yes. The day I failed with my compass. So then I said, 'Salute Rashid from me', and he smiled. Then the pain came back and he closed his eyes again. Just as I was lifting the revolver once more to his head he said 'God will give you peace'. Then I fired. The Turks were already coming out of the blockhouse.

(*Pause.*)

AUDA: The memory of it will not always be so sharp.

LAWRENCE: I once said the same to Hamed. He didn't believe it then and nor do I now.

AUDA: You must think of other things. Think of Damascus and what we must do there.

LAWRENCE: Yes.

AUDA: And all that we must do after Damascus. Only now does our fight truly begin. (*Anxiously*) You will go on fighting with us and for us, el Aurans? For Allah knows we will need you in peace even more than we have in war.

LAWRENCE: Yes. I suppose I must try and make amends —

AUDA: Amends?

LAWRENCE: To the people I've misled.

(*Pause.*)

AUDA: By Allah, I think your victories have made you mad. Have you misled us all from Mecca to Damascus – a thousand miles and more – against an enemy many times our strength?

LAWRENCE: Forgive me, Auda. It was a feeble joke.

AUDA: You will fight for us in peace as you fought for us in war?

LAWRENCE: Yes. To the limits of my strength. Can I say more?

AUDA: No. For what limits are there to the strength of el Aurans?

LAWRENCE: Some, I think.

AUDA: None, I know. (*He embraces* LAWRENCE) I have lost many sons – yes, and grandsons – but for none of them did I grieve so much as I did for you – that day when you left us and went to Gaza and we thought you had gone for ever. What time tonight?

LAWRENCE: Midnight. We shall be in Damascus by dawn.

(BARRINGTON *comes on hurriedly*.)

BARRINGTON: Ah, Lawrence. Good. I'm glad I've found you. You really ought to leave clearer indications about the exact site of your headquarters. You see —

(AUDA, *under the stress of an evidently stormy emotion, clutches* BARRINGTON'S *tunic, and pulls him to him*.)

AUDA: Who are you?

BARRINGTON: My name's Barrington. General Barrington – GHQ.

AUDA (*fiercely*): Tell them, GHQ, tell them in England what I Auda Abu Tayi say of el Aurans. Of Manhood (*he shakes* BARRINGTON) the man. Of Freedom (*he shakes him again*) free. A spirit (*he shakes him a third time*) without equal. I see no flaw in him. And if any offal-eating traitor should ever deny the greatness of that man (*pointing to* LAWRENCE) may the curse of Auda fall upon his dung-filled head.

(*He shakes* BARRINGTON *a fourth time, then releases him abruptly and strides out*.)

BARRINGTON: One of your chaps?

LAWRENCE: Yes.

BARRINGTON: The Bedouin are excitable people. Far too excitable.

LAWRENCE: How did you get up here?

BARRINGTON: By armoured car from Deraa. I was with the Fourth Cavalry Division when they entered the town this morning. The GOC sent me here to find you and bring you down there to him at once.

LAWRENCE: Oh? Under arrest?

BARRINGTON (*impatiently*): No, of course not, but he's raging – absolutely raging – and God knows – after the sights I saw this morning – I don't blame him. Apparently some of your wogs sneaked into the place last night—

LAWRENCE: May we make our language more official, General? A contingent of Prince Feisal's Arab forces, acting under my orders, last night captured the important road and rail centre of Deraa —

BARRINGTON: Yes, I daresay that's how it'll go down in your report. Listen, I'm a fairly hardened soldier, Lawrence, but in all my life I've never seen anything like it. It's utterly sickening. They've been burning and looting everything Turkish they can find — massacring the garrison — there are only a handful of survivors. We've even had to surround the military hospital. It's a dangerous situation, and, as you seem to be the only person who can control these savages, you've got to come down with me now at once —

LAWRENCE (*coldly*): I'm sorry, but I'm afraid I can't spare the time.

(*Pause.*)

BARRINGTON (*wide-eyed*): Shall I report that to the GOC?

LAWRENCE: You will anyway, so why ask me? You can also tell the GOC that I suggest he orders his troops out of a town which was captured and is now being securely held by mine. And now — General — if you don't mind, I have an important operation planned for tonight, and I must prepare for it —

(*He turns to go.* BARRINGTON *runs to bar his way.*)

BARRINGTON: I'm getting pretty tired of these schoolboy jokes of yours, Lawrence.

LAWRENCE (*amused*): Schoolboy jokes? How interesting. I've grown up a bit since we first met at Abdullah's camp. Or hadn't you noticed?

BARRINGTON: Your suggestion is serious?

(LAWRENCE *shrugs.*)

That Deraa be left in the hands of those savages?

LAWRENCE (*quietly*): It may be that some of those savages come from a village called Tafas. We followed the Turks into it two days ago. Outside the village we saw a child with a bayonet wound in his neck — but he was still alive.

When I bent over him, he screamed 'Don't hit me, Baba.' Then he ran away from us until he fell over and died. That was only the first thing we saw. When we went into the village and saw the bodies of eighteen women, all bayoneted obscenely, two of them pregnant, I said 'The best of you brings me the most Turkish dead.' I note, General, with interest that my wishes were apparently carried out last night in Deraa. (*A thought striking him*) In Deraa? How stupid! I hadn't realized. In Deraa? (*He laughs softly.*)

> (*He makes a move to go.* BARRINGTON *stops him forcibly.*)

BARRINGTON: Are you quite lost to all human feeling?

> (LAWRENCE *laughs again, with now a different note.*)

LAWRENCE: Do you know, General, I think you're right. That's exactly what I am.

> (*His laugh grows louder, with a shade of hysteria in it.*)

Quite lost to all human feeling.

BARRINGTON (*appalled*): I think you're a callous, soulless, sadistic little brute.

LAWRENCE (*still laughing, eagerly*): Yes, yes, oh yes. Especially soulless.

BARRINGTON: You sicken me.

> (*He pushes* LAWRENCE *away violently so that he falls down, still laughing, but weakly now.* BARRINGTON *goes out.*)

LAWRENCE (*calling after him*): I sicken myself. That's the joke. Not a schoolboy joke. Just – a – joke.

> (*The laughter is no longer laughter, but the sound continues.*)

Lawrence of Arabia – the soulless wonder —

> (*Suddenly a quiet, clear voice (actual not recorded) cuts through the sound that* LAWRENCE *is making.*)

HAMED'S VOICE: God will give you peace.

LAWRENCE (*struggling to his feet*): No, Hamed, never. Never in this life.

> (*He goes out unsteadily.*)

HAMED'S VOICE (*as* LAWRENCE *disappears*): God will give you peace.

> (*The lights fade on the tent. Loud and clear comes a bugle call, playing the reveille.*)
> THE LIGHTS COME UP ON THE NEXT SCENE

SCENE VII

The FLIGHT LIEUTENANT'S *office. He is sitting at the desk, looking up in bewilderment at an RAF* CORPORAL.

F/LT: What? But I don't understand. The Group Captain coming to see me? Are you sure?

CPL: On his way, sir.

F/LT: But why didn't he tell me to come and see him?

CPL: Don't know, sir.

F/LT: Well, it's very odd. Thank you.

> (*He begins hastily to clear up his desk, moving a few documents from the 'In' tray to the 'Out' tray, and emptying an overfull ashtray. There is a peremptory knock.*)

(*Nervously*) Come in.

> (*The* GROUP CAPTAIN *comes in. He is only half dressed and looks dishevelled and harassed. The* CORPORAL *springs to attention.*)

Why, sir. This is a surprise. I don't often have the honour —

G/C: Corporal, tell the Flight Sergeant of B Flight to report to me here immediately.

CORPORAL: Yes, sir.

> (*He goes out.*)

G/C (*hoarsely*): Do you keep any drink here?

F/LT: A little – er – medicinal, sir.

> (*He opens a cupboard and takes out half a bottle of whisky and a glass.*)

G/C: I need it. My office has become a nightmare. The telephone hasn't stopped since six this morning, when the duty officer woke me with the news. (*Taking the glass*) Now I'm not at all sure it isn't being tapped. Probably the *Daily*

Mirror. They were the first on. Thanks. Cheers. (*He takes another swig and hands the glass back to the bewildered* FLIGHT LIEUTENANT) Now, listen, we've got to get this fellow off the station within an hour —

F/LT: Which fellow?

G/C (*impatiently*): Ross, of course. Air Ministry are most insistent that there aren't any photographs, so I suggest we smuggle him through my private gate. Agreed?

F/LT: Er — excuse me, sir, I'm just the least little bit behind. Do I agree that we smuggle Aircraftman Ross off the station, through your own private gate? That was the question, wasn't it?

G/C: Oh, my God! You don't know? No, I suppose you wouldn't. We're trying to keep it as dark as possible, though everyone will know tonight —

F/LT (*patiently*): Has it anything to do with the charge I put him on for hearing by you this morning?

G/C: You put him on a charge?

F/LT: Yes, sir. Gross insubordination.

G/C: Who to?

F/LT: Me.

(*Pause.*)

G/C (*solicitously*): I think you'd better have a nip of your own whisky.

F/LT (*virtuously*): Never touch it in the morning.

G/C: Well, I will. (*Muttering*) A charge? God. If the *Mirror* got hold of that.

(*He takes another glass from the* FLIGHT LIEUTENANT.) You know who it was you've charged with insubordination? Lawrence of Arabia.

F/LT (*after a pause, confidently*): Oh no. Oh no. That can't be. I mean —

G/C: How exactly was he insubordinate?

F/LT: He was late on pass. I asked him who he'd been with, that night. He said the Archbishop of Canterbury (*his voice begins to falter*), Lord and Lady Astor, and Mr and Mrs George Bernard — oh my God!

G/C (*holding out the bottle*): Here.

F/Lt (*taking it*): But it's unbelievable. Why has he done it?

G/C: Well, that's the question. It's very difficult to get anything out of him. I had an hour with him, nearly. A bit awkward. I had to ask him to sit, of course.

F/Lt: Of course.

G/C: Kept on using the one word. The RAF was his refuge.

F/Lt: From what?

G/C: God knows. From himself and his reputation, he said. He wanted a number, not a name. Very insistent about his number. Lets him lose his identity. One of a mass. Fellow's a bit screwy, if you ask me.

F/Lt (*excitedly*): It wouldn't be a public protest about the Arabs being let down at Versailles?

G/C: No. Asked him that.

F/Lt: Or the Palestine question?

G/C: No. Welcomes a Jewish State.

    (*He takes out a piece of paper.*)

He fought for – er – yes, here it is. (*Reading*) He fought for the whole Semitic race, irrespective of religion. He has no grievance at all about either Arabia or Palestine. Churchill's recent settlement of the Middle East has brought us out with clean hands. Those were his exact words.

F/Lt: Really? His exact words?

G/C (*glowering*): Yes, but don't you quote them.

F/Lt: No, sir.

G/C: Queer little fellow. If he wasn't who he is, you might feel quite sorry for him.

F/Lt: What's going to happen to him?

G/C: Air Ministry are turning him out pronto. They're flaming mad. They're being badgered already by foreign embassies. Going to be questions in the House too. Oh no. I mean, you can't have the Service turned into a rest home for war heroes. Army too.

F/Lt: Legally *can* they turf him out?

G/C: Oh yes. Entered under false name and false particulars.

(*There is a knock on the door.*)

F/LT: Come in.

(*The* FLIGHT SERGEANT *comes in and salutes.*)

F/SGT: Flight Sergeant Thompson, B Flight, reporting, sir.

G/C: Yes, Flight. It's about a man in your Flight. Aircraftman Ross.

F/SGT: Yes, sir.

G/C: He has to be off this station within an hour.

F/SGT: Yes, sir.

G/C: You knew about it?

F/SGT: He told me, sir.

G/C: Did he tell you why?

F/SGT: Yes, sir.

G/C: Oh, well, don't tell the rest of the Flight.

F/SGT: They all know, sir. I told them.

G/C: Oh God! (*To* FLIGHT LIEUTENANT) It'll be all round the camp by now —

F/LT (*to* FLIGHT SERGEANT, *curiously*): Exactly what did he tell you, Flight?

F/SGT: What the Group Captain said to him, sir. That he was the wrong type for the RAF. Didn't fit in. Was too old. Couldn't do the job — so he was being hoof — discharged the Service.

(*Pause.*)

F/LT: That's all he told you, Flight?

F/SGT: Yes, sir.

G/C: Nothing else at all?

F/SGT (*trying to remember*): No, sir. Except that he didn't know — what he was going to do with himself now.

G/C: That's all right, Flight. (*Dismissing him*) Thank you.

F/SGT: Leave to speak, sir.

(*The* GROUP CAPTAIN *nods.*)

I've known this airman ten weeks. He's not an ideal recruit, but then who is? In fact he's not a bad little – (*he bites the word off*) chap at all. I think – if you only let him stay, sir – I can see to it that he won't get into no more trouble. And I'm sure, some day, he'll make an airman.

(*Pause.*)

G/C: I'm sorry, Flight – but it's all settled.

F/Lt (*with a faint smile*): He doesn't fit in.

F/Sgt: Yes, sir. It's just that it takes all sorts, sir – that's what I always say —

G/C (*sharply*): That's enough, Flight. See that he's off the station by nine hundred hours —

F/Sgt: Yes, sir.

(*He salutes, marches to the door and turns.*)

Forgive forthrightness, sir. It's just I don't believe there's anyone in this world who can't be made to fit in somehow —

G/C: Yes, Flight. Thank you.

F/Sgt: Trust I have given no offence.

G/C: No offence. It's just that Ross happens to be a special case. (*To* FLIGHT LIEUTENANT) A very special case.

F/Sgt: Yes, sir.

(*He salutes and goes.*)

THE LIGHTS FADE

Scene VIII

Hut fourteen. LAWRENCE, *in civilian clothes, is packing a kitbag. He is looking out of the window, whence we hear the sound of a bugle. When it stops he turns back to his task.* EVANS *comes in.*

EVANS (*embarrassed, but with false joviality*): Hullo, Rossie, boy. How's the world?

LAWRENCE: All right. Break on?

EVANS: Yes.

LAWRENCE: No cocoa and biscuits this morning?

EVANS: Not hungry. Rossie —

(*He holds out some money.*)

LAWRENCE: No. You keep that.

EVANS: Oh, but I couldn't.

(*He puts the money on the bed.*)

You'll be needing it more than me now, anyway.

LAWRENCE (*realizing resistance is useless*): Thank you, Taff. I must give you back the half crown.

EVANS (*as* LAWRENCE *holds it out*): Keep it, man. No, keep it. It's not much, but it could help out there. What are you going to do?

LAWRENCE (*putting the money away*): No idea, Taff.

EVANS: Got a job to go to?

LAWRENCE: No.

EVANS: It's terrible this unemployment. Terrible. I wouldn't be in this place if it weren't for that, I can tell you. No fear. You got a girl?

LAWRENCE: No.

EVANS (*smiling*): Lucky man.

LAWRENCE: Yes. I suppose so.

EVANS: One comfort – you don't have to tell her you got hoofed. Anyone to tell?

LAWRENCE: No.

EVANS: I'll write to anyone if you'll give me the address. Say what bad luck it was you got on the wrong side of the Station Commander. Just unreasonable, I'll say he was —

(PARSONS *comes in quickly.*)

PARSONS: Listen – I don't want no noes about this, because I've talked to all the others – except Taff here and he'll say yes like the rest, I know – won't you, Taff?

EVANS (*plaintively*): I don't know what it is, yet.

PARSONS (*snarling*): I'm telling you, aren't I?

EVANS: Sorry.

PARSONS: We're writing a document – quite dignified – most respectful – dear sir – we have the honour – all that cock – and we're all signing it and sending it to the Group Captain – and what we're going to say is that we all think that the way they're treating you is the most dirtiest, bleed-ingest trick that even those bastards have ever pulled on one of us – and that's saying something.

LAWRENCE (*quietly*): On one of us?

PARSONS: Yes – of course – but what I said just now – we must make it respectful – B Flight suggest there has been some slight misapprehension regarding Airman Ross not fitting in (*warming to his subject*) because if he can fit into B Flight he can bloody well fit into the RAF or into any other bloody Service you can bloody well think of – sir. (*Thoughtfully*) Trouble is, we're really going to need you to write this for us. Got the time?

LAWRENCE: No. Besides you mustn't send it.

PARSONS: Don't worry. We're sending it. Aren't we, Taff?

EVANS: I'm game – if all the others are. Are they really, Sailor?

PARSONS (*fiercely*): What kind of a mug do you think I am? In this sort of lark it's all or no one – see. One single blackleg – just one, and they'll beat us. There aren't no blacklegs on this.

LAWRENCE: Dickinson?

PARSONS: He's in. Thinks it's a joke, mind you, hasn't got no proper social conscience – officer class, you see – but he's in all right and glad to be. So you're in too, Taff – right?

EVANS: Right.

PARSONS (*to* LAWRENCE): That's all of us, chum. So it's settled —

LAWRENCE (*shaking his head, gently*): No.

PARSONS: Why not?

LAWRENCE: It can only mean trouble.

PARSONS (*contemptuously*): Nah. What can they do? Hoof the whole Flight and have the papers talk about a mutiny at Uxbridge? Put us all on jankers, and have the story round the whole camp. No. Worst they'll do is collective reprimand. (*In his 'officer' voice*) 'None of you understand Service ways, my boys. That's your trouble.' (*He makes a face*) *Best* they can do is reconsider —

LAWRENCE: They won't do that.

PARSONS (*obviously agreeing*): Well, it's a chance. There's always a chance, as the bishop said to the housemaid.

LAWRENCE: Don't send it until tomorrow.

PARSONS: Well — we thought — the sooner the better —

LAWRENCE: No. Not until tomorrow.

PARSONS: All right. Well, goodbye, Rossie.

LAWRENCE (*taking his outstretched hand*): Goodbye, Sailor.

PARSONS (*muttering*): The bastards! I could bloody well murder them — I could go up to each and every one of them and collectively or individually screw all their —

(*He has disappeared.* EVANS *also puts his hand out.*)

EVANS: Goodbye, Rossie.

LAWRENCE: Goodbye, Taff.

EVANS: Good luck for the future.

LAWRENCE: Thank you. The same to you. And thank you for the (*remembering the slang*) half-dollar.

(EVANS *makes a deprecating gesture and is going out as the* FLIGHT SERGEANT *comes in.*)

F/SGT: What do you think you're doing, young Evans? Think the break lasts all morning?

EVANS: I was talking to Ross.

F/SGT (*roaring*): I don't care if you were talking to the Aga Khan, get back on fatigue —

EVANS: Yes, Flight. Sorry, Flight —

(*He flees. The* FLIGHT SERGEANT *comes up to* LAWRENCE.)

F/SGT: Ready, boy?

LAWRENCE: Nearly.

(*He turns to collect some books. The* FLIGHT SERGEANT, *sitting on the bed, pulls out of the nearly filled kitbag* LAWRENCE's *ornamental dagger.*)

F/SGT: What's this?

LAWRENCE (*carelessly*): Oh — sort of keepsake. Would you like to have it?

F/Sgt: Well, thanks. I'll give it to the wife to hang on the wall. She loves stuff like that. I'm telling you, son, you'd have made an airman if the bleeders had only let you be. I told 'em that just now – head bleeder and all.

Lawrence: Thank you, Flight, I'm grateful.

F/Sgt: Didn't work, though. They got it in for you proper, son – don't know why. Something to do with your past, shouldn't wonder.

Lawrence: Yes. It may be.

F/Sgt: Well, listen here, my boy, don't let them get you down. What's past is past, see, and finished and dead. What you got to think about is the future. (*Looking at his watch*) Well – are you ready now?

Lawrence (*pulling his kitbag closed and tying it*): Just about.

F/Sgt: What are you going to do? Any idea?

Lawrence (*head bent over kitbag*): Yes. I think I have. I'm going to get back into the RAF as soon as I can.

F/Sgt (*surprised*): Think you can do that?

Lawrence: Well, I'll have to change my name, I suppose. Ross won't do any more.

(*He points to the name 'Ross' painted on his kitbag.*)
Shaw. I thought of that this morning. How do you like it?

F/Sgt: All right.

Lawrence: But it's not the name that matters. It's the number.

F/Sgt (*wonderingly*): The number? What number?

Lawrence: Oh, any number. Just provided it's one of a lot of others – like this.

(*He points to the number on his kitbag.*)

F/Sgt: I don't know what you're talking about. Do you really want another dose of all this?

(*He indicates the hut.*)

Lawrence: More than anything else I can think of.

F/Sgt: You're a glutton for punishment, aren't you?

Lawrence (*smiling*): It rather looks like it.

F/Sgt: I've got to sneak you out through the Group Cap-

tain's private entrance. Gawd knows why. I'll get the key.
You know his house?

    (LAWRENCE *nods*.)

I'll meet you over there.

    (*He goes out.* LAWRENCE *finishes tying his kitbag, his head bent over it.*)

  LAWRENCE: God will give you peace.

    (*He looks round the hut for the last time and then, shouldering his kitbag, he follows the* FLIGHT SERGEANT *out. A distant bugle call is sounding as the* CURTAIN FALLS.)

THE ROYAL HUNT OF THE SUN

By Peter Shaffer

For
ALAN and PAULA
with love

NOTE

The Royal Hunt of the Sun was first presented by the National Theatre at Chichester on July 7th, 1964, with the following cast:

MARTIN RUIZ	Robert Lang
MARTIN RUIZ as a Boy	Roy Holder
FRANCISCO PIZARRO	Colin Blakely
DIEGO DE TRUJILLO	Mike Gambon
SALINAS	Dan Meaden
RODAS	Rod Beacham
FRAY VINCENTE DE VALVERDE	Peter Cellier
VASCA	Robert Russell
DOMINGO	Lewis Fiander
JUAN CHAVEZ	Christopher Timothy
PEDRO CHAVEZ	Gerald McNally
HERNANDO DE SOTO	Michael Turner
FELIPILLO	Derek Jacobi
FRAY MARCOS DE NIZZA	Edward Caddick
MIGUEL ESTETE	James Mellor
MANCO	Neil Fitzpatrick
ATAHUALLPA	Robert Stephens
VILLAC UMU	Edward Petherbridge
CHALLCUCHIMA	Edward Hardwicke
PEDRO DE CANDIA	Frank Wylie
CHIEFTAIN	Peter John
HEADMAN	Bruce Purchase
INTI COUSSI	Louise Purnell
OELLO	Jeanette Landis

PERUVIAN INDIANS

Michael Byrne, Christopher Chittell, Kurt Christian, Anton Darby, Nicholas Edmett, William Hobbs, Alan Ridgway, John Rogers, Clive Rust

Production by

JOHN DEXTER, DESMOND O'DONOVAN

Scenery and Costumes by Michael Annals

Music by Marc Wilkinson

Movement by Claude Chagrin

Lighting by John Read

CHARACTERS
The Spaniards

The Officers

Francisco Pizarro	Commander of the Expedition
Hernando de Soto	Second-in-Command
Miguel Estete	Royal Veedor, or Overseer
Pedro de Candia	Commander of Artillery
Diego de Trujillo	Master of Horse

The Men

Martin Ruiz
Young Martin   Pizarro's Page: Old Martin as
                         a boy

Salinas	Blacksmith
Rodas	Tailor
Vasca	
Domingo	
Juan Chavez	
Pedro Chavez	

The Priests

Fray Vincente de Valverde	Chaplain to the Expedition (Dominican)
Fray Marcos de Nizza	Franciscan Friar

The Indians

Atahuallpa	Sovereign Inca of Peru
Villac Umu	High Priest of Peru
Challcuchima	An Inca General
A Chieftain	
A Headman of a Thousand Families	
Felipillo	An Indian boy, employed by Pizarro as Interpreter
Manco	A Chasqui, or Messenger
Inti Coussi ⎱ non-	Step-sister of Atahuallpa
Oello ⎰ speaking	A wife of Atahuallpa

Spanish Soldiers and Peruvian Indians

PLACE—*Apart from two early scenes in Spain and Panama, the play is set in the Upper Province of the Inca Empire: what is now South Ecuador and North Western Peru. The whole of Act II takes place in the town of Cajamarca.*

TIME: *June 1529–August 1533*

Act I—THE HUNT   Act II—THE KILL

AUTHOR'S NOTES

The Text

Each Act contains twelve sections, marked by Roman numerals. These are solely for reference, and do not indicate pauses or breaks of any kind. The action is continuous.

The Set

In this version of the play I refer throughout to the set used by the National Theatre Company at the Chichester Festival, 1964. Essentially, all that is required for a production of *The Royal Hunt of the Sun* is a bare stage and an upper level. However, the setting by Michael Annals was so superb, and so brilliantly succeeded in solving the visual problems of the play, that I wish to recall it here in print.

Basically this design consisted of a huge aluminium ring, twelve feet in diameter, hung in the centre of a plain wooden back-wall. Around its circumference were hinged twelve petals. When closed, these interlocked to form a great medallion on which was incised the emblem of the Conquistadors; when opened, they formed the rays of a giant golden sun, emblem of the Incas. Each petal had an inlay of gold magnetized to it: when these inlays were pulled out (in Act II, Scene vi) the great black frame remaining symbolized magnificently the desecration of Peru. The centre of this sun formed an acting area above the stage, which was used in Act I to show Atahuallpa in majesty, and in Act II served for his prison and subsequently for the treasure chamber.

This simple but amazing set was for me totally satisfying on all levels: scenically, aesthetically, and symbolically.

The Music

The musical excerpts at the end of the play represent the three most easily detached pieces from the remarkable score composed for the play by Marc Wilkinson. This extraordinary music I believe to be an integral part of any production of *The Royal Hunt of the Sun*. It embraces bird cries; plainchant; a fantasia for organ; freezing sounds for the Mime of the Great Ascent, and frightening ones for the Mime of the Great Massacre. To me its most memorable items are the exquisitely doleful lament which opens Act II, and, most amazing of all, the final Chant of Resurrection, to be whined and whispered, howled and hooted, over Atahuallpa's body in the darkness, before the last sunrise of the Inca Empire.

The full score can be obtained from London Authors, 8 Upper Brook Street, London, W.1.

THE PRODUCTION

There are, no doubt, many ways of producing this play, as there are of setting it. My hope was always to realize on stage a kind of 'total' theatre, involving not only words but rites, mimes, masks and magics. The text cries for illustration. It is a director's piece, a pantomimist's piece, a musician's piece, a designer's piece, and of course an actor's piece, almost as much as it is an author's. In this edition, as with the set, I have included as many details of the Chichester production as possible, partly because I was deeply involved in its creation, but mainly as a tribute to the superb achievement of John Dexter.

P.S.

ACT I – THE HUNT

A bare stage. On the back wall, which is of wood, hangs a huge metal medallion, quartered by four black crucifixes, sharpened to resemble swords.

Scene I

Darkness.

OLD MARTIN, *grizzled, in his middle fifties, appears. He wears the black costume of a Spanish hidalgo in the mid-sixteenth century.*

OLD MARTIN: Save you all. My name is Martin. I'm a soldier of Spain and that's it. Most of my life I've spent fighting for land, treasure and the cross. I'm worth millions. Soon I'll be dead and they'll bury me out here in Peru, the land I helped ruin as a boy. This story is about ruin. Ruin and gold. More gold than any of you will ever see even if you work in a counting house. I'm going to tell you how one hundred and sixty-seven men conquered an empire of twenty-four million. And then things that no one has ever told: things to make you groan and cry out I'm lying. And perhaps I am. The air of Peru is cold and sour like in a vault, and wits turn easier here even than in Europe. But grant me this: I saw him closer than anyone, and had cause only to love him. He was my altar, my bright image of salvation, Francisco Pizarro! Time was when I'd have died for him, or for any worship.

(YOUNG MARTIN enters duelling an invisible opponent with a stick. He is Old Martin as an impetuous boy of fifteen.)

If you could only imagine what it was like for me at the beginning, to be allowed to serve him. But boys don't dream like that any more — service! Conquest! Riding down Indians in the name of Spain. The inside of my head was one vast plain for feats of daring. I used to lie up in the hayloft for hours reading my Bible — Don Cristobal on the rules of Chivalry. And then he came and made them real. And the only wish of my life is that I had never seen him.

(FRANCISCO PIZARRO *comes in. He is a man in late middle age: tough, commanding, harsh, wasted, secret. The gestures are blunt and often violent; the expression intense and energetic, capable of fury and cruelty, but also of sudden melancholy and sardonic humour. At the moment he appears more neatly than he is ever to do again: hair and beard are trimmed, and his clothes quite grand, as if he is trying to make a fine impression.*

He is accompanied by his Second-in-Command, HERNANDO DE SOTO, *and the Dominican* FRAY VINCENTE DE VALVERDE. DE SOTO *is an impressive figure in his forties: his whole air breathes an unquestioning loyalty — to his profession, his faith, and to accepted values. He is an admirable soldier and a staunch friend.* VALVERDE *on the other hand is a peasant Priest whose zeal is not greatly tempered by intelligence, nor sweetened by any anxiety to please.*)

PIZARRO: I was suckled by a sow. My house is the oldest in Spain — the pig-sty.

OLD MARTIN: He'd made two expeditions to the New World already. Now at over sixty years old he was back in Spain, making one last try. He'd shown the King enough gold to get sole right of discovery in Peru and the title of Viceroy over anything he conquered. In return he was to fit out an army at his own expense. He started recruiting in his own birthplace, Trujillo.

(*Lights up below as he speaks. Several Spanish villagers have entered, among them* SALINAS, *a blacksmith*, RODAS, *a tailor*, VASCA, DOMINGO *and the* CHAVEZ *brothers.* PIZARRO *addresses* DIEGO, *a young man of twenty-five.*)

PIZARRO: What's your name?

DIEGO: Diego, sir.

PIZARRO: What do you know best?

DIEGO: Horses I suppose, if I was to name anything.

PIZARRO: How would you feel to be Master of Horse, Diego?

DIEGO (*eagerly*): Sir!

PIZARRO: Go over there. Who's smith here?

SALINAS: I am.

PIZARRO: Are you with us?

SALINAS: I'm not against you.

PIZARRO: Who's your friend?

RODAS: Tailor, if it's your business.

PIZARRO: Soldiers never stop mending and patching. They'll be grateful for your assistance.

RODAS: Well, find some other fool to give it to them. I'm resting here.

PIZARRO: Rest. (*To* YOUNG MARTIN) Who's this?

DIEGO: Martin Ruiz, sir. A good lad. He knows all his codes of Chivalry by heart. He's aching to be a page, sir.

PIZARRO: How old?

OLD MARTIN: Seventeen.

PIZARRO: Don't lie.

YOUNG MARTIN: Fifteen, sir.

(OLD MARTIN *goes off.*)

PIZARRO: Parents?

YOUNG MARTIN: Dead, sir.

PIZARRO: Can you write?

YOUNG MARTIN: Two hundred Latin words. Three hundred Spanish.

PIZARRO: Why do you want to come?

YOUNG MARTIN: It's going to be glorious, sir.

PIZARRO: Look you, if you served me you'd be Page to an old slogger: no titles, no traditions. I learnt my trade as a mercenary, going with who best paid me. It's a closed book to me, all that chivalry. But then, not reading or writing, all books are closed to me. If I took you you'd have to be my reader and writer, both.

YOUNG MARTIN: I'd be honoured, my Lord. Oh, please my Lord!

PIZARRO: General will do. Let's see your respect. Greet me. (*The boy bows*) Now to the Church. That's Brother Valverde, our Chaplain.

VALVERDE: The blessing of God on you, my son. And on all who come with us to alter the heathen.

PIZARRO: Now to our Second-in-Command, Cavalier de Soto. I'm sure you all know the Cavalier well by reputation: a great soldier. He has fought under Cordoba! No expedition he seconds can fail. (*He takes a roll of cloth, woven with the design of a llama, from* DE SOTO) Now look at this! Indian stuff! Ten years ago standing with the great Balboa, I saw a chieftain draw this beast on the leaf of an aloe. And he said to me: Where this roams is uncountable wealth!

RODAS: Oh, yes, uncountable! Ask Sanchez the farrier about that. He listened to talk like that from him five years ago.

DIEGO: Who cares about him?

RODAS: Uncountable bloody wealth? It rained six months and his skin rotted on him. They lost twenty-seven out of fifty.

PIZARRO: And so we may again. What do you think I'm offering? A walk in the country? Jellies and wine in a basket, your hand round your girl? No, I'm promising you swamps. A forest like the beard of the world. Sitting half-buried in earth to escape the mouths of insects. You may live for weeks on palm tree buds and soup made out of leather straps. And at night you will sleep in thick wet darkness with snakes hung over your heads like bell ropes – and black men in that blackness: men that eat each other. And why should you endure all this? Because I believe that beyond this terrible place is a kingdom, where gold is as common as wood is here! I took only two steps in and found cups and pans made out of it solid.

(*He claps his hands.* FELIPILLO *comes in. He is a slim,
delicate Indian from Ecuador, loaded with golden ornaments. In actuality* FELIPILLO *is a treacherous and hysterical creature, but at the moment, under his master's
eye, he sways forward before the stupefied villagers with
a demure grace.*)

I present Felipillo, captured on my last trip. Look close at
his ornaments. To him they are no more than feathers are
to us, but they are all gold, my friends. Examine him. Down!

(*The villagers examine him.*)

VALVERDE: Look at him well. This is a heathen. A being
condemned to eternal flame unless you help him. Don't think
we are merely going to destroy his people and lift their
wealth. We are going to take from them what they don't
value, and give them instead the priceless mercy of heaven.
He who helps me lift this dark man into light I absolve of all
crimes he ever committed.

PIZARRO: Well?

SALINAS: That's gold right enough.

PIZARRO: And for your taking. I was like you once.
Sitting the afternoon away in this same street, drunk in the
inn, to bed in the sty. Stink and mud and nothing to look
for. Even if you die with me, what's so tender precious to
hold you here?

VASCA: You're hissing right!

PIZARRO: I tell you, man: over there you'll be the masters
– that'll be your slave.

VASCA: Well, there's a thought: talk about the slave of
slaves!

DOMINGO (*timidly*): Do you think it's true?

PIZARRO: Do you say I lie?

DOMINGO: Oh, no, sir. . .

VASCA: Even if he does, what's to keep you here? You're a
cooper: how many casks have you made this year? That's
no employment for a dog.

PIZARRO: How about you? You're brothers aren't you?

DIEGO: That's the Chavez brothers, Juan and Pedro.

JUAN: Sir.

PEDRO: Sir.

PIZARRO: Well, what d'you say?

JUAN: I say right, sir.

PEDRO: Me too.

VASCA: And me. I'm going to get a slave or two like him.

DOMINGO: And me. Vasca's right, you can't do worse than stay here.

RODAS: Well not me, boys. Just you catch Rodas marching through any hissing jungle!

SALINAS: Oh, shut your ape's face. Are you going to sit here for ever and pick fleas? He'll come, sir.

PIZARRO: Make your way to Toledo for the muster. Diego, enrol them all and take them along.

DIEGO: Sir!

> (YOUNG MARTIN *makes to go off with the rest*. PIZARRO *stays him*.)

PIZARRO: Boy.

YOUNG MARTIN: Sir.

> (*A pause*.)

PIZARRO: Muster me the names of all officers and men so far listed.

YOUNG MARTIN: Oh, sir! Yes, sir! Thank you, sir!

PIZARRO: You're a page now, so act like one. Dignity at all times.

YOUNG MARTIN (*bowing*): Yes, sir.

PIZARRO: Respect.

YOUNG MARTIN (*bowing*): Yes, sir.

PIZARRO: And obedience.

YOUNG MARTIN (*bowing*): Yes, sir.

PIZARRO: And it isn't necessary to salute every ten seconds.

YOUNG MARTIN (*bowing*): No, sir.

VALVERDE: Come, my son, there's work to do.

> (*They go off*.)

PIZARRO: Strange sight, yourself, just as you were in this very street.

DE SOTO: Do you like it?

PIZARRO: No, I was a fool. Dreamers deserve what they get.

DE SOTO: And what are you dreaming about now?

PIZARRO: Gold.

DE SOTO: Oh, come. Gold is not enough lodestone for you, not any more to drag you back to the new world.

PIZARRO: You're right. At my age things become what they really are. Gold turns into metal.

DE SOTO: Then why? You could stay here now and be hero for a province. What's left to endure so much for — especially with your infirmity? You've earned the right to comfort. Your country would gladly grant it to you for the rest of your life.

PIZARRO: My country, where is that?

DE SOTO: Spain, sir.

PIZARRO: Spain and I have been strangers since I was a boy. The only spot I know in it is here — this filthy village. This is Spain to me. Is this where you wish me comfort? For twenty-two years I drove pigs down this street because my father couldn't own to my mother. Twenty-two years without one single day of hope. When I turned soldier and dragged my arquebus along the roads of Italy, I was so famished I was beyond eating. I got nothing and I gave nothing, and though I groaned for that once I'm glad with it now. Because I owe nothing . . . Once the world could have had me for a petty farm, two rocky fields and a Senor to my name. It said 'No'. Ten years on it could have had me for double — small estate, fifty oranges and a Sir to them. It said 'No'. Twenty years more and it could still have had me cheap: Balboa's trusty lieutenant, marched with him into the Pacific and claimed it for Spain: State Pension and dinner once a week with the local Mayor. But the world said 'No'. Said 'No' and said 'No'. Well, now it's going to know me. If I live this next year I'm going to get me a name that won't ever be forgotten. A name to be sung here for centuries in your ballads, out there under the cork trees where I sat as a boy with bandages for shoes. I amuse you.

De Soto: Surely you see you don't.

Pizarro: Oh, yes, I amuse you, Cavalier de Soto. The old pigherd lumbering after fame. You inherited your honour – I had to root for mine like the pigs. It's amusing.

Scene II

Lights whiter, colder.
He kneels. An organ sounds: the austere polyphony of Spanish celebration. Valverde *enters, bearing an immense wooden Christ. He is accompanied by his assistant,* Fray Marcos de Nizza, *a Franciscan, a man of far more serene temper and intellectual maturity. All the villagers come in also, wearing the white cloaks of chivalry and carrying banners. Among them is* Pedro de Candia, *a Venetian captain, wearing a pearl in one ear and walking with a lazy stealth that at once suggests danger.* Old Martin *comes in.*

Old Martin: On the day of St John the Evangelist, our weapons were consecrated in the Cathedral Church of Panama. Our muster was one hundred and eighty-seven, with horses for twenty-seven.

Valverde: You are the huntsmen of God. The weapons you draw are sacred! Oh, God, invest us all with the courage of Thy unflinching Son. Show us our way to beat the savage out of his dark forests on to the broad plain of Thy Grace.

De Nizza: And comfort, we pray, all warriors that shall be in affliction from this setting out.

Old Martin: Fray Marcos de Nizza, Franciscan, appointed to assist Valverde.

De Nizza: You are the bringers of food to starving peoples. You go to break mercy with them like bread, and outpour gentleness into their cups. You will lay before them the inexhaustible table of free spirit, and invite to it all who have dieted on terror. You will bring to all tribes the nourishment of pity. You will sow their fields with love, and teach them to harvest the crop of it, each yield in its season. Remember this always: we are their New World.

VALVERDE: Approach all and be blessed.

(*During this, the men kneel and are blessed.*)

OLD MARTIN: Pedro de Candia, Cavalier from Venice, in charge of weapons and artillery. These villagers you know already. There were many others of course. Almagro, the General's partner, who stayed to organize reinforcements and follow in three months. Riquelme the Treasurer. Pedro of Ayala and Blas of Atienza. Herrada the Swordsman and Gonzales of Toledo. And Juan de Barbaran whom everyone called the good servant out of love for him. And many smaller men. Even its youngest member saw himself with a following of Indians and a province for an orchard. It was a tumbled company, none too noble but ginger for wealth.

(*Enter* ESTETE: *a stiff, haughty man, dressed in the black of the Spanish court.*)

And chiefly there was —

ESTETE: Miguel Estete. Royal Veedor, and Overseer in the name of King Carlos the Fifth. You should not have allowed anyone to be blessed before me.

PIZARRO: Your pardon, Veedor, I don't understand affairs of before and after.

ESTETE: That is evident. General, on this expedition my name is the law: it is spoken with the King's authority.

PIZARRO: Your pardon, but on this expedition *my* name is the law: there will be no other.

ESTETE: In matters military.

PIZARRO: In all matters.

ESTETE: In all that do not infringe the majesty of the King.

PIZARRO: What matters could?

ESTETE: Remember your duty to God, sir, and to the throne, sir, and you will not discover them.

PIZARRO (*furious*): De Soto! In the name of Spain our Holy country, I invest you as Second-in-Command to me.

Subject only to me. In the name of Spain our Holy country — I — I — . (*He falters, clutching his side in pain. A pause. The men whisper among themselves*) Take the banners out. . .

DE SOTO: Take up your banners. March!

    (*The organ music continues: all march out, leaving* PIZARRO *and his* PAGE *alone on the stage. Only when all the rest are gone does the General collapse. The boy is frightened and concerned.*)

YOUNG MARTIN: What is it, sir?

PIZARRO: A wound from long ago. A knife to the bone. A savage put it into me for life. It troubles me at times . . . You'll start long before me with your wounds. With your killing too. I wonder how you'll like that.

YOUNG MARTIN: You watch me, sir.

PIZARRO: I will. You deal in deaths when you are a soldier, and all your study should be to make them clean, what scratches kill and how to cut them.

YOUNG MARTIN: But surely, sir, there's more to soldiering than that?

PIZARRO: You mean honour, glory – traditions of the service?

YOUNG MARTIN: Yes, sir.

PIZARRO: Dungballs. Soldiers are for killing: that's their reason.

YOUNG MARTIN: But, sir —

PIZARRO: What?

YOUNG MARTIN: It's not just killing.

PIZARRO: Look, boy: know something. Men cannot just stand as men in this world. It's too big for them and they grow scared. So they build themselves shelters against the bigness, do you see? They call the shelters Court, Army, Church. They're useful against loneliness, Martin, but they're not true. They're not real, Martin. Do you see?

YOUNG MARTIN: No, sir. Not truthfully, sir . . .

PIZARRO: No, sir. Not truthfully sir! Why must you be so young? Look at you. Only a quarter formed. A colt the

134

world will break for its sightless track. Listen once. Army loyalty is blasphemy. The world of soldiers is a yard of ungrowable children. They play with ribbons and make up ceremonies just to keep out the rest of the world. They add up the number of their blue dead and their green dead and call that their history. But all this is just the flower the bandit carves on his knife before shoving it into a man's side . . . What's Army Tradition? Nothing but years of Us against Them. Christ-men against Pagan-men. Men against men. I've had a life of it, boy, and let me tell you it's nothing but a nightmare game, played by brutes to give themselves a reason.

YOUNG MARTIN: But sir, a noble reason can make a fight glorious.

PIZARRO: Give me a reason that stays noble once you start hacking off limbs in its name. There isn't a cause in the world to set against this pain. Noble's a word. Leave it for the books.

YOUNG MARTIN: I can't believe that, sir.

PIZARRO: Look at you — hope, lovely hope, it's on you like dew. Do you know where you're going? Into the forest. A hundred miles of dark and screaming. The dark we all came out of, hot. Things flying, fleeing, falling dead — and their death unnoticed. Take your noble reasons there, Martin. Pitch your silk flags in that black and wave your crosses at the wild cats. See what awe they command. Be advised, boy. Go back to Spain.

YOUNG MARTIN: No, sir. I'm coming with you. I can learn, sir.

PIZARRO: You will be taught. Not by me. The forest.
(*He stumps out.*)

SCENE III

The boy is left alone. The stage darkens and the huge medallion high on the back wall begins to glow. Great cries of 'Inca!' are heard. The boy bolts off stage. Exotic music mixes with the chanting. Slowly the medallion opens outwards to form a huge golden sun with twelve great rays. In the centre stand ATAHUALLPA, *sovereign Inca of Peru, masked, crowned, and dressed in gold. When he speaks, his voice, like the voices of all the Incas, is strangely formalized.*

Enter below the Inca court: VILLAC UMU, *the High Priest,* CHALLCUCHIMA, MANCO *and others, all masked, and robed in terracotta. They prostrate themselves.*

MANCO: Atahuallpa! God!

ATAHUALLPA: God hears.

MANCO: Manco your Chasqui speaks. I bring truth from many runners what has been seen in the Farthest Province. White men sitting on huge sheep. The sheep are red! Everywhere their leader shouts aloud 'Here is God!'

ATAHUALLPA: The White God!

VILLAC UMU: Beware, beware Inca!

ATAHUALLPA: All-powerful spirit who left this place before my ancestors ruled you. The White God returns!

CHALLCUCHIMA: You do not know this.

ATAHUALLPA: He has been long waited for. If he comes, it is with blessing. Then my people will see I did well to take the Crown.

VILLAC UMU: Ware you! Your mother Moon wears a veil of green fire. An eagle fell on to the temple in Cuzco.

MANCO: It is true, Capac. He fell out of the sky.

VILLAC UMU: Out of a green sky.

CHALLCUCHIMA: On to a house of gold.

VILLAC UMU: When the world ends, small birds grow sharp claws.

ATAHUALLPA: Cover your mouth. (*All cover their mouths*) If the White God comes to bless me, all must see him.

   (*The Court retires.* ATAHUALLPA *remains on stage, motionless in his sunflower. He stays in this position until the end of Scene VII.*)

SCENE IV

Mottled light.
Province of Tumbes. Screams and whoops of alarm
imitating tropical bird cries. A horde of Indians rushes
across the stage pursued by soldiers.

DE CANDIA: Grab that one! That's the chief.

(*They capture the Chieftain. At the sight of this, all*
the Indians fall silent and passive. DE CANDIA ap-
proaches him with drawn sword.)

Now, you brownie bastard, show us gold.

PIZARRO: Gently, De Candia. You'll get nothing from
him in terror.

DE CANDIA: Let's see.

PIZARRO: God's wounds! Put up! Felipillo, ask for gold.

(FELIPILLO *adopts a set of stylized gestures for his*
interpreting, in the manner of sign language.)

CHIEF: We have no gold. All was taken by the great
King in his war.

PIZARRO: What King?

CHIEF: Holy Atahuallpa, Inca of earth and sky. His
Kingdom is the widest in the world.

DE SOTO: How wide?

CHIEF: A man can run in it every day for a year.

DE SOTO: More than a thousand miles.

ESTETE: Poor savage, trying to impress us with his little
tribe.

PIZARRO: I think we've found more than a little tribe,
Veedor. Tell me of this King. Who did he fight?

CHIEF: His brother Huascar. His father the great Inca
Huayana grew two sons. One by a wife, one by a not-wife.
At his death he cut the Kingdom in two for them. But
Atahuallpa wanted all. So he made war, and killed his
brother. Now he is lord of earth and sky.

PIZARRO: And he's the bastard?

(*All the Indians cry out.*)

Answer! He's the bastard?

CHIEF: He is Son of the Sun. He needs no wedded mother. He is God.

INDIANS (*chanting*): Sapa Inca! Inca Capac!

PIZARRO: God?

CHIEF: God!

PIZARRO: God on earth?

VALVERDE: Christ defend us!

DE SOTO: Do you believe this?

CHIEF: It is true. The sun is God. Atahuallpa is his child sent to shine on us for a few years of life. Then he will return to his father's palace and live for ever.

PIZARRO: God on earth!

VALVERDE: Oh, my brothers, where have we come? The land of Anti-Christ! Do your duty, Spaniards! Take each an Indian and work to shift his soul. Go to them. Show them rigour! No softness to gentle idolatry. (*To the* INDIANS) The cross, you pagan dust!

(*They try to escape.*)

Stay them!

(*The Spaniards ring them with swords.*)

Repeat. Jesus Christ Inca!

INDIANS (*uncertainly*): Jesus Christ Inca!

ESTETE: Jesus Christ Inca!

INDIANS: Jesus Christ Inca!

(*The soldiers herd them off stage. Their cries punctuate the end of the scene. All go off after them, save* PIZARRO *and* DE SOTO.)

ATAHUALLPA: He surely is a god. He teaches my people to praise him.

PIZARRO: He's a god all right. They're scared to hell of him. And a bastard too. That's civil war — bastards against bastards!

ATAHUALLPA: I will see him. Let no one harm these men.

PIZARRO: Let's see you, then. What's it look like to be Son of the Sun?

DE SOTO: That's something in Europe no one's ever dared call himself.

PIZARRO: God on earth, living for ever!

DE SOTO: He's got a shock coming.

(*He goes off.*)

PIZARRO: Do you hear that, God? You're not going to like that! Because we've got a God worth a thousand of yours. A gentle God with gentle priests, and a couple of big cannon to blow you out of the sky!

VALVERDE (*off*): Jesus Christ Inca!

PIZARRO: Christ the Merciful, with his shackles and stakes! So enjoy yourself while you can. Have a glorious shine. (*He makes the sign of the cross*) Take that, Anti-Christ!

(*He runs off, laughing.*)

VALVERDE (*off*): Jesus Christ Inca!

(*Indians* (*off*) *cry out.*)

(*Enter* VILLAC UMU *and* CHALLCUCHIMA.)

VILLAC UMU: Your people groan.

ATAHUALLPA: They groan with my voice.

CHALLCUCHIMA: Your people weep.

ATAHUALLPA: They weep with my tears.

CHALLCUCHIMA: He searches all the houses. He seeks your crown. Remember the prophecy! The twelfth Lord of the Four Quarters shall be the last. Inca, ware you!

VILLAC UMU: Inca, ware you!

ATAHUALLPA (*to* CHALLCUCHIMA): Go to him. Take him my word. Tell him to greet me at Cajamarca, behind the great mountains. If he is a god he will find me. If he is no god, he will die.

(*Lights down on him. Priest and noblemen retire.*)

SCENE V

Night. Wild bird cries. DOMINGO *and* VASCA *on sentry duty.*

VASCA: There must be a hissing thousand of 'em, every night we halt.

DOMINGO: Why don't they just come and get us?

VASCA: They're waiting.

DOMINGO: What for?

VASCA: Maybe they're cannibals and there's a feast day coming up.

DOMINGO: Very funny . . . Six weeks in this hissing forest and not one smell of gold. I think we've been had.

VASCA: Unless they're hiding it, like the General says.

DOMINGO: I don't believe it. God-damned place. I'm starting to rust.

VASCA: We all are. It's the damp. Another week and we'll have to get the blacksmith to cut us out.

(*Enter* ESTETE *with* DE CANDIA *carrying an arquebus.*)

VASCA: Who's there?

DE CANDIA: Talk on duty again and *I'll* cut you out.

DOMINGO: Yes, sir.

VASCA: Yes, sir.

(*They separate and go off.*)

DE CANDIA: They're right. Everything's rusting. Even you, my darling. (*The gun*) Look at her, Strozzi's most perfect model. She can stop a horse at five hundred paces. You're too good for brownies, my sweet.

ESTETE: What are they waiting for? Why don't they just attack and be done with it?

DE CANDIA: They'd find nothing against them. A hundred and eighty terrified men, nine of these and two cannon. If your King wasn't so mean we might just stand a chance out here.

ESTETE: Hold your tongue, De Candia.

DE CANDIA: Good: loyalty. That's what I like to see. The only thing that puzzles me is what the hell you get out of it. They tell me Royal Overseers get nothing.

ESTETE: Any man without self-interest must puzzle a Venetian. If you serve a King you must kill personal ambition. Only then can you become a channel between the people and its collective glory – which otherwise it would never feel. In Byzantium Court officials were castrated to resemble the Order of Angels. But I don't expect you to understand.

DE CANDIA: You Spaniards! You men with missions! You just can't bear to think of yourselves as the thieves you are.

ESTETE: How dare you, sir!

(*Enter* PIZARRO *and* YOUNG MARTIN.)

DE CANDIA: Our noble General. They say in the Indies he traded his immortal part to the Devil.

ESTETE: For what, pray? Health? Breeding? Handsomeness?

DE CANDIA: That they don't tell.

ESTETE: I daresay not. I only wonder His Majesty could give command to such a man. I believe he's mad.

DE CANDIA: No, but still dangerous.

ESTETE: What do you mean?

DE CANDIA: I've served under many men: but this is the first who makes me afraid. Look into him, you'll see a kind of death.

(*Bird cries fill the forest.*)

PIZARRO: Listen to them. There's the world. The eagle rips the condor; the condor rips the crow. And the crow would blind all the eagles in the sky if once it had the beak to do it. The clothed hunt the naked; the legitimates hunt the bastards, and put down the word Gentleman to blot up the blood. Your Chivalry rules don't govern me, Martin. They're for belonging birds – like them: legitimate birds with claws trim on the perch their feathers left to them. Make no error; if I could once peck them off it, I'd tear them into gobbets to feed cats. Don't ever trust me, boy.

YOUNG MARTIN: Sir? I'm your man.

PIZARRO: Don't ever trust me.

YOUNG MARTIN: Sir?

PIZARRO: Or if you must, never say I deceived you. Know me.

YOUNG MARTIN: I do, sir. You are all I ever want to be.

PIZARRO: I am nothing you could ever want to be, or any

141

man alive. Believe this: if the time ever came for you to harry me, I'd rip you too, easy as look at you. Because you belong too, Martin.

YOUNG MARTIN: I belong to you, sir!

PIZARRO: You belong to hope. To faith. To priests and pretences. To dipping flags and ducking heads; to laying hands and licking rings; to powers and parchments; and the whole vast stupid congregation of crowners and cross-kissers. You're a worshipper, Martin. A groveller. You were born with feet but you prefer your knees. It's you who make Bishops – Kings – Generals. You trust me, I'll hurt you past believing. (*A pause*) Have the sentries changed?

YOUNG MARTIN: Not yet, sir.

PIZARRO: Little Lord of Hope, I'm harsh with you. You own everything I've lost. I despise the keeping, and I loathe the losing. Where can a man live, between two hates?

(*He goes towards the two officers.*)
Gentlemen.

ESTETE: How is your wound tonight, General?

PIZARRO: The calmer for your inquiring, Veedor.

DE CANDIA: Well, and what's your plan, sir?

PIZARRO: To go on until I'm stopped.

DE CANDIA: Admirable simplicity.

ESTETE: What kind of plan is that?

PIZARRO: You have a better? It's obvious they've been ordered to hold off.

ESTETE: Why?

PIZARRO: If it's wickedness I'm sure the crown can guess it as soon as the Army.

ESTETE: Sir, I know your birth hasn't fitted for much civility, but remember, in me speaks your King.

PIZARRO: Well, go and write to him. Set down more about my unfitness in your report. Then show it to the birds.

(*He goes off.* ESTETE *goes off another way.* DE CANDIA *laughs and follows him.*)

Scene VI

Light brightens to morning.
Enter OLD MARTIN.

OLD MARTIN: We were in the forest for six weeks, but at last we escaped and found on the other side our first witness of a great empire. There was a road fifteen feet wide, bordered with mimosa and blue glories, with walls on both sides the height of a man. We rode it for days, six horses abreast: and all the way, far up the hillsides, were huge fields of corn laid out in terraces, and a net of water in a thousand canals. (*Exit.*)

(*Lights up on* ATAHUALLPA, *above.*)

MANCO: Manco your Chasqui speaks. They move on the road to Ricaplaya.

ATAHUALLPA: What do they do?

MANCO: They walk through the field terraces. They listen to toil-songs. They clap their hands at fields of llama.

(*Enter groups of* INDIANS, *singing a toil-song and miming their work of sowing and reaping.* PIZARRO, *the* PRIESTS, FELIPILLO *and* SOLDIERS, *among them* DE SOTO, DE CANDIA, DIEGO, ESTETE *and* YOUNG MARTIN, *enter and stand watching.* YOUNG MARTIN *carries a drum.*)

DE NIZZA: How beautiful their tongue sounds.

YOUNG MARTIN: I'm trying to study it but it's very hard. All the words seem to slip together.

FELIPILLO: Oh, very hard, yes. But more hard for Indian to learn Spanish.

DE NIZZA: I'm sure. See how contented they look.

DIEGO: It's the first time I've ever seen people glad at working.

DE SOTO: This is their Headman.

PIZARRO: You are the Lord of the Manor?

(FELIPILLO *interprets.*)

HEADMAN: Here all work together in families: fifty, a hundred, a thousand. I am head of a thousand families. I give out to all food. I give out to all clothes. I give out to all confessing.

DE NIZZA: Confessing?

HEADMAN: I have priest power. . . . I confess my people of all crimes against the laws of the sun.

DE NIZZA: What laws are these?

HEADMAN: It is the seventh month. That is why they must pick corn.

ATAHUALLPA (*intoning*): In the eighth month you will plough. In the ninth, sow maize. In the tenth, mend your roofs.

HEADMAN: Each age also has its tasks.

ATAHUALLPA: Nine years to twelve, protect harvests. Twelve to eighteen, care for herds. Eighteen to twenty-five, warriors for me – Atahuallpa Inca!

FELIPILLO: They are stupid; always do what they are told.

DE SOTO: This is because they are poor?

FELIPILLO: Not poor. Not rich. All same.

ATAHUALLPA: At twenty-five all will marry. All will receive one tupu of land.

HEADMAN: What may be covered by one hundred pounds of maize.

ATAHUALLPA: They will never move from there. At birth of a son one more tupu will be given. At birth of a daughter, half a tupu. At fifty all people will leave work for ever and be fed in honour till they die.

DE SOTO: I have settled several lands. This is the first I've entered which shames our Spain.

ESTETE: Shames?

PIZARRO: Oh, it's not difficult to shame Spain. Here shames every country which teaches we are born greedy for possessions. Clearly we're made greedy when we're assured it's natural. But there's a picture for a Spanish eye! There's nothing to covet, so covetousness dies at birth.

DE SOTO: But don't you have any nobles or grand people?

HEADMAN: The King has great men near him to order the country. But they are few.

De Soto: How then can he make sure so many are happy over so large a land?

Headman: His messengers run light and dark, one after one, over four great roads. No one else may move on them. So he has eyes everywhere. He sees you now.

Pizarro: Now?

Atahuallpa: Now!

(Challcuchima *enters with* Manco, *bearing the image of the Sun on a pole.*)

Challcuchima: I bring greeting from Atahuallpa Inca, Lord of the Four Quarters, King of the earth and sky.

Estete: I will speak with him. A King's man must always greet a King's man. We bring greeting from King Carlos, Emperor of Spain and Austria. We bring blessing from Jesus Christ, the Son of God.

Atahuallpa: Blessing!

Challcuchima: *I* am sent by the son of God. He orders *you* to visit him.

Estete: Orders? Does he take us for servants?

Challcuchima: All men are his servants.

Estete: Does he think so? He's got awakening coming.

Challcuchima: Awakening?

Pizarro: Veedor, under pardon, let my peasant tongue have a word. Where is your King?

Challcuchima: Cajamarca. Behind the great mountains. Perhaps they are too high for you.

Estete: There isn't a hill in your whole country a Spaniard couldn't climb in full armour.

Challcuchima: That is wonderful.

Pizarro: How long should we march before we find him?

Challcuchima: One life of Mother Moon.

Felipillo: A month.

Pizarro: For us, two weeks. Tell him we come.

Atahuallpa: He gives his word with no fear.

Challcuchima: Ware you! It is great danger to take back your word.

Pizarro: I do not fear danger. What I say I do.

CHALLCUCHIMA: So. Do.

(CHALLCUCHIMA *and* MANCO *go off.*)

ATAHUALLPA: He speaks with a God's tongue. Let us take his blessing.

DE SOTO: Well, God help us now.

DE CANDIA: He'd better. I don't know who else will get us out of this. Certainly not the artillery.

FELIPILLO (*imitating* CHALLCUCHIMA'S *walk and voice*): So! Do!

DE SOTO: Be still. You're too free.

ESTETE: My advice to you now is to wait for the reinforcements.

PIZARRO: I thank you for it.

DE SOTO: There's no telling when they'll come, sir. We daren't stay till then.

PIZARRO: But *you* of course will.

ESTETE: I?

PIZARRO: I cannot hazard the life of a Royal officer.

ESTETE: My personal safety has never concerned me, General. My Master's service is all I care for.

PIZARRO: That's why we must ensure its continuance. I'll give you twenty men. You can make a garrison.

ESTETE: I must decline, General. If you go – I go also.

PIZARRO: I'm infinitely moved, Veedor – but my orders remain. You stay here. (*To his* PAGE) Call Assembly.

YOUNG MARTIN (*banging his drum*): Assembly! Assembly!

SCENE VII

The Company pelts on. ESTETE *goes off angrily.*

PIZARRO: We are commanded to court by a brown King, more powerful than any you have ever heard of, sole owner of all the gold we came for. We have three roads. Go back, and he kills us. Stay here, and he kills us. Go on, and he still may kill us. Who fears to meet him can stay here with the

Veedor and swell a garrison. He'll have no disgrace, but no gold neither. Who stirs?

RODAS: Well, I hissing stir for one. I'm not going to be chewed up by no bloody heathen king. What do you say, Vasca lad?

VASCA: I don't know. I reckon if he chews us first, he chews you second. We're the eggs and you're the stew.

RODAS: Ha, ha, day of a hundred jokes!

SALINAS: Come on friend, for God's sake. Who's going to sew us up if you desert?

RODAS: You can all rot for all I care, breeches and what's bloody in 'em.

SALINAS: Bastard!

RODAS: To hell with the lot of you!
        (*He walks off.*)

PIZARRO: Anyone else?

DOMINGO: Well, I don't know. . . . Maybe he's right.

JUAN: Hey, Pedro, what do you think?

PEDRO: Hell, no! Vasca's right. It's as safe to go as stay here.

SALINAS: That's right.

VASCA: Anyway, I didn't come to keep no hissing garrison.

PEDRO: Nor me. I'm going on.

JUAN: Right, boy.

SALINAS: And me.

DOMINGO: Well, I don't know . . .

VASCA: Oh, close your mouth. You're like a hissing girl. (*To* PIZARRO) We're coming. Just find us the gold.

PIZARRO: All right then. (*To* YOUNG MARTIN) You stay here.

YOUNG MARTIN: No, sir. The place of a squire is at all times by his Knight's side. Laws of Chivalry.

PIZARRO (*touched*): Get them in rank. *Move!*

YOUNG MARTIN: Company in rank. Move!
        (*The soldiers form up in rank.*)

PIZARRO: Stand firm. Firmer! . . . Look at you, you could be dead already. If he sees you like that you will be. Make no error, he's watching every step you take. You're not men any longer, you're Gods now. Eternal Gods, each one of you. Two can play this immortality game, my lads. I want to see you move over his land like figures from a Lent Procession. He must see Gods walk on earth. Indifferent! Uncrushable! No death to be afraid of. I tell you, one shiver dooms the lot of us. One yelp of fright and we'll never be heard of again. He'll serve us like cheeseworms you crush with a knife. So come on you tattered trash – shake out the straw. Forget your village magic: fingers in crosses, saints under your shirts. You can grant prayers now – no need to answer them. Come on! Fix your eyes! Follow the pig-boy to his glory! I'll have an Empire for my farm. A million boys driving in the pigs at night. And each one of you will own a share – juicy black earth a hundred mile apiece – and golden ploughs to cut it! Get up you God-boys – March!

> (MARTIN *bangs his drum. The Spaniards begin to march in slow motion. Above, masked Indians move on to the upper level.*)

MANCO: They move, Inca! they come! One hundred and sixty and seven.

ATAHUALLPA: Where?

MANCO: Zaran.

VILLAC UMU: Ware! Ware Inca!

MANCO: They move all in step. Not fast, not slow. They keep straight on from dark to dark.

VILLAC UMU: Ware! Ware, Inca!

MANCO: They are at Motupe, Inca! They do not look on left or right.

VILLAC UMU: Ware! this is great danger.

ATAHUALLPA: No danger. He is coming to bless me. A god and all his priests. Praise Father Sun!

ALL ABOVE (*chanting*): Viracoch'an Atiesi.

ATAHUALLPA: Praise Sapa Inca!

ALL ABOVE: Sapa Inca! Inca Capac!

ATAHUALLPA: Praise Inti Cori!

ALL ABOVE: Caylla, int'i cori!

CHALLCUCHIMA: They come to the mountains.

VILLAC UMU: Kill them now.

ATAHUALLPA: Praise Atahuallpa.

VILLAC UMU: Destroy them! Teach them death!

ATAHUALLPA: *Praise Atahuallpa!*

ALL ABOVE: Atahuallpa! Sapa Inca! Huaccha Cuyak!

ATAHUALLPA (*crying out*): Let them see my mountains!

(*A crash of primitive instruments. The lights snap out and, lit from the side, the rays of the metal sun throw long shadows across the wooden wall. All the Spaniards fall down. A cold blue light fills the stage.*)

DE SOTO: God in heaven!

(*Enter* OLD MARTIN.)

OLD MARTIN: You call them the Andes. Picture a curtain of stone hung by some giant across your path. Mountains set on mountains: cliffs on cliffs. Hands of rock a hundred yards high, with flashing nails where the snow never moved, scratching the gashed face of the sun. For miles around the jungle lay black in its shadow. A freezing cold fell on us.

PIZARRO: Up, my godlings. Up, my little gods. Take heart, now. He's watching you. *Get to your feet!* (*To* DIEGO) Master, what of the horses?

DIEGO: D'you need them, sir?

PIZARRO: They're vital, boy.

DIEGO: Then you'll have 'em, sir. They'll follow you as we will.

PIZARRO: Up we go, then! We're coming for you, Atahuallpa. Show me the toppest peak-top you can pile — show me the lid of the world — I'll stand tiptoe on it and pull you right out of the sky. I'll grab you by the legs, you Son of the Sun, and smash your flaming crown on the rocks. Bless them, Church!

VALVERDE: God stay you, and stay with you all.

DE NIZZA: Amen.

(*Whilst* PIZARRO *is calling his last speech to the Inca, the silent King thrice beckons to him, and retires backwards out of the sun into blackness. In the cold light there now ensues*:)

Scene VIII

The Mime of the Great Ascent

As Old Martin *describes their ordeal, the men climb the Andes. It is a terrible progress; a stumbling, tortuous climb into the clouds, over ledges and giant chasms, performed to an eerie, cold music made from the thin whine of huge saws.*

Old Martin: Have you ever climbed a mountain in full armour? That's what we did, him going first the whole way up a tiny path into the clouds, with drops sheer on both sides into nothing. For hours we crept forward like blind men, the sweat freezing on our faces, lugging skittery leaking horses, and pricked all the time for the ambush that would tip us into death. Each turn of the path it grew colder. The friendly trees of the forest dropped away, and there were only pines. Then they went too, and there just scrubby little bushes standing up in ice. All round us the rocks began to whine with cold. And always above us, or below us, those filthy condor birds, hanging on the air with great tasselled wings.

(*It grows darker. The music grows colder yet. The men freeze and hang their heads for a long moment, before resuming their desperate climb.*)

Then night. We lay down twos and threes together on the path, and hugged like lovers for warmth in that burning cold. And most cried. We got up with cold iron for bones and went on. Four days like that: groaning, not speaking; the breath a blade in our lungs. Four days, slowly, like flies on a wall; limping flies, dying flies, up an endless wall of rock. A tiny army lost in the creases of the moon.

Indians (*off: in echo*): Stand!

(*The Spaniards whirl round.* Villac Umu *and his attendants appear, clothed entirely in white fur. The High Priest wears a snow-white llama head on top of his own.*)

150

VILLAC UMU: You see Villac Umu. Chief Priest of the Sun. Why do you come?

PIZARRO: To see the Great Inca.

VILLAC UMU: Why will you see him?

PIZARRO: To give him blessing.

VILLAC UMU: Why will you bless him?

PIZARRO: He is a God. I am a God.

VALVERDE (*sotto voce*): General!

PIZARRO: Be still.

VILLAC UMU: Below you is the town of Cajamarca. The Great Inca orders: rest there. Tomorrow early he will come to you. Do not move from the town. Outside it is his anger.

(*He goes off with his attendants.*)

VALVERDE: What have you done, sir?

PIZARRO: Sent him news to amaze him.

VALVERDE: I cannot approve blasphemy.

PIZARRO: To conquer for Christ, one can surely usurp his name for a night, Father. Set on.

SCENE IX

A dreary light.

The Spaniards fan out over the stage. DE SOTO *goes off.*

OLD MARTIN: So down we went from ledge to ledge, and out on to a huge plain of eucalyptus trees, all glowing in the failing light. And there, at the other end, lay a vast white town with roofs of straw. As night fell, we entered it. We came into an empty square, larger than any in Spain. All round it ran long white buildings, three times the height of a man. Everywhere was grave quiet. You could almost touch the silence. Up on the hill we could see the Inca's tents, and the lights from his fires ringing the valley. (*Exit.*)

(*Some sit. All look up at the hillside.*)

DIEGO: How many do you reckon there's up there?

DE CANDIA: Ten thousand.

DE SOTO (*re-entering*): The town's empty. Not even a dog.

DOMINGO: It's a trap. I know it's a trap.

PIZARRO: Felipillo! Where's that little rat? Felipillo!

FELIPILLO: General, Lord.

PIZARRO: What does this mean?

FELIPILLO: I don't know. Perhaps it is order of welcome. Great people. Much honour.

VALVERDE: Nonsense, it's a trick, a brownie trick. He's got us all marked for death.

DE NIZZA: He could have killed us at any time. Why should he take such trouble with us?

PIZARRO: Because we're Gods, Father. He'll change soon enough when he finds out different.

DE SOTO: Brace up, boy! It's what you came for, isn't it? Death and glory?

YOUNG MARTIN: Yes, sir.

PIZARRO: De Soto. De Candia. (*They go to him*) It's got to be ambush. That's our only hope.

DE SOTO: Round the square?

PIZARRO: Lowers the odds. Three thousand at most.

DE CANDIA: Thirty to one. Not low enough.

PIZARRO: It'll have to do. We're not fighting ten thousand or three. One man: that's all. Get him, the rest collapse.

DE SOTO: Even if we can, they'll kill us all to get him back.

PIZARRO: If there's a knife at his throat? It's a risk, sure. But what do worshippers do when you snatch their God?

DE CANDIA: Pray to you instead.

DIEGO: It's wonderful. Grab the King, grab the Kingdom!

DE NIZZA: It would avoid bloodshed.

PIZARRO: What do you say?

DE CANDIA: It's the only way. It could work.

DE SOTO: With God's help.

PIZARRO: Then pray all. Disperse. Light fires. Make confession. Battle orders at first light.

(*Most disperse. Some lie down to pray and sleep.*)

DE NIZZA (*to* DE CANDIA): Shall I hear your confession now, my son?

DE CANDIA: You'd best save all that for tomorrow, Father. For the men who are left. What have we got to confess tonight but thoughts of murder?

DE NIZZA: Then confess those.

DE CANDIA: Why? Should I feel shame for them? What would I say to God if I refused to destroy His enemies?

VALVERDE: More Venetian nonsense!

DE NIZZA: God has no enemies, my son. Only those nearer to Him or farther from Him.

DE CANDIA: Well, my job is to aim at the far ones. I'll go and position the guns. Excuse me.

(*He goes off.*)

PIZARRO: Diego, look to the horses. I know they're sorry, but we'll need them brisk.

VALVERDE: Come my brother, we'll pray together.

(*They go too.*)

PIZARRO: The cavalry will split and hide in the buildings, there and there.

DE SOTO: And the infantry in file — there, and round there.

PIZARRO: Perfect. Herrada can command one flank, de Barbaran the other. Everyone hidden.

DE SOTO: They'll suspect then.

PIZARRO: No, the Church will greet them.

DE SOTO: We'll need a watchword.

PIZARRO: San Jago.

DE SOTO: San Jago. Good.

(*The old man comes upon his* PAGE, *who is sitting huddled by himself.*)

PIZARRO: Are you scared?

YOUNG MARTIN: No, sir. Yes, sir.

PIZARRO: You're a good boy. If ever we get out of this, I'll make you a gift of whatever you ask me. Is that chivalrous enough for you?

YOUNG MARTIN: Being your page is enough, sir.

PIZARRO: And there's nothing else you want?

YOUNG MARTIN: A sword, sir.

PIZARRO: Of course . . . Take what rest you can. Call Assembly at first light.

YOUNG MARTIN: Yes, sir. Goodnight, sir.

DE SOTO: Goodnight, Martin. Try and sleep.

(*The boy lies down to sleep. The singing of prayers is heard, off, all around.*)

PIZARRO: Hope, lovely hope. A sword's no mere bar of metal for him. His world still has sacred objects. How remote . . .

DIEGO: Holy Virgin, give us victory. If you do, I'll make you a present of a fine Indian cloak. But you let us down, and I'll leave you for the Virgin of the Conception, and I mean that.

(*He lies down also. The prayers die away. Silence.*)

SCENE X

Semi-darkness.

PIZARRO: This is probably our last night. If we die, what will we have gone for?

DE SOTO: Spain. Christ.

PIZARRO: I envy you, Cavalier.

DE SOTO: For what?

PIZARRO: Your service. God. King. It's all simple for you.

DE SOTO: No, sir, it's not simple. But it's what I've chosen.

PIZARRO: Yes. And what have I chosen?

DE SOTO: To be a King yourself. Or as good, if we win here.

PIZARRO: And what's that at my age? Not only swords turn into bars of metal. Sceptres too. What's left, De Soto?

DE SOTO: What you told me in Spain. A name for ballads. The man of Honour has three good lives: The Life Today. The Life to Come. The Life of Fame.

PIZARRO: Fame is long. Death is longer . . . Does anyone ever die for anything? I thought so once. Life was fierce with feeling. It was all hope, like on that boy. Swords shone and armour sang, and cheese bit you, and kissing burned and Death — ah, death was going to make an exception in my case. I couldn't believe I was ever going to die. But once you know it — really know it — it's all over. You know you've been cheated, and nothing's the same again.

DE SOTO: Cheated?

PIZARRO: Time cheats us all the way. Children, yes — having children goes some steps to defeating it. Nothing else. It would have been good to have a son.

DE SOTO: Did you never think to marry?

PIZARRO: With my parentage? The only women who would have had me weren't the sort you married. Spain's a pile of horsedung . . . When I began to think of a world here, something in me was longing for a new place like a country after rain, washed clear of all the badges and barriers, the pebbles men drop to tell them where they are on a plain that's got no landmarks. I used to look after women with hope, but they didn't have much time for me. One of them said — what was it? — my soul was frostbitten. That's a word for you — Frostbitten. How goes it, man?

VASCA (off): A clear night, sir. Everything clear.

PIZARRO: I had a girl once, on a rock by the Southern Ocean. I lay with her one afternoon in winter, wrapped up in her against the cold, and the sea-fowl screaming, and it was the best hour of my life. I felt then that sea-water, and bird-droppings and the little pits in human flesh were all linked together for some great end right out of the net of words to catch. Not just my words, but anyone's. Then I lost it. Time came back. For always.

(He moves away, feeling his side.)

DE SOTO: Does it pain you?

PIZARRO: Oh, yes: *that's* still fierce.

DE SOTO: You should try to sleep. We'll need our strength.

PIZARRO: Listen, listen! Everything we feel is made of Time. All the beauties of life are shaped by it. Imagine a fixed sunset: the last note of a song that hung an hour, or a kiss for half of it. Tray and halt a moment in our lives and it becomes maggoty at once. Even that word 'moment' is wrong, since that would mean a speck of time, something you could pick up on a rag and peer at . . . But that's the awful trap of life. You can't escape maggots unless you go with Time, and if you go, they wriggle in you anyway.

DE SOTO: This is gloomy talk.

(YOUNG MARTIN *groans in his sleep.*)

PIZARRO: For a gloomy time. You were talking women. I loved them with all the juice in me – but oh, the cheat in that tenderness. What is it but a lust to own their beauty, not them, which you never can: like trying to own the beauty of a goblet by paying for it. And even if you could it would become you and get soiled . . . I'm an old man, Cavalier, I can explain nothing. What I mean is: Time whipped up the lust in me and Time purged it. I was dandled on Time's knee and made to gurgle, then put to my sleep. I've been cheated from the moment I was born because there's death in everything.

DE SOTO: Except in God.

(*A pause.*)

PIZARRO: When I was young, I used to sit on the slope outside the village and watch the sun go down, and I used to think: if only I could find the place where it sinks to rest for the night, I'd find the source of life, like the beginning of a river. I used to wonder what it could be like. Perhaps an island, a strange place of white sand, where the people never died. Never grew old, or felt pain, and never died.

DE SOTO: Sweet fancy.

PIZARRO: It's what your mind runs to when it lacks instruction. If I had a son, I'd kill him if he didn't read his book. . . . Where does the sun rest at night?

DE SOTO: Nowhere. It's a heavenly body set by God to move round the earth in perpetual motion.

PIZARRO: Do you know this?

DE SOTO: All Europe knows it.

PIZARRO: What if they were wrong? If it settled here each evening, somewhere in those great mountains, like a God laid down to sleep? To a savage mind it must make a fine God. I myself can't fix anything nearer to a thought of worship than standing at dawn and watching it fill the world. Like the coming of something eternal, against going flesh. What a fantastic wonder that anyone on earth should dare to say: 'That's my father. My father: the sun!' It's silly – but tremendous . . . You know – strange nonsense: since first I heard of him I've dreamed of him every night. A black king with glowing eyes, sporting the sun for a crown. What does it mean?

DE SOTO: I've no skill with dreams. Perhaps a soothsayer would tell you: 'The Inca's your enemy. You dream his emblem to increase your hate.'

PIZARRO: But I feel no enemy.

DE SOTO: Surely you do.

PIZARRO: No. Only that of all meetings I have made in my life, this with him is the one I have to make. Maybe it's my death. Or maybe new life. I feel just this: all my days have been a path to this one morning.

OLD MARTIN: The sixteenth of November, 1532. First light, sir.

Scene XI

Lights brighten slowly.

VALVERDE (*singing, off*): Exsurge Domine.

SOLDIERS (*singing in unison*): Exsurge Domine.
  (*All the company comes on, chanting.*)

VALVERDE: Deus meus eripe me de manu peccatoris.

SOLDIERS: Deus meus eripe me de manu peccatoris.
  (*All kneel, spread across the stage.*)

VALVERDE: Many strong bulls have compassed me.

DE NIZZA: They have gaped upon me with their mouths, as a lion ravening.

VALVERDE: I am poured out like water, and all my bones are scattered.

DE NIZZA: My heart is like wax, melting in the midst of

my bowels. My tongue cleaves to my jaws, and thou hast brought me into the dust of death.

(*All freeze.*)

OLD MARTIN: The dust of death. It was in our noses. The full scare came to us quickly, like plague.

(*All heads turn.*)

The men were crammed in buildings all round the square.

(*All stand.*)

They stood there shivering, making water where they stood. An hour went by. Two. Three.

(*All remain absolutely still.*)

Five. Not a move from the Indian camp. Not a sound from us. Only the weight of the day. A hundred and sixty men in full armour, cavalry mounted, infantry at the ready, standing in dead silence – glued in a trance of waiting.

PIZARRO: Hold fast now. Come on – you're Gods. Take heart. Don't blink your eyes, that's too much noise.

OLD MARTIN: Seven.

PIZARRO: Stiff. Stiff. You're your own masters, boys. Not peasant any more. This is your time. Own it. Live it.

OLD MARTIN: Nine. Ten hours passed. There were few of us then who didn't feel the cold begin to crawl.

PIZARRO (*whispering*): Send him, send him, send him, send him.

OLD MARTIN: Dread comes with the evening air. Even the priest's arm fails.

PIZARRO: The sun's going out!

OLD MARTIN: No one looks at his neighbour. Then, with the shadow of night already running towards us —

YOUNG MARTIN: *They're coming!* Look, down the hill —

DE SOTO: How many?

YOUNG MARTIN: Hundreds, sir.

DE CANDIA: Thousands – two or three.

PIZARRO: Can you see *him*?

DE CANDIA: No, not yet.

DOMINGO: What's that? – out there in front – they're doing something.

VASCA: Looks like sweeping —

DIEGO: They're sweeping the road!

DOMINGO: For *him*! They're sweeping the road for him! Five hundred of 'em sweeping the road!

SALINAS: God in Heaven!

PIZARRO: Are they armed?

DE CANDIA: To the teeth!

DE SOTO: How? —

DE CANDIA: Axes and spears.

YOUNG MARTIN: They're all glittering, glittering red! —

DIEGO: It's the sun! Like someone's stabbed it! —

VASCA: Squirting blood all over the sky!

DOMINGO: It's an omen! —

SALINAS: Shut up.

DOMINGO: It must be. The whole country's bleeding. Look for yourself. It's an omen!

VALVERDE: This is the day foretold you by the Angel of the Apocalypse. Satan reigns on the altars, jeering at the true God. The earth teems with corrupt kings.

DOMINGO: Oh God! Oh God! Oh God! Oh God!

DE SOTO: Control yourself!

DE CANDIA: They're stopping!

YOUNG MARTIN: They're throwing things down, sir!

PIZARRO: What things?

DE CANDIA: Weapons.

PIZARRO: No!

DIEGO: Yes, sir. I can see. All their weapons. They're throwing them down in a pile.

VASCA: They're laying down their arms.

SALINAS: I don't believe it!

VASCA: They are. They are leaving everything!

DOMINGO: It's a miracle.

DE SOTO: Why? *Why?*

PIZARRO: Because we're Gods. You see? You don't approach Gods with weapons.

(*Strange music faintly in the distance. Through all the ensuing it grows louder and louder.*)

De Soto: What's that?

Young Martin: It's *him*. He's coming, sir.

Pizarro: Where?

Young Martin: *There*, sir.

Diego: Oh, look, *look*. God Almighty, it's not happening! . . .

De Soto: Steady man.

Pizarro: You're coming. Come on then! *Come on!*

De Soto: General, it's time to hide.

Pizarro: Yes, quick now. No one must be seen but the priests. Out there in the middle, Fathers: everyone else in hiding.

De Soto: Quick! jump to it!

(*Only now do the men break, scatter and vanish.*)

Pizarro (*to* Young Martin): You too.

Young Martin: Until the fighting, sir?

Pizarro: All the time for you, fighting or no.

Young Martin: Oh no, sir!

Pizarro: Do as I say. Take him, de Soto.

De Soto: Save you, General.

Pizarro: And you, de Soto. San Jago!

De Soto: San Jago! Come on.

De Candia: There are seven gunners on the roof. And three over there.

Pizarro: Watch the cross-fire.

De Candia: I'll wait for your signal.

Pizarro: Then sound yours.

De Candia: You'll hear it.

Pizarro (*to* Felipillo): Felipillo! Stand there! Now . . . now . . . NOW!

(*He hurries off.*)

Scene XII

The music crashes over the stage as the Indian procession enters in an astonishing explosion of colour. The King's attendants — many of them playing musical instruments:

reed pipes, cymbals, and giant marracas — are as gay as parrots. They wear costumes of orange and yellow, and fantastic headdresses of gold and feathers, with eyes embossed on them in staring black enamel. By contrast, ATAHUALLPA INCA *presents a picture of utter simplicity. He is dressed from head to foot in white: across his eyes is a mask of jade mosaic, and round his head a circlet of plain gold. Silence falls. The King glares about him.*

ATAHUALLPA (*haughtily*): Where is the God?

VALVERDE (*through* FELIPILLO): I am a Priest of God.

ATAHUALLPA: I do not want the priest. I want the God. Where is he? He sent me greeting.

VALVERDE: That was our General. Our God cannot be seen.

ATAHUALLPA: *I* may see him.

VALVERDE: No. He was killed by men and went into the sky.

ATAHUALLPA: A God cannot be killed. See my father. You cannot kill him. He lives for ever and looks over his children every day.

VALVERDE: I am the answer to all mysteries. Hark, pagan, and I will expound.

OLD MARTIN: And so he did, from the Creation to Our Lord's ascension.

(*He goes off.*)

VALVERDE (*walking among the Indians to the right*): And when he went he left the Pope as Regent for him.

DE NIZZA (*walking among the Indians to the left*): And when he went he left the Pope as Regent for him.

VALVERDE: He has commanded our King to bring all men to belief in the true God.

DE NIZZA: He has commanded our King to bring all men to belieff in the true God.

VALVERDE ⎫
DE NIZZA ⎭ (*together*): In Christ's name therefore I charge you: yield yourself his willing vassal.

ATAHUALLPA: I am the vassal of no man. I am the greatest

Prince on earth. Your King is great. He has sent you far across the water. So he is my brother. But your Pope is mad. He gives away countries that are not his. His faith also is mad.

VALVERDE: Beware!

ATAHUALLPA: Ware you! You kill my people: you make them slaves. By what power?

VALVERDE: By this. (*He offers a Bible*) The Word of God.

(ATAHUALLPA *holds it to his ear. He listens intently. He shakes it.*)

ATAHUALLPA: No word.

(*He smells the book, and then licks it. Finally he throws it down impatiently.*)

God is angry with your insults.

VALVERDE: Blasphemy!

ATAHUALLPA: God is angry.

VALVERDE: Francisco Pizarro, do you stay your hand when Christ is insulted? Let this pagan feel the power of your arm. I absolve you all! San Jago!

(PIZARRO *appears above with drawn sword, and in a great voice sings out his battle-cry.*)

PIZARRO: SAN JAGO Y CIERRA ESPAÑA!

(*Instantly from all sides the soldiers rush in, echoing the great cry.*)

SOLDIERS: SAN JAGO!

(*There is a tense pause. The Indians look at this ring of armed men in terror. A violent drumming begins, and there ensues:*

THE MIME OF THE GREAT MASSACRE

To a savage music, wave upon wave of Indians are slaughtered and rise again to protect their lord who stands bewildered in their midst. It is all in vain. Relentlessly the Spanish soldiers hew their way through the ranks of feathered attendants towards their quarry. They surround him. SALINAS *snatches the crown off his head and tosses it up to* PIZARRO, *who catches it and to a great shout crowns himself. All the Indians cry out in horror. The drum hammers on relentlessly while* ATAHUALLPA *is led off at sword-point by the whole band of Spaniards. At the same time, dragged from the middle of the sun by howling Indians, a vast bloodstained cloth bellies out over the stage. All rush off; their screams fill the theatre.*

The lights fade out slowly out on the rippling cloth of blood.

ACT II – THE KILL

SCENE I

Darkness. A bitter Inca lament is intoned, above.
Lights up a little. The bloodstained cloth still lies over
the stage. In the sun chamber ATAHUALLPA *stands in*
chains, his back to the audience, his white robe dirty
with blood. Although he is unmasked, we cannot yet see
his face, only a tail of black hair hanging down his neck.

    (OLD MARTIN *appears. From opposite,* YOUNG MARTIN
    comes in, stumbling with shock. He collapses on his
    knees.)

OLD MARTIN: Look at the warrior where he struts. Glory
on his sword. Salvation in his new spurs. One of the knights
at last. The very perfect knight Sir Martin, tender in virtue,
bodyguard of Christ. Jesus, we are all eased out of kids'
dreams; but who can be ripped out of them and live loving
after? Three thousand Indians we killed in that square. The
only Spaniard to be wounded was the General, scratched by
a sword whilst protecting his Royal prisoner. That night, as
I knelt vomiting into a canal, the empire of the Incas stopped.
The spring of the clock was snapped. For a thousand miles
men sat down not knowing what to do.

    (*Enter* DE SOTO.)

DE SOTO: Well, boy, what is it? They weren't armed, is
that it? If they had been we could be dead now.

YOUNG MARTIN: Honourably dead! Not alive and shamed.

DE SOTO: And Christ would be dead here too, scarcely
born. When I first breathed blood it was in my lungs for
days. But the time comes when you won't even sniff when it
pours over your feet. See, boy, here and now it's kill or get

164

killed. And if we go, we betray Christ, whose coming we are here to make.

YOUNG MARTIN: You talk as if we're butlers, sent to open the door for him.

DE SOTO: So we are.

YOUNG MARTIN: No! He's with us now – at all times – or never.

DE SOTO: He's with us, yes, but not with them. After he is, there will be time for mercy.

YOUNG MARTIN: When there is no danger! Some mercy!

DE SOTO: Would you put Christ in danger, then?

YOUNG MARTIN: He can look after himself.

DE SOTO: He can't. That's why he needs servants.

YOUNG MARTIN: To kill for him?

DE SOTO: If necessary. And it was. My parish priest used to say: There must always be dying to make new life. I think of that whenever I draw the sword. My constant thought is: I must be winter for Our Lord to be Spring.

YOUNG MARTIN: I don't understand.

(PIZARRO *and* FELIPILLO *come in.*)

PIZARRO: Stand up when the Second addresses you. What are you, a defiled girl? (*To* DE SOTO) I've sent De Candia back to the Garrison. Reinforcements should be there presently. Come now: let's meet this King.

SCENE II

Lights up more.
They move upstage and bow. Above OELLO *and* INTI
COUSSI *come in and kneel on either side of the* INCA, *who
ignores the embassy below.*

My lord, I am Francisco Pizarro, General of Spain. It is an honour to speak with you. (*Pause*) You are very tall, my lord. In my country are no such tall men. (*Pause*) My lord, won't you speak?

(ATAHUALLPA *turns. For the first time we see his face,*

carved in a mould of serene arrogance. His whole bearing displays the most entire dignity and natural grace. When he moves or speaks, it is always with the consciousness of his divine origin, his sacred function and his absolute power.)

ATAHUALLPA (*to* FELIPILLO): Tell him I am Atahuallpa Capac, Son of the Sun, Son of the Moon, Lord of the Four Quarters. Why does he not kneel?

FELIPILLO: The Inca says he wishes he had killed you when you first came.

PIZARRO: Why didn't he?

ATAHUALLPA: He lied to me. He is not a God. I came for blessing. He sharpened his knives on the shoulders of my servants. I have no word for *him* whose word is evil.

FELIPILLO: He says he wants to make slaves of your best warriors, then kill all the others. Especially you he would kill because you are old; no use as slave.

PIZARRO: Tell him he will live to rue those intentions.

FELIPILLO: You make my master angry. He will kill you tomorrow. Then he will give that wife (*he indicates* OELLO) to me for my pleasure.

(OELLO *rises in alarm.*)

ATAHUALLPA: How dare you speak this before my face?

YOUNG MARTIN: General.

PIZARRO: What?

YOUNG MARTIN: Excuse me, sir, but I don't think you're being translated aright.

PIZARRO: You don't?

YOUNG MARTIN: No, sir. Nor the King to you. I know a little of the language and he said nothing about slaves.

PIZARRO: You! What are you saying?

FELIPILLO: General Lord. This boy know nothing how to speak.

YOUNG MARTIN: I know more than you think. I know you're lying. . . . He's after the woman, General. I saw him before, in the square, grabbing at her.

PIZARRO: Is that true?

YOUNG MARTIN: As I live, sir.

PIZARRO: What do you say?

FELIPILLO: General Lord, I speak wonderful for you. No one speak so wonderful.

PIZARRO: What about that girl?

FELIPILLO: You give her as present to me, yes?

PIZARRO: The Inca's wife?

FELIPILLO: Inca has many wives. This one small, not famous.

PIZARRO: Get out.

FELIPILLO: General Lord!

PIZARRO: You work another trick like this and I'll swear I'll hang you. Out!

(FELIPILLO *spits at him and runs off.*)

PIZARRO: Could you take his place?

YOUNG MARTIN: With work, sir.

PIZARRO: Work, then. Come, let's make a start. Ask him his age.

YOUNG MARTIN: My lord, (*hesitantly*) how old are him? I mean 'you' . . .

ATAHUALLPA: I have been on earth thirty and three years. What age is your master?

YOUNG MARTIN: Sixty-three.

ATAHUALLPA: All those years have taught him nothing but wickedness.

YOUNG MARTIN: That's not true.

PIZARRO: What does he say?

YOUNG MARTIN: I don't quite understand, my lord . . .

(*Exit* YOUNG MARTIN.)

OLD MARTIN: So it was I became the General's interpreter and was privy to everything that passed between them during the next months. The Inca tongue was very hard, but to please my adored master I worked at it for hours, and with each passing day found out more of it.

(PIZARRO *leaves, followed by* DE SOTO.)

Scene III

Re-enter Young Martin *above.* Old Martin *watches below before going off.*

Young Martin: Good day, my lord. I have a game here to amuse you. No Spaniard is complete without them. I take half and you take half. Then we fight. These are the Churchmen with their pyxes. The Nobility with their swords. The Merchants with their gold, and the Poor with their sticks.

Atahuallpa: What are the poor?

Young Martin: Those who've got no gold. They suffer for this.

Atahuallpa (*crying out*): Aiyah!

Young Martin: What are you thinking, my lord?

Atahuallpa: That my people will suffer.

(*Enter* Pizarro *and* De Soto.)

Pizarro: Good day, my lord. How are you this morning?

Atahuallpa: You want gold. That is why you came here.

Pizarro: My lord —

Atahuallpa: You can't hide from me. (*Showing him the card of the Poor*) You want gold. I know. Speak.

Pizarro: You have gold?

Atahuallpa: It is the sweat of the sun. It belongs to me.

Pizarro: Is there much?

Atahuallpa: Make me free. I would fill this room.

Pizarro: Fill?

De Soto: It's not possible.

Atahuallpa: I am Atahuallpa and I say it.

Pizarro: How long?

Atahuallpa: Two showings of my Mother Moon. But it will not be done.

Pizarro: Why not?

Atahuallpa: You must swear to free me and you have no swear to give.

Pizarro: You wrong me, my lord.

Atahuallpa: No, it is in your face, no swear.

PIZARRO: I never broke word with you. I never promised you safety. If once I did, you would have it.

ATAHUALLPA: Do you now?

DE SOTO: Refuse, sir. You could never free him.

PIZARRO: It won't come to that.

DE SOTO: It could.

PIZARRO: Never. Can you think how much gold it would take? Even half would drown us in riches.

DE SOTO: General, you can only give your word where you can keep it.

PIZARRO: I'll never have to break it. It's the same case.

DE SOTO: It's not.

PIZARRO: Oh, God's wounds, your niceties! He's offering more than any conqueror has ever seen. Alexander, Tamberlaine, or who you please. I mean to have it.

DE SOTO: So. At your age gold is no lodestone!

PIZARRO: No more is it. I promised my men gold. Yes? He stands between them and that gold. If I don't make this bargain now he'll die; the men will demand it.

DE SOTO: And what's that to you if he does?

PIZARRO: I want him alive. At least for a while.

DE SOTO: You're thinking of how you dreamed of him.

PIZARRO: Yes. He has some meaning for me, this Man-God. An immortal man in whom all his people live completely. He has an answer for time.

DE SOTO: If it was true.

PIZARRO: Yes, if . . .

DE SOTO: General, be careful. I don't understand you in full but I know this: what you do now can never be undone.

PIZARRO: Words, my dear Cavalier. They don't touch me. This way I'll have gold for my men and him there safe. That's enough for the moment. (*To* ATAHUALLPA) Now you must keep the peace meanwhile, not strive to escape, nor urge your men to help you. So swear.

ATAHUALLPA: I swear!

PIZARRO: Then I swear too. Fill that room with gold and I will set you free.

DE SOTO: General!

PIZARRO: Oh, come, man! He never will.

DE SOTO: I think this man performs what he swears. Pray God we don't pay bitterly for this.

(*He goes off. Enter* OLD MARTIN.)

PIZARRO: My lord — (ATAHUALLPA *ignores him*) — well spoken, lad. Your services increase every day.

YOUNG MARTIN: Thank you, sir.

(*The General leaves the stage and the boy goes out of the Sun chamber, leaving* ATAHUALLPA *alone in it.*)

OLD MARTIN: The room was twenty-two feet long by seventeen feet wide. The mark on the wall was nine feet high.

(*The* INCA *adopts a pose of command. Drums mark each name.*)

ATAHUALLPA: Atahuallpa speaks! (*A crash of instruments*) Atahuallpa needs. (*Crash*) Atahuallpa commands. (*Crash*) Bring him gold. From the palaces. From the temples. From all buildings in the great places. From walls of pleasure and roofs of omen. From floors of feasting and ceilings of death. Bring him the gold of Quito and Pachamacac! Bring him the gold of Cuzco and Coricancha! Bring him the gold of Vilcanota! Bring him the gold of Colae! Of Aymaraes and Arequipa! Bring him the gold of the Chimu! Put up a mountain of gold and free your Sun from his prison of clouds.

(*Lights down above.* ATAHUALLPA *leaves the chamber.*)

OLD MARTIN: It was agreed that the gold collected was not to be melted beforehand into bars, so that the Inca got the benefit of the space between them. Then he was moved out of his prison to make way for the treasure and given more comfortable state.

SCENE IV

Lights fade above, and brighten below.
Slowly the great cloth of blood is dragged off by two Indians as ATAHUALLPA *appears. He advances to the*

middle of the stage. He claps his hands, once. Immedi-
ately a gentle hum is heard and Indians appear with
new clothing. From their wrists hang tiny golden
cymbals and small bells; to the soft clash and tinkle of
these little instruments his servants remove the Inca's
bloodstained garments and put on him clean ones.

OLD MARTIN: He was allowed to audience his nobles. The
little loads they bore were a sign of reverence.

(VILLAC UMU *and* CHALLCUCHIMA *come in.*)

He was dressed in his royal cloak, made from the skins of
vampire birds, and his ears were hung again with the weight
of noble responsibility.

(ATAHUALLPA *is cloaked, a collar of turquoises is placed*
round his neck and heavy gold rings are placed in his
ears. While this is happening there is a fresh tinkling and
more Indians appear, carrying his meal in musical dishes
— plates like tambourines from whose rims hang bells, or
in whose lower shelves are tiny golden balls. The stage
is filled with chimes and delicate clatter, and above it
the perpetual humming of masked servants.)

OLD MARTIN: His meals were served as they always had
been. I remember his favourite food was stewed lamb,
garnished with sweet potatoes.

(*The food is served to the* INCA *in this manner.* OELLO
takes meat out of a bowl, places it in her hands and
ATAHUALLPA *lowers his face to it, while she turns her*
own face away from him out of respect.)

OLD MARTIN: What he didn't eat was burnt, and if he
spilled any on himself, his clothes were burnt also. (*Exit.*)

(OELLO *rises and quietly removes the dish. Suddenly*
FELIPILLO *rushes on and knocks it violently from her*
hand.)

FELIPILLO: You're going to burn it? Why? Because your
husband is a God? How stupid! stupid! stupid!

(*He grabs her and flings her to the ground. A general*
cry of horror.)

(*To* ATAHUALLPA) Yes, I touch her! Make me dead! You

171

are a God. Make me dead with your eyes!

VILLAC UMU: What you have said kills you. You will be buried in the earth alive.

(*A pause. For a moment* FELIPILLO *half believes this. Then he laughs and kisses the girl on the throat. As she screams and struggles,* YOUNG MARTIN *rushes in.*)

YOUNG MARTIN: Felipillo, stop it!

(VALVERDE *comes in from another side; with* DE NIZZA.)

VALVERDE: Felipillo! Is it for this we saved you from Hell? Your old God encouraged lust. Your new God will damn you for it. Leave him!

(FELIPILLO *runs off*.)

(*To the Indians*) Go!

(*A pause. No one moves until* ATAHAULLPA *claps his hands twice. Then all the servants bow and leave.*)

Now, my lord, let us take up our talk again. Tell me – I am only a simple priest – as an undoubted God, do you live forever here on earth?

VILLAC UMU: Here on earth Gods come one after another, young and young again, to protect the people of the Sun. Then they go up to his great place in the sky, at his will.

VALVERDE: What if they are killed in battle?

VILLAC UMU: If it is not the Sun's time for them to go, he will return them to life again in the next day's light.

VALVERDE: How comforting. And has any Inca so returned?

VILLAC UMU: No.

VALVERDE: Curious.

VILLAC UMU: This means only that all Incas have died in the Sun's time.

VALVERDE: Clever.

VILLAC UMU: No. True.

VALVERDE: Tell me this, how can the Sun have a child?

VILLAC UMU: How can your God have a Child, since you say he has no body?

VALVERDE: He is spirit – inside us.

VILLAC UMU: Your God is inside you? How can this be?

ATAHUALLPA: They eat him. First he becomes a biscuit, and then they eat him. (*The Inca bares his teeth and laughs soundlessly*) I have seen this. At praying they say 'This is the body of our God'. Then they drink his blood. It is very bad. Here in my empire we do not eat men. My family forbade it many years past.

VALVERDE: You are being deliberately stupid.

VILLAC UMU: Why do you eat your God? To have his strength?

DE NIZZA: Yes, my lord.

VILLAC UMU: But your God is weak. He fights with no man. That is why he was killed.

DE NIZZA: He wanted to be killed, so he could share death with us.

ATAHUALLPA: So he needed killers to help him, though you say killing is bad.

VALVERDE: This is the devil's tongue.

DE NIZZA: My lord must see that when God becomes man, he can no longer act perfectly.

ATAHUALLPA: Why?

DE NIZZA: He joins us in the prison of our sin.

ATAHUALLPA: What is sin?

DE NIZZA: Let me picture it to you as a prison cell, the bars made of our imperfections. Through them we glimpse a fair country where it is always morning. We wish we could walk there, or else forget the place entirely. But we cannot snap the bars, or if we do, others grow in their stead.

ATAHUALLPA: All your pictures are of prisons and chains.

DE NIZZA: All life is chains. We are chained to food, and fire in the winter. To innocence lost but its memory unlost. And to needing each other.

ATAHUALLPA: I need no one.

DE NIZZA: That is not true.

ATAHUALLPA: I am the Sun. I need only the sky.

DE NIZZA: That is not true, Atahuallpa. The sun is a ball of fire. Nothing more.

ATAHUALLPA: How?

DE NIZZA: Nothing more.

(*With terrible speed, the* INCA *rises to strike* DE NIZZA.)

VALVERDE: Down! Do you dare lift your hand against a priest? Sit! Now!

(ATAHUALLPA *does not move.*)

DE NIZZA: You do not feel your people, my lord, because you do not love them.

ATAHUALLPA: Explain love.

DE NIZZA: It is not known in your kingdom. At home we can say to our ladies: 'I love you', or to our native earth. It means we rejoice in their lives. But a man cannot say this to the woman he must marry at twenty-five; or to the strip of land allotted to him at birth which he must till till he dies. Love must be free, or else it alters away. Command it to your court: it will send a deputy. Let God order it to fill our hearts, it becomes useless to him. It is stronger than iron: yet in a fist of force it melts. It is a coin that sparkles in the hand: yet in the pocket it turns to rust. Love is the only door from the prison of ourselves. It is the eagerness of God to enter that prison, to take on pain, and imagine lust, so that the torn soldier, or the spent lecher, can call out in his defeat: 'You know this too, so help me from it'.

(*A further music of bells and humming. Enter* OLD MARTIN.)

THE FIRST GOLD PROCESSION

Guarded closely by Spanish soldiers, a line of Indian porters comes in, each carrying a stylized gold object — utensils and ornaments. They cross the stage and disappear. Almost simultaneously, above, similar objects are hung up by Indians in the middle of the sun.

OLD MARTIN (*during this*): The first gold arrived. Much of it was in big plates weighing up to seventy-five pounds, the rest in objects of amazing skill. Knives of ceremony;

collars and fretted crowns; funeral gloves, and red-stained death masks, goggling at us with profound enamel eyes. Some days there were things worth thirty or forty gold pesos – but we weren't satisfied with that. (*Exit*.)

(*Enter* PIZARRO *and* DE SOTO.)

PIZARRO: I find you wanting in honesty. A month has passed: the room isn't a quarter full.

ATAHUALLPA: My kingdom is great; porters are slow. You will see more gold before long.

PIZARRO: The rumour is we'll see a rising before long.

ATAHUALLPA: Not a leaf stirs in my kingdom without my leave. If you do not trust me send to Cuzco, my capital. See how quiet my people sit.

PIZARRO (*to* DE SOTO): Good. You leave immediately with a force of thirty.

CHALLCUCHIMA: God is tied by his word, like you. But if he raised one nail of one finger of one hand, you would all die that same raising.

PIZARRO: So be it. If you play us false, both these will die before us.

ATAHUALLPA: There are many Priests, many Generals. These can die.

VALVERDE: Mother of God! There's no conversion possible for this man.

DE SOTO: You cannot say that, sir.

VALVERDE: Satan has many forms and there sits one. As for his advisers, it is you, Priest, who stiffen him against me. You, General, who whisper revolt.

CHALLCUCHIMA: You lie.

VALVERDE: Leave him!

(*As before they do not move until* ATAHUALLPA *has clapped his hands twice. Then, immediately, the two Indians bow and leave.*)

Pagan filth.

DE SOTO: I'll make inspection. Goodbye, my lord, we'll meet in a month.

(*Exit* DE SOTO.)

VALVERDE: Beware, Pizarro. Give him the slack, he will destroy us all.

(*He goes out another way.*)

DE NIZZA: The Father has great zeal.

PIZARRO: Oh, yes, great zeal to see the devil in a poor dark man.

DE NIZZA: Not so poor, General. A man who is the soul of his kingdom. Look hard, you *will* find Satan here, because here is a country which denies the right to hunger.

PIZARRO: You call hunger a right?

DE NIZZA: Of course, it gives life meaning. Look around you: happiness has no feel for men here since they are forbidden unhappiness. They have everything in common so they have nothing to give each other. They are part of the seasons, no more; as indistinguishable as mules, as predictable as trees. All men are born unequal: this is a divine gift. And want is their birthright. Where you deny this and there is no hope of any new love; where tomorrow is abolished, and no man ever thinks 'I can change myself', there you have the rule of Anti-Christ. Atahuallpa, I will not rest until I have brought you to the true God.

ATAHUALLPA: No! He is not true! Where is he? There is my father-Sun! You see now only by his wish; yet try to see into him and he will darken your eyes for ever. With hot burning he pulls up the corn and we feed. With cold burning he shrinks it and we starve. These are his burnings and our life. Do not speak to me again of your God: he is nowhere.

(PIZARRO *laughs. Hurriedly* DE NIZZA *leaves.*)

SCENE V

PIZARRO: You said you'd hear the Holy Men.

ATAHUALLPA: They are fools.

PIZARRO: They are not fools.

ATAHUALLPA: Do you believe them?

PIZARRO: For certain.

ATAHUALLPA: Look into me.

PIZARRO: Your eyes are smoking wood.

ATAHUALLPA: You do not believe them.

PIZARRO: You dare not say that to me . . .

ATAHUALLPA: You do not believe them. Their God is not in your face.

    (PIZARRO *retreats from* ATAHUALLPA, *who begins to sing in a strange voice*):

> You must not rob, O little finch.
> The harvest maize, O little finch.
> The trap is set, O little finch.
> To seize you quick, O little finch.
>
> Ask that black bird, O little finch.
> Nailed on a branch, O little finch.
> Where is her heart, O little finch.
> Where are her plumes, O little finch.
>
> She is cut up, O little finch.
> For stealing grain, O little finch.
> See, see the fate, O little finch.
> Of robber birds, O little finch.

This is a harvest song. For you.

PIZARRO: For me?

ATAHUALLPA: Yes.

PIZARRO: Robber birds.

ATAHUALLPA: Yes.

PIZARRO: You're a robber bird yourself.

ATAHUALLPA: Explain this.

PIZARRO: You killed your brother to get the throne.

ATAHUALLPA: He was a fool. His body was a man. His head was a child.

PIZARRO: But he was the rightful king.

ATAHUALLPA: I was the rightful God. My Sky Father shouted 'Rise up! In you lives your Earth Father, Huayana the Warrior. Your brother is fit only to tend herds but you were born to tend my people.' So I killed him, and the land smiled.

PIZARRO: That was my work long ago. Tending herds.

ATAHUALLPA: It was not your work. You are a warrior. It is in your face.

PIZARRO: You see much in my face.

ATAHUALLPA: I see my father.

PIZARRO: You do me honour, lad.

ATAHUALLPA: Speak true. If in your home your brother was King, but fit only for herds, would you take his crown?

PIZARRO: If I could.

ATAHUALLPA: And then you would kill him.

PIZARRO: No.

ATAHUALLPA: If you could not keep it for fear of his friends, unless he was dead, you would kill him.

PIZARRO: Let me give you another case. If I come to a country and seize the King's crown, but for fear of his friends cannot keep it unless I kill him, what do I do?

ATAHUALLPA: So.

PIZARRO: So.

(ATAHUALLPA *moves away, offended*.)

Oh, it is only a game we play. Tell me – did you hate your brother?

ATAHUALLPA: No. He was ugly like a llama, like his mother. My mother was beautiful.

PIZARRO: I did not know my mother. She was not my father's wife. She left me at the church door for anyone to find. There's talk in the village still, how I was suckled by a sow.

ATAHUALLPA: You are not then . . . ?

PIZARRO: Legitimate? No, my lord, no more than you.

ATAHUALLPA: So.

PIZARRO: So.

(*A pause*.)

ATAHUALLPA: To be born so is a sign for a great man.

PIZARRO (*smiling*): I think so too.

(ATAHUALLPA *removes one of his golden earings and hangs it on* PIZARRO'*s ear*.)

And what is that?

ATAHUALLPA: The sign of a nobleman. Only the most important men may wear them. The most near to me.

YOUNG MARTIN: Very becoming, sir. Look.

(*He hands him a dagger. The General looks at himself in the blade.*)

PIZARRO: I have never seemed so distinguished to myself. I thank you.

ATAHUALLPA: Now you must learn the dance of the aylu.

YOUNG MARTIN: The dance of a nobleman, sir.

ATAHUALLPA: Only he can do this. I will show you.

(PIZARRO *sits.* ATAHUALLPA *dances a ferocious mime of a warrior killing his foes. It is very difficult to execute, demanding great litheness and physical stamina. As suddenly as it began, it is over.*)

ATAHUALLPA: You dance.

PIZARRO: I can't dance, lad.

ATAHUALLPA (*sternly*): You dance.

(*He sits to watch. Seeing there is no help for it,* PIZARRO *rises and clumsily tries to copy the dance. The effect is so grotesque that* YOUNG MARTIN *cannot help laughing. The General tries again, lunges, slips, slides, and finally starts to laugh himself. He gives up the attempt.*)

PIZARRO (*to* ATAHUALLPA): You make me laugh! (*In sudden wonder*) You make me laugh!

(ATAHUALLPA *consults his young interpreter, who tries to explain. The* INCA *nods gravely. Tentatively* PIZARRO *extends his hand to him.* ATAHUALLPA *takes it and rises. Quietly they go off together.*)

SCENE VI

Enter OLD MARTIN.

OLD MARTIN: Slowly the pile increased. The army waited nervously and licked its lips. Greed began to rise in us like a tide of sea.

(*A music of bells and humming.*)

THE SECOND GOLD PROCESSION *and*
THE RAPE OF THE SUN

*Another line of Indian porters comes in, bearing gold
objects. Like the first, this instalment of treasure is
guarded by Spanish soldiers, but they are less disciplined
now. Two of them assault an Indian and grab his headdress. Another snatches a necklace at sword's point.
Above, in the chamber, the treasure is piled up as before.
DIEGO and the CHAVEZ brothers are seen supervising.
They begin to explore the sun itself, leaning out of the
chamber and prodding at the petals with their halberds.
Suddenly DIEGO gives a cry of triumph, drives his
halberd into a slot in one of the rays, and pulls out the
gold inlay. The sun gives a deep groan, like the sound
of a great animal being wounded. With greedy yelps,
all the soldiers below rush at the sun and start pulling it
to bits; they tear out the gold inlays and fling them on
the ground, while terrible groans fill the air. In a
moment only the great gold frame remains; a broken,
blackened sun.*

　　(*Enter* DE SOTO.)

DIEGO: Welcome back, sir.

DE SOTO: Diego, it's good to see you.

DIEGO: What's it like, sir? Is there trouble?

DE SOTO: It's grave quiet. Terrible. Men just standing in
fields for hundreds of miles. Waiting for their God to come
back to them.

DIEGO: Well, if he does they'll be fighters again and we're
for the limepit.

DE SOTO: How's the General?

DIEGO: An altered man. No one's ever seen him so easy.
He spends hours each day with the King. He's going to find
it hard when he has to do it.

DE SOTO: Do what?

DIEGO: Kill him, sir.

DE SOTO: He can't do that. Not after a contract witnessed before a whole army.

DIEGO: Well, he can't let him go, that's for certain . . . Never mind, he'll find a way. He's as cunning as the devil's granddad, save your pardon, sir.

DE SOTO: No, you're right, boy.

DIEGO: Tell us about their capital, then. What's it like?

(During the preceding, a line of Indians, bent double, has been loaded with the torn-off petals from the sun. Now, as DE SOTO describes Cuzco, they file slowly round the stage and go off, staggering under the weight of the great gold slabs. When he reaches the account of the garden, the marvellous objects he tells of appear in the treasure chamber above, borne by Indians, and are stacked up until they fill it completely. The interior of the sun is now a solid mass of gold.)

DE SOTO: Completely round. They call it the navel of the earth and that's what it looks like. In the middle was a huge temple, the centre of their faith. The walls were plated with gold, enough to blind us. Inside, set out on tables, golden platters for the sun to dine off. Outside, the garden: acres of gold soil planted with gold maize. Entire apple trees in gold. Gold birds on the branches. Gold geese and ducks. Gold butterflies in the air on silver strings. And — imagine this — away in a field, life-size, twenty golden llamas grazing with their kids. The garden of the Sun at Cuzco. A wonder of the earth. Look at it now.

DIEGO *(rushing in below)*: Hey! The room's full!

DOMINGO: It isn't!

SALINAS: It is. Look!

JUAN: He's right. It's full!

DIEGO: We can start the share-out now. *(Cheers.)*

PEDRO: What'll you do with your lot, Juan, boy?

JUAN: Buy a farm.

PEDRO: Me, too. I don't work for nobody ever again.

DOMINGO: Ah, you can buy a palace, easy, with a share of that. Never mind a hissing farm! What d'you say, Diego?

DIEGO: Oh, I want a farm. A good stud farm, and a stable of Arabs just for me to ride! What will you have, Salinas?

SALINAS: Me? A bash-house! (*Laughter*) Right in the middle of Trujillo, open six to six, filled with saddle-backed little fillies from Andalusia ...

(*Enter* VASCA *rolling a huge gold sun, like a hoop.*)

VASCA: Look what I got, boys! The sun! He ain't public any more, the old sun. He's private property!

DOMINGO: There's no private property, till share-out.

VASCA: Well, here's the exception. I risked my life to get this a hundred feet up.

JUAN: Dungballs!

VASCA: I did! Off the temple roof.

PEDRO: Come on, boy, get it up there with the rest.

VASCA: No. Finding's keepings. That's the law.

JUAN: What law?

VASCA: My law. Do you think you'll see any of this once the share-out starts? Not on your hissing life. You leave it up there, boy, you won't see nothing again.

PEDRO (*to his brother*): He's right there.

JUAN: Do you think so?

VASCA: Of course. Officers first, then the Church. You'll get hissing nothing. (*A pause.*)

SALINAS: So let's have a share-out now, then!

DOMINGO: Why not? We're all entitled.

VASCA: Of course we are.

JUAN: All right. I'm with you.

PEDRO: Good boy!

SALINAS: Come on, then.

(*They all make a rush for the Sun Chamber.*)

DE SOTO: Where do you think you're going? ... You know the General's orders. Nothing till share-out. Penalty for breach, death. Disperse now. I'll go and see the General.

(*They hesitate.*)

(*Quietly*) Get to your posts.

(*Reluctantly, they disperse.*)

And keep a sharp watch. The danger's not over yet.

DIEGO: I'd say it had only just begun, sir.
(*He goes.* DE SOTO *remains.*)

SCENE VII

(*Enter* PIZARRO *and* ATAHUALLPA *duelling furiously;*
YOUNG MARTIN *behind. The Inca is a magnificent
fighter and launches himself vigorously on the old man,
finally knocking the sword from his hand.*)

PIZARRO: Enough! You exhaust me . . .

ATAHUALLPA: I fight well — 'ye-es'?

(*From the difficulty he has with this word, it is evident
that it is in Spanish.*)

PIZARRO (*imitating him*): 'Ye-es! . . . Like a hidalgo!

YOUNG MARTIN: Magnificent, my lord.

PIZARRO: I'm proud of you.

ATAHUALLPA: Chica!

YOUNG MARTIN: Maize wine, sir.

PIZARRO: De Soto! — A drink, my dear second.

DE SOTO: With pleasure, General, the room is full.

PIZARRO (*casually*): I know it.

DE SOTO: My advice to you is to share out right away.
The men are just on the turn.

PIZARRO: I think so too.

DE SOTO: We daren't delay.

PIZARRO: Agreed. Now I shall astound you, Cavalier.
Atahuallpa, you have learnt how a Spaniard fights. Now you
will learn his honour. Martin, your pen. (*Dictating*) 'Let
this be known throughout my army. The Inca Atahuallpa
has today discharged his obligation to General Pizarro. He
is therefore a free man.'

DE SOTO (*toasting him*): My lord, your freedom!

(ATAHUALLPA *kneels. Silently he mouths words of
gratitude to the sun.*)

ATAHUALLPA: Atahuallpa thanks the lord De Soto, the
lord Pizarro, all lords of honour. You may touch my joy.

(*He extends his arms. Both Spaniards help to raise him.*)

DE SOTO: What happens now?

PIZARRO: I release him. He must swear first, of course, not to harm us.

DE SOTO: Do you think he will?

PIZARRO: For me he will.

ATAHUALLPA (*to the boy*): What is that you have done?

YOUNG MARTIN: Writing, my lord.

ATAHUALLPA: Explain this.

YOUNG MARTIN: These are signs: This is 'Atahuallpa', and this is 'ransom'.

ATAHUALLPA: You put this sign, and he will see and know 'ransom'?

YOUNG MARTIN: Yes.

ATAHUALLPA: No.

YOUNG MARTIN: Yes, my lord. I'll do it again.

ATAHUALLPA: Here, on my nail. Do not say what you put.

(YOUNG MARTIN *writes on his nail.*)

YOUNG MARTIN: Now show it to Cavalier De Soto.

(*He does so.* DE SOTO *reads and whispers the word to* ATAHUALLPA.)

ATAHUALLPA (*to the boy*): What is put?

YOUNG MARTIN: God.

ATAHUALLPA (*amazed*): God! . . . (*He stares at his nail in fascination then bursts into delighted laughter, like a child.*) Show me again! Another sign!

(*The boy writes on another nail.*)

PIZARRO: Tell Salinas to take five hundred Indians and melt everything down.

DE SOTO: Everything?

PIZARRO: We can't transport it as it is.

DE SOTO: But there are objects of great beauty, sir. In all my service I've never seen treasure like this. Work subtler than anything in Italy.

PIZARRO: You're a tender man.

ATAHUALLPA (*extending his nail to* PIZARRO): What is put?

PIZARRO (*who of course cannot read*): Put?

ATAHUALLPA: Here.

PIZARRO: This is a foolish game.

YOUNG MARTIN: The General never learnt the skill, my lord. (*An embarrassed pause*) A soldier does not need it.

(ATAHUALLPA *stares at him.*)

ATAHUALLPA: A King needs it. There is great power in these marks. You are the King in this room. You must teach us two. We will learn together – like brothers.

PIZARRO: You would stay with me here, to learn?

(*Pause.*)

ATAHUALLPA: No. Tomorrow I will go.

PIZARRO: And then? What will you do then?

ATAHUALLPA: I will not hurt you.

PIZARRO: Or my army?

ATAHUALLPA: That I do not swear.

PIZARRO: You must.

ATAHUALLPA: You do not say this till now.

PIZARRO: Well, now I say it. Atahuallpa, you must swear to me that you will not hurt a man in my army if I let you go.

ATAHUALLPA: I will not swear this.

PIZARRO: For my sake.

ATAHUALLPA: Three thousand of my servants they killed in the square. Three thousand, without arms. I will avenge them.

PIZARRO: There is a way of mercy, Atahuallpa.

ATAHUALLPA: It is not my way. It is not your way.

PIZARRO: Well, show it to me, then.

ATAHUALLPA: Keep your swear first.

PIZARRO: That I cannot do.

ATAHUALLPA: Cannot?

PIZARRO: Not immediately . . . you must see: you are many, we are few.

ATAHUALLPA: This is not important.

PIZARRO: To me it is.

(ATAHUALLPA *hisses with fury. He strides across the*

room and before PIZARRO's *face makes a violent gesture with his hand between their two mouths.*)

ATAHUALLPA (*violently*): You gave a word!

PIZARRO: And will keep it. Only not now. Not today.

ATAHUALLPA: When?

PIZARRO: Soon.

ATAHUALLPA: When?

PIZARRO: Very soon.

ATAHUALLPA (*falling on his knees and beating the ground*): *When?*

PIZARRO: As soon as you promise not to hurt my army.

ATAHUALLPA (*with wild rage*): I will kill every man of them! I will make drums of their bodies! I will beat music on them at my great feasts!

PIZARRO (*provoked*): Boy — what have I put?

YOUNG MARTIN: 'He is therefore a free man.'

PIZARRO: Continue: 'But for the welfare of the country, he will remain for the moment as guest of the army.'

DE SOTO: What does that mean?

ATAHUALLPA: What does he say?

PIZARRO: Don't translate.

DE SOTO: So it's started. My warning was nothing to you.

PIZARRO: Well, gloat, gloat!

DE SOTO: I don't gloat.

ATAHUALLPA: What does he say?

PIZARRO: Nothing.

ATAHUALLPA: There is fear in his face!

PIZARRO: *Be quiet!* . . . (*To* DE SOTO) I want all the gold in blocks. Leave nothing unmelted. Attend to it yourself, personally!

> (DE SOTO *goes abruptly.* OLD MARTIN *appears in the background.* PIZARRO *is trembling.*)

(*To the* PAGE) Well, what are you staring at, Little Lord Chivalry? Get out!

YOUNG MARTIN: He trusts you, sir.

PIZARRO: Trust: what's that? Another word? Honour . . . glory . . . trust: your word — Gods!

YOUNG MARTIN: You can see it, sir. He trusts you.

PIZARRO: I told you: out.

YOUNG MARTIN (*greatly daring*): You can't betray him, sir. You can't.

PIZARRO: Damn you – impertinence!

YOUNG MARTIN: I don't care, sir. You just can't! (*He stops.*)

PIZARRO: In all your study of those admirable writers, you never learned the duty a page owes his master. I am sorry you have not better fulfilled your first office. There will be no other.

(*The* BOY *makes to go out.*)

A salute, if you please.

(*He bows.*)

Time was when we couldn't stop you.

(YOUNG MARTIN *leaves.* PIZARRO *stares after him, shaking.*)

OLD MARTIN: I went out into the night – the cold high night of the Andes, hung with stars like crystal apples – and dropped my first tears as a man. My first and last. That was my first and last worship too. Devotion never came again. (*Exit.*)

(*With a moan,* PIZARRO *collapses on the floor and lies writhing in pain.* ATAHUALLPA *contemplates his captor with surprised disdain. But slowly, as the old man's agony continues, contempt in the King is replaced by a gentler emotion. Curious, he kneels. Uncertain what to do, he extends his hands, first to the wound, and then to* PIZARRO's *head, which he holds with a kind of remote tenderness. The lights go down all around them.*)

PIZARRO: Leave it now. There's no cure or more easing for it. Death's entered the house you see. It's half down already, like an old barn. What can you know about that? Youth's in you like a spring of blood, to spurt for ever. Your skin is singing: 'I will never get old.' But you will. Time is stalking you, as I did. That gold flesh will cold and blacken. Your eyes will curdle, those wet living eyes . . . They'll make a mummy of your body – I know the custom – and wrap you in robes of vicuna wool, and carry you through all your Empire down to Cuzco. And then they'll fold you in two and sit you on a chair in darkness . . . Atahuallpa, I'm going to die! And the thought of that dark has for years rotted everything for me, all simple joy in life. All through old age, which is so much longer and more terrible than anything in youth, I've watched the circles of nature with hatred. The leaves pop out, the leaves fall. Every year it's piglet time, calving time, time for children in a gush of blood and water. Women dote on this. A birth, any birth, fills them with love. They clap with love, and my soul shrugs. Round and round is all I see: an endless sky of birds, flying and ripping and nursing their young to fly and rip and nurse their young – *for what?* Listen, boy. That prison the Priest calls Sin Original, I know as Time. And seen in time everything is trivial. Pain. Good. God is trivial in that seeing. Trapped in this cage we cry out 'There's a gaoler; there must be. At the last, last, last of lasts he will let us out. He will! He will!' . . . But, oh my boy, no one will come for all our crying. (*Pause*) I'm going to kill you, Atahuallpa. What does it matter? Words kept, words broken, it all means nothing. Nothing. You go to sleep earlier than me, that's all. Do you see? Look at your eyes, like coals from the sun, glowing forever in the deep of your skull. Like my dream . . . Sing me your little song. (*Singing*) O little finch. . . .

    (ATAHUALLPA *intones a few lines of the song.*)
Nothing. Nothing . . . (*In sudden anguish, almost hatred*) O, lad, what am I going to do with you?

Scene VIII

A red light up above.
OLD MARTIN *appears above in the Sun Chamber. Violent music, the sound of destruction. The light fades and comes up on stage where the soldiers assemble.*
OLD MARTIN: Nine forges were kept alight for three

weeks. The masterwork of centuries was banged down into fat bars, four hundred and forty pounds each day. The booty exceeded all other known in history: the sack of Genoa, Milan or even Rome. Share-out started at once. (*Exit*.)

DIEGO: General Francisco Pizarro, 57,220 gold pesos. Hernando De Soto, 17,740 gold pesos. The Holy church, 2,220 gold pesos.

(*Enter* ESTETE *and* DE CANDIA.)

ESTETE: And a fifth of everything, of course, to the Crown.

PIZARRO: You come in good time, Veedor.

ESTETE: So it seems! Cavalier.

DE SOTO: Veedor.

PIZARRO: Welcome, De Candia.

DE CANDIA: Thank you. (*Indicating the ear-ring*) I see the living's become soft here already. The men hung with jewels like fops at Court.

PIZARRO: You set the fashion: I only follow.

DE CANDIA: I'm flattered.

PIZARRO: What news of the reinforcements?

DE CANDIA: None.

ESTETE: I sent runners back to the coast. They saw nothing.

PIZARRO: So we're cut off, here. How's my garrison?

DE CANDIA: Spanish justice reigns supreme. They hang Indians for everything. How's your royal friend? When do we hang him?

(*Pause.* PIZARRO *tears off his ear-ring and flings it on the floor.*)

PIZARRO: Finish the share-out.

(*Violently he leaves them. The men stare after him.*)

DE SOTO: Go on, Diego. Tell us the rest ... *Go on,* man!

DIEGO: The remainder – cavalry, infantry, clerks, farriers, coopers and the like – will divide a total of 971,000 gold pesos!

(*Cheers. Enter* RODAS.)

SALINAS: Well, look. Our little tailor! How are you, friend?

RODAS: Hungry. What do I get?

SALINAS: A kick up the tunnel.

RODAS: Ha, ha. Day of a hundred jokes! I got a right to a share.

DOMINGO: What for?

RODAS: I stayed behind and guarded your hissing rear, that's what for.

DE SOTO: You've no right, Rodas. As far as you cared we could all rot, remember? Well, now you get nothing; the proper wage for cowardice.

(*General agreement. The men settle upstage to a game of dice.*)

(*To* ESTETE) I must wait on the General.

ESTETE: I am sorry to see him still subject to distress. I had hoped that victory would have brought him calmer temper.

DE CANDIA: It must be his new wealth, Veedor, So much, so sudden, must be a great burden to him.

DE SOTO: The burdens of the General, sir, are care for his men, and for our present situation. Let us try to lighten them for him as we can.

(*He goes off.*)

DE CANDIA: Let us indeed. One throat cut and we're all lightened.

ESTETE: It would much relieve the Crown if you'd cut it.

DE CANDIA: If I . . .? You mean I'm not Spanish, I don't have to trouble with honour.

ESTETE: You're not a subject. It could be disowned by my King. And you have none.

DE CANDIA: So the Palace of Disinterest has a shithouse after all. Look man, you're the overseer here, so do your job. Go to the General and tell him the brownie must go. And add this from me: if Spain waits any longer, Venice will act for herself.

(*They go off. Enter* OLD MARTIN.)

Scene IX

A scene of tension and growing violence. The soldiers, now dirty almost beyond recognition, but wearing ornaments, ear-rings and headdresses stolen from the treasure, dice for gold. They are watched silently from above by a line of masked Indians carrying instruments for making bird noises. A drum begins to beat. PIZARRO *stumbles in, and during the whole ensuing scene limps to and fro across the stage like a caged animal, ignoring everything but his own mental pain.*

OLD MARTIN: Morale began to go fast. Day after day we watched his private struggle, and the brownies watched us, waiting one sign from the frozen boy to get up and kill the lot of us.

DOMINGO: Play up, then!

PEDRO: Two fours.

(JUAN *throws successfully.*)

JUAN (*grabbing a gold bar belonging to* PEDRO): That's mine, boy.

PEDRO: No – Juan!

JUAN: Give it. (*He snatches it.*)

DOMINGO: They say there's an army gathering in the mountains. At least five thousand of them.

VASCA: I heard that too.

DOMINGO: Blas says there's some of them cannibals.

(*Bird cries.*)

SALINAS: That's just stories. Hissing stupid stories. You don't want to listen to 'em.

RODAS: I'd like to see you when they tie you to the spit.

VASCA (*rolling the dice*): Turn up! Turn up! Turn up!

RODAS: Come on boys, cut me in.

VASCA: Hiss off! No stake, no play.

RODAS: Bloody bastards!

DOMINGO: They say it's led by the Inca's top general. The brownies are full of his name.

VASCA: What is it? Rumi . . . Rumi . . .?

DOMINGO: That's it. Ruminagui, something like that.

(*The Indians above repeat the name in a low menacing chant:* RU-MIN-Ā-GUI! *The soldiers look fearfully about them. The bird cries sound again.*)

SALINAS: Come on, then, let's play.

VASCA: What for? The sun?

SALINAS: The sun!

VASCA: Turn up! Turn up! Turn up! Turn up! King and ten. Beat that!

SALINAS: Holy Mary, mother of Christ. Save my soul and bless my dice. (*He throws*) Two Kings . . . I did it! I'm sorry, lads, but that's your sun gone.

VASCA: Go on, then. Let's see you pick it up.

(SALINAS *bends and tries to shift it.* VASCA *laughs. The bird cries grow wilder.*)

RODAS: He can't even lift it, but I can't play!

SALINAS: I'll settle for these.

(*He picks up three gold bars and walks off with them.* RODAS *trips him up and he goes sprawling.*)

Christ damn you, Rodas – that's the hissing last I take from you.

(*He springs at* RODAS *and clouts him with a gold bar. The tailor howls, picks up another, and a fight starts between them which soon becomes a violent free-for-all. The men shout; the birds scream; the General paces to and fro, ignoring everything. Finally* DE SOTO *rushes on just in time as* SALINAS *tries to strangle* RODAS. *He is followed by* ESTETE *and the two priests, who attend to the wounded.*)

DE SOTO: *Stop this!* . . . Do you want to start it all off?

(*Silence. All the Indians rise, above. Uneasily the soldiers stare up at them.*)

You – night watch. You, you go with him. You take the East Gate. The rest to quarters. Move!

(*They disperse.* ESTETE *and the priests remain.*)

Scene X

De Soto (*to* Pizarro): Mutiny's smoking. Act now or it'll be a blaze you'll not put out.

Pizarro: What do I do?

De Soto: Take our chances, what else can we do? You have to let him go.

Pizarro: And what happens then? A tiny army is wiped out in five minutes, and the whole story lost for always. Later someone else will conquer Peru and no one will even remember my name.

De Soto: What kind of name will they remember if you kill him?

Pizarro: A conqueror. That at least.

De Soto: A man who butchered his prisoner after giving his word. There's a name for your ballads.

Pizarro: I'll never live to hear them. What do I care? What does it matter? Whatever I do, what does it matter?

De Soto: Nothing, if you don't feel it. But I think you do.

Pizarro: Let me understand you. As Second-in-Command, you counsel certain death for this army?

De Soto: I'll not counsel his.

Pizarro: Then you counsel the death of Christ in this country, as you told my page boy months ago?

De Soto: That's not known.

Pizarro: As good.

De Soto: No. Christ is love. Love is —

Pizarro: What? *What?*

De Soto: Now in him. He trusts you, trust him. It's all you can do.

Pizarro: Have you gone soft in the head? What's this chorus now? 'Trust! trust!' You know the law out here: kill or get killed. You said it yourself. The mercies come later.

De Soto: Not for you. I wish to God you'd never made

this bargain. But you did. Now you've no choice left.

PIZARRO: No, this is my kingdom. In Peru I am absolute. I have choice always.

DE SOTO: You had it. But you made it.

PIZARRO: Then I'll take it back.

DE SOTO: Then you never made it. I'm not playing words, General. There's no choice where you don't stick by it.

PIZARRO: I can *choose* to take it back.

DE SOTO: No, sir. That would only be done on orders from your own fear. That's not choosing.

ESTETE: May the Crown be allowed a word?

PIZARRO: I know your word. Death.

ESTETE: What else can it be?

VALVERDE: Your army is in terror. Do you care nothing for them?

PIZARRO: Well, Cavalier. Do you?

DE SOTO: I care for them. But less than I care for you ... God knows why.

(*He goes off.*)

ESTETE: The issue is simple. You are Viceroy here ruling in the name of the King who sent you. You have no right to risk his land for any reason at all.

PIZARRO: And what did this King ever do for me? Granted me salary if I found money to pay it. Allowed me governance if I found land to govern. Magnificent! For years I strove to make this expedition, years of scars and hunger. While I sweated your Holy Roman vulture turned away his beak till I'd shaken out enough gold to tempt his greed. If I'd failed this time he'd have cast me off with one shrug of his royal feathers. Well, now I cast him. Francisco Pizarro casts off Carlos the Fifth. Go and tell him.

ESTETE: This is ridiculous.

PIZARRO: No doubt, but you'll have to give me better argument before I give him up.

ESTETE: Perverse man, what is Atahuallpa to you?

PIZARRO: Someone I promised Life.

ESTETE: Promised life? How quaint. The sort of chivalry

idea you pretend to despise. If you want to be an absolute king, my man, you must learn to act out of personal will. Break your word just *because* you gave it. Till then, you're only a pig-man trying to copy his betters.

(PIZARRO *rounds on him angrily*.)

VALVERDE: My son, listen to me. No promise to a pagan need bind a Christian. Simply think what's at stake: the lives of a hundred and seventy of the faithful. Are you going to sacrifice them for one savage?

PIZARRO: You know lives have no weight, Father. Ten can't be added up to outbalance one.

VALVERDE: Ten good can against one evil. And this man is evil. His people kiss his hands as the source of life.

PIZARRO: As we do yours. All your days you play at being God. You only hate my Inca because he does it better.

VALVERDE: *What?*

PIZARRO: Dungballs to all churches that are or ever could be! How I hate you. 'Kill who I bid you kill and I will pardon it.' YOU with your milky fingers forcing in the blade. How dare you priests bless any man who goes slicing into battle? But no. You slice with him. 'Rip!' you scream, 'Tear! blind! in the name of Christ!' Tell me, soft Father, if Christ was here now, do you think he would kill my Inca? . . . Well, Brother De Nizza, you're the lord of answers: let's hear you. Do I kill him?

DE NIZZA: Don't try and trap me. I know as well as you how terrible it is to kill. But worse is to spare evil. When I came here first I thought I had found Paradise. Now I know it is Hell. A country which castrates its people. What are your Inca's subjects? A population of eunuchs, living entirely without choice.

PIZARRO: And what are your Christians? Unhappy hating men. Look: I'm a peasant. I want value for money. If I go marketing for Gods, who do I buy? The God of Europe with all its death and blooding, or Atahuallpa of Peru? His spirit keeps an Empire sweet and still as corn in the field.

DE NIZZA: And you're content to be a stalk of corn?

PIZARRO: Yes, yes! They're no fools, these sun men. They know what cheats you sell on your barrow. Choice. Hunger. Tomorrow. They've looked at your wares and passed on. They live here as part of nature, no hope and no despair.

DE NIZZA: And no life. Why must you be so dishonest? You are not only part of nature, and you know it. There is something in you at war with nature; there is in all of us. Something that does not belong in you the animal. What do you think it is? What is this pain in you that month after month makes you hurl yourself against the cage of time? . . . This is God, driving you to accept divine eternity. Take it, General: not this pathetic copy of eternity the Incas have tried to make on earth. Peru is a sepulchre of the soul. For the sake of the free spirit in each of us it must be destroyed.

PIZARRO: So there is Christian charity. To save my own soul I must kill another man!

DE NIZZA: To save love in the world you must kill lovelessness.

PIZARRO: Hail to you, sole judge of love! No salvation outside your church: and no love neither. Oh, you arrogance! . . . (*Simply*) I do not know love, Father, but what can I ever know, if I feel none for him?

DIEGO (*rushing on*): Sir! Sir! Another fight broke out, sir. There's one dead.

PIZARRO: Who?

DIEGO: Blas. He drew a knife. I only meant to spit his leg, but he slipped and got it through the guts.

PIZARRO: You did well to punish fighting.

DIEGO: May I speak free, sir?

PIZARRO: What? I've got to kill him, is that it?

DIEGO: What other way is there? The men are out of their wits. They feel death all round them.

PIZARRO: So it is and let them face it. I promised them gold, not life. Well, they've got gold. The cripples have gold crutches. The coughers spit gold snot. The bargain's over.

DIEGO: No, sir, not with me. To me you're the greatest General in the world. And we're the greatest company.

PIZARRO: Pizarro's boys, is that it?

DIEGO: Yes, sir. Pizarro's boys.

PIZARRO: Ah, the old band. The dear old regiment. Fool! Look, you were born a man. Not a Blue man, or a Green man, but A MAN. You are able to feel a thousand separate loves unordered by fear or solitude. Are you going to trade them all in for Gang-love? Flag-love? Carlos-the-Fifth-love? Jesus-the-Christ-love? All that has been tied on you; it is only this that makes you bay for death.

VALVERDE: I'll give you death. When I get back to Spain, a commission will hale you to the stake for what you have said today.

PIZARRO: If I let the Inca go, Father, you'll never get back to Spain.

ESTETE: You madman: see here, you put him underground by sunset or I'll take the knife to him myself.

PIZARRO: ATAHUALLPA!

(ATAHUALLPA *enters with* YOUNG MARTIN.)

They ache for your death. They want to write psalms to their God in your blood. But they'll all die before you — that I promise. (*He binds* ATAHUALLPA's *arm to his own with a long cord of rope last used to tie some gold*) There. No, no, some here. Now no one will kill you unless they kill me first.

ESTETE: De Candia!

(*Enter* DE CANDIA, *with a drawn sword.*)

DE CANDIA: A touching game — gaolers and prisoners. But it's over now. General, do you think I'm going to die so that you can dance with a darkie?

(PIZARRO *pulls the sword from* YOUNG MARTIN's *scabbard.*)

DIEGO (*drawing*): Sorry, sir, but it's got to be done.

ESTETE (*drawing*): There's nothing you can do, Pizarro. The whole camp's against you.

PIZARRO: De Soto!

DE CANDIA: If De Soto raises his sword, he'll lose the arm that swings it.

PIZARRO: You'll lose yours first. Come on!

(*He rushes at* DE CANDIA *but* ATAHUALLPA *gives a growl and pulls him back by the rope. A pause.*)

ATAHUALLPA: I have no eyes for you. You are nothing.

PIZARRO: I command here still. They will obey me.

ATAHUALLPA: They will kill me though you cry curses of earth and sky. (*To them all*) Leave us. I will speak with him.

(*Impressed by the command in his voice, all leave, save the General — now roped to his prisoner — and* YOUNG MARTIN.)

SCENE XI

ATAHUALLPA: It is no matter. They cannot kill me.

PIZARRO: Cannot?

ATAHUALLPA: Man who dies cannot kill a God who lives forever.

PIZARRO: I wouldn't bet on it, my lord.

ATAHUALLPA: Only my father can take me from here. And he would not accept me killed by men like you. Men with no word. You may be King in this land, but never God. I am God of the Four Quarters and if you kill me tonight I will rise at dawn when my Father first touches my body with light.

PIZARRO: You believe this?

ATAHUALLPA: All my people know it — it is why they have let me stay with you.

PIZARRO: They knew you could not be harmed . . .

ATAHUALLPA: So.

PIZARRO: Was this the meaning? The meaning of my dream? You were choosing me?

YOUNG MARTIN: My lord, it's just a boast. Beyond any kind of reason.

PIZARRO: Is it?

YOUNG MARTIN: How can a man die, then get up and walk away?

PIZARRO: Let's hear your creed, boy. 'I believe in Jesus

Christ, the Son of God, that He suffered under Pontius Pilate, was crucified, dead and buried' . . . and what?

YOUNG MARTIN: Sir?

PIZARRO: What?

YOUNG MARTIN: 'He descended into Hell, and on the third day He rose again from the dead . . .'

PIZARRO: You don't believe it!

YOUNG MARTIN: I do! On my soul! I believe with perfect faith.

PIZARRO: But Christ's to be the only one, is that it? What if it's possible, here in a land beyond all maps and scholars, guarded by mountains up to the sky, that there were true Gods on earth, creators of true peace? Think of it! Gods, free of time.

YOUNG MARTIN: It's impossible, my lord.

PIZARRO: It's the only way to give life meaning! To blast out of time and live forever, *us,* in our own persons. This is the law: die in despair or be a God yourself! . . . Look at him: always so calm as if the teeth of life never bit him . . . or the teeth of death. What if it was really true, Martin? That I've gone God-hunting and caught one. A being who can renew his life over and over?

YOUNG MARTIN: But how can he do that, sir? How could any man?

PIZARRO: By returning over and over again to the source of life — *to the Sun!*

YOUNG MARTIN: No, sir . . .

PIZARRO: Why not? What else is a God but what we know we can't do without? The flowers that worship it, the sunflowers in their soil, are us after night, after cold and lightless days, turning our faces to it, adoring. The sun is the only God I know! We eat you to walk. We drink you to sing. Our reins loosen under you and we laugh. Even I laugh, here!

YOUNG MARTIN: General, you need rest, sir.
    (*Pause.*)

PIZARRO: Yes. Yes . . . yes. (*Bitterly*) How clever. He's

understood everything I've said to him these awful months
– all the secret pain he's heard – and this is his revenge.
This futile joke. How he must hate me. (*Tightening the
rope*) Oh, yes, you cunning bastard! Look, Martin – be-
hold, my God. I've got the Sun on a string! I can make it
rise (*He pulls the Inca's arm up*) – or set!

    (*He throws the Inca to his knees.*)

YOUNG MARTIN: General . . . !

PIZARRO: I'll make you set forever! Two can joke as well
as one. You want your freedom? All right, you're Free!
(*He starts circling round* ATAHUALLPA) Walk out of the
camp! They may stop you, but what's that to you? You're
invulnerable. They'll knock you down but your father the
Sun will pick you up again. Go on! Get up! . . . Go on! . . .
Get up! . . . Go on! . . . Go on! . . . Go on! . . . Go on!
. . . Go on! . . . Go on!

    (*He breaks into a frantic gallop round and round the
    Inca, the rope at full stretch,* ATAHUALLPA *turning with
    him, somersaulting, then holding him, his teeth bared
    with the strain, as if breaking a wild horse, until the old
    man tumbles exhausted to the ground. Silence follows,
    broken only by deep moaning from the stricken man.
    Quietly the Inca pulls in the rope. Then at last he speaks.*)

ATAHUALLPA: Pizarro. You will die soon and you do not
believe in your God. That is why you tremble and keep
no word. Believe in me. I will give you a word and fill
you with joy. For you I will do a great thing. I will swallow death and spit it out of me.

    (*Pause. This whole scene stays very still.*)

PIZARRO (*whispering*): You cannot.

ATAHUALLPA: Yes, if my father wills it.

PIZARRO: How if he does not?

ATAHUALLPA: He will. His people still need me. Believe.

PIZARRO: Impossible.

ATAHUALLPA: Believe.

PIZARRO: How? . . . How? . . .

ATAHUALLPA: First you must take my priest power.

PIZARRO (*quietly*): Oh, no! you go or not as you choose, but I take nothing more in this world.

ATAHUALLPA: Take my word. Take my peace. I will put water to your wound, old man. Believe.

(*A long silence. The lights are now fading round them.*)

PIZARRO: What must I do?

(*Enter* OLD MARTIN.)

OLD MARTIN: How can I speak now and hope to be believed? As night fell like a hand over the eye, and great white stars sprang out over the snow-rim of our world, Atahuallpa confessed Pizarro. He did it in the Inca manner. He took Ichu grass and a stone. Into the Ichu grass the General spoke for an hour or more. None heard what he said save the King, who could not understand it. Then the King struck him on the back with the stone, cast away the grass, and made the signs for purification.

PIZARRO: If any blessing is in me, take it and go. Fly up, my bird, and come to me again.

(*The Inca takes a knife from* YOUNG MARTIN *and cuts the rope. Then he walks upstage. All the* OFFICERS *and* MEN *enter. During the following a pole is set up above, in the sun, and* ATAHUALLPA *is hauled up into it.*)

SCENE XII

OLD MARTIN: The Inca was tried by a court quickly mustered. He was accused of usurping the throne and killing his brother; of idolatry and of having more than one wife. On all these charges he was found —

ESTETE: Guilty.

VALVERDE: Guilty.

DE CANDIA: Guilty.

DIEGO: Guilty.

OLD MARTIN: Sentence to be carried out the same night.

ESTETE: Death by burning.

(*Lights up above in the sun.*)

(ATAHUALLPA *gives a great cry.*)

PIZARRO: No! He must not burn! His body must stay in one piece.

VALVERDE: Let him repent his idolatry and be baptized a Christian. He will receive the customary mercy.

OLD MARTIN: Strangling instead.

PIZARRO: You must do it! Deny your Father! If you don't, you will be burnt to ashes. There will be no flesh left for him to warm alive at dawn.

(YOUNG MARTIN *screams and runs from the stage in horror.*)

You must do it.

(*In a gesture of surrender the* INCA *king kneels.*)

OLD MARTIN: So it was that Atahuallpa came to Christ.

(*Enter* DE NIZZA, *above, with a bowl of water.*)

DE NIZZA: I baptize you Juan de Atahuallpa, in honour of Juan the Baptist, whose sacred day this is.

ESTETE: The twenty-ninth of August, 1533.

VALVERDE: And may Our Lord and His angels receive your soul with joy!

SOLDIERS: Amen!

(*The* INCA *suddenly raises his head, tears off his clothes and intones in a great voice.*)

ATAHUALLPA: INTI! INTI! INTI!

VALVERDE: What does he say?

PIZARRO (*intoning also*): The Sun. The Sun. The Sun.

VALVERDE: *Kill him!*

(*Soldiers haul* ATAHUALLPA *to his feet and hold him to the stake.* RODAS *slips a string over his head and while all the Spaniards recite the Latin Creed below, and great howls of 'Inca!' come from the darkness, the Sovereign King of Peru is garrotted. His screams and struggles subside; his body falls slack. His executioners hand the corpse down to the soldiers below, who carry it to the centre of the stage and drop it at* PIZARRO's *feet. Then all leave save the old man, who stands as if turned to stone. A drum beats. Slowly, in semi-darkness, the stage fills with all the Indians, robed in black and*

*terracotta, wearing the great golden funeral masks of
ancient Peru. Grouped round the prone body, they
intone a strange Chant of Resurrection, punctuated by
hollow beats on the drums and by long, long silences
in which they turn their immense triangular eyes enquiringly up to the sky. Finally, after three great cries
appear to summon it, the sun rises. Its rays fall on the
body.* ATAHUALLPA *does not move. The masked men
watch in amazement — disbelief — finally, despair.
Slowly, with hanging, dejected heads, they shuffle away.*
PIZARRO *is left alone with the dead King. He contemplates him. A silence. Then suddenly he slaps it vici-
ously, and the body rolls over on its back.*)

PIZARRO: Cheat! You've cheated me! Cheat . . .

(*For a moment his old body is racked with sobs;
then, surprised, he feels tears on his cheek. He examines
them. The sunlight brightens on his head.*)

What's this? What is it? In all your life you never made one
of these, I know, and I not till this minute. Look. (*He
kneels to show the dead Inca*) Ah, no. You have no eyes
for me now, Atahuallpa: they are dusty balls of amber I
can tap on. You have no peace for me, Atahuallpa: the
birds still scream in your forest. You have no joy for me,
Atahuallpa, my boy: the only joy is in death. I lived between two hates: I die between two darks: blind eyes and a
blind sky. And yet you saw once. The sky sees nothing, but
you saw. Is there comfort there? The sky knows no feeling,
but we know them, that's sure. Martin's hope, and De Soto's
honour, and your trust — your trust which hunted me: we
alone make these. That's some marvel, yes, some marvel. To
sit in a great cold silence, and sing out sweet with just our
own warm breath: that's some marvel, surely. To make
water in a sand world: surely, surely . . . God's just a name
on your nail; and naming begins cries and cruelties. But to
live without hope of after, and make whatever God there is,
oh, that's some immortal business surely . . . I'm tired. Where
are you? You're so cold. I'd warm you if I could. But

there's no warming now, not ever now. I'm colding too. There's a snow of death falling all round us. You can almost see it. It's over, lad, I'm coming after you. There's nothing but peace to come. We'll be put into the same earth, father and son in our own land. And that sun will roam uncaught over his empty pasture.

OLD MARTIN: So fell Peru. We gave her greed, hunger and the Cross: three gifts for the civilized life. The family groups that sang on the terraces are gone. In their place slaves shuffle underground and they don't sing there. Peru is a silent country, frozen in avarice. So fell Spain, gorged with gold; distended; now dying.

PIZARRO (*singing*): 'Where is her heart, O little finch' . . .

OLD MARTIN: And so fell you, General, my master, whom men called the Son of His Own Deeds. He was killed later in a quarrel with his partner who brought up the reinforcements. But to speak truth, he sat down that morning and never really got up again.

PIZARRO (*singing*): 'Where are her plumes, O little finch' . . .

OLD MARTIN: I'm the only one left now of that company: landowner – slaveowner – and forty years from any time of hope. It put out a good blossom, but it was shaken off rough. After that I reckon the fruit always comes sour, and doesn't sweeten up much with age.

PIZARRO (*singing*): 'She is cut up, O little finch. For stealing grain, O little finch' . . .

OLD MARTIN: General, you did for me, and now I've done for you. And there's no joy in that. Or in anything now. But then there's no joy in the world could match for me what I had when I first went with you across the water to find the gold country. And no pain like losing it. Save you all.

(*He goes out.* PIZARRO *lies beside the body of* ATA-HUALLPA *and quietly sings to it.*)

PIZARRO (*singing*):

> See, see the fate, O little finch,
> Of robber birds, O little finch.

(*The sun glares at the audience.*)

LIST OF MUSIC IN SCORE

1. Recorded Organ Music (4 min. 45 sec.)
2. Opening of the Sun (35–40 sec.) – orchestra and chants
3. End of the Court scene (15–45 sec.) – orchestral
4. Atahuallpa's invitation to Pizarro – orchestral
5. The bird cries in the forest (up to 6 min.) – 4 tracks of recorded bird cries plus Indians on 'bird flutes' and guerros
6. Introduction to 'Toil Song' – orchestral
7. 'Toil Song' – Indian singing with small marracas and small drum
8. Villac Umu's Embassy: arrival (5 sec.) exit (5 sec.) } orchestral
9. Indian Chants of Praise – orchestra and chants
10. Offstage Spanish Te Deum – recorded Spanish chanting
11. Climbing of the Andes (up to 6 min.)–orchestral (2 flexatons)
12. Procession into Cajamarca (1 min.–1 min. 20 sec.) – orchestra, plus Indians playing bells, cymbals, 'thumb pianos', marracas (large)
13. The Massacre (1 min.–1 min. 30 sec.) – orchestra plus bells on Indians
14. 1st Indian Lament – chant
15. Atahuallpa's Command for Gold (35 sec.) – orchestral
16. Clothing of Atahuallpa and his meal – Indians hum and play crotales, 'musical plates' and 'thumb pianos'
17. 1st Gold Procession – orchestra plus Indian humming
18. 'Little Finch' sòng – Atahuallpa sings
19. 2nd Gold Procession – orchestra plus Indian humming
20. The Dice Scene – orchestra plus Indian menaces; Indians play bird flutes and guerros
21. The Garrotting of Atahuallpa – orchestra
22. The Death Chant

INSTRUMENTATION OF SCORE

(Orchestra: four percussionists)

Indians play the following on stage
2 drums (Indian 'tablas' or 2 pairs of bongos)
2 suspended cymbals on 'Indian handles'

2 pairs very large marracas
1 pair very small marracas on long handles
4 guerros
2 dozen bamboo 'bird flutes' (slide recorders) (these can be obtained from any shop specializing in folk craft from India)
2 'thumb pianos' (cigar box type sounding board with spring steel tongues which should be hit with light, hard sticks)

Orchestral instruments, divided between four percussion players
6 suspended cymbals
4 pairs of bongos
1 big drum
1 xylophone
1 glockenspiel
2 lion roar drums (string drums)
2 guerros
5 triangles
3 pairs crotales (small cymbals)
2 sets of sleigh bells
1 woodblock
4 slapsticks
1 large flexaton (musical saw; blade approximately 5 ft. 6 in. long)
1 small flexaton

THE MASSACRE

All Indians have small bells sewn along their sleeves in the Massacre (and the Procession into Cajamarca). Insofar as their movements are rhythmed, and in time with the orchestral music, this helps to keep the centre of musical (as well as dramatic) attention on stage. There is a section in the orchestral score of the Massacre which is almost completely silent, to enhance this effect.

THE BIRD CRIES IN THE FOREST (1st Act)

THE DICE SCENE (*Ruminagui*) (2nd Act)

In both these scenes the Indians play loud interjections to word cues on both 'bird flutes' and guerros, as a counterpoint either to the recording of bird cries, or the orchestral music, to bring closer the sense of threat and danger to the centre of dramatic attention.

TOIL SONG

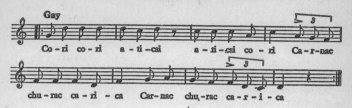

As the Indians come on the stage they all hum this tune, accompanied by the two women, one woman playing small marracas (one marraca to each beat), the other beating the exact rhythm on a small drum (perhaps a 'tabla' wood drum). When work commences the two women sing the song twice, then all resume humming as the Spaniards speak until all workers are off stage.

LITTLE FINCH

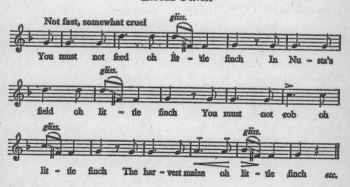

This should be sung very simply with no 'rubato'. Accentuation and dynamics must depend on the meaning of the words. The glissandi should be as the swooping of a bird of prey.

THE HUMMINGS

Atahuallpa's Dressing Scene and meal:

All Indians should hum this tune throughout the scene.

The Indians who help to dress Atahuallpa all have one pair of suspended crotales (ancient Chinese cymbals) hanging from each wrist (about 15 inches of string to each crotale). The Indians who bring on food and feed Atahuallpa have no crotales, but the gold plates should have many small bells hanging below the rims. The plates should also have double bottoms (the lower ones are drum skins). Dried peas or gravel should be inserted between the two bottoms, thus turning the plates into rattles. These plates should be 'played' as they are carried onstage and until Atahuallpa receives his first morsel of food. During Atahuallpa's meal, plates and crotales are silent, the humming continues accompanied by two 'thumb pianos' (pitch ad libitum, to the rhythm of the 'Toil song')

THE GOLD PROCESSIONS

Hum the TOIL SONG tune at a lower pitch, *slow*.

BILLY LIAR

By

Keith Waterhouse

and

Willis Hall

This play was first presented at the Cambridge Theatre, London, on September 13th, 1960, with the following cast:

FLORENCE BOOTHROYD	Ethel Griffies
GEOFFREY FISHER	George A. Cooper
ALICE FISHER	Mona Washbourne
BILLY FISHER	Albert Finney
ARTHUR CRABTREE	Trevor Bannister
BARBARA	Ann Beach
RITA	Juliet Cooke
LIZ	Jennifer Jayne

The play is set in Stradhoughton, an industrial town in the North of England, today

Act I: Saturday Morning

Act II: Afternoon of the same day

Act III: Later the same evening

Directed by Lindsay Anderson

NOTE

ACT I

*The set consists of a living-room, entrance hall and a
section of the garden of* GEOFFREY FISHER'S *house.
It is a typical lower middle-class detached house in an
industrial town in the North of England. To the left of
the stage is the garden containing a small garden seat.
The entrance to the house from the garden leads directly
into the hallway with stairs going up to the bedrooms.
Through the hallway is the living-room where most of
the action of the play takes place. There is also a door
in the living-room R., leading into the kitchen. The
room is furnished with an uncut moquette three-piece
suite and a dining-room suite in dark oak. The furniture
is quite new, but in dreadful taste — as are also the plas-
ter ornaments and the wall plaques with which the room
is overdressed. Above the fireplace is the usual collection
of family photographs on the mantelpiece, and above the
mantelpiece is a large brass-studded circular mirror. The
room also contains a cheap and flashy cocktail cabinet, a
large television and also a sideboard with two cupboards.*

As the curtain rises we discover FLORENCE BOOTHROYD
*sitting on the couch. She is Alice Fisher's mother, an
old lady in her eighties, who finds it impossible to accus-
tom herself to the modern way of life. She continually
talks to herself and when she cannot be heard her lips
continue to move. She is in the habit of addressing her
remarks to inanimate objects. At the moment she is
going through the contents of her large handbag. The
handbag is open on her knee and as she takes out each
object she examines it and then puts it down on the
couch beside her, making a neat display. She has already*

taken out a few odd possessions and, at the moment, she is holding her old age pension book. She addresses the sideboard.

FLORENCE: I don't know. . . . They haven't stamped my book now. . . . They haven't sent it up. It should have gone up last week but they haven't sent it up. (*She puts down the pension book and takes a white hospital appointment card from her handbag*) That's not right, either. Doctor Blakemore? I've never seen Doctor Blakemore. Which is Doctor Blakemore? I bet it's that blackie. Else it's the lady doctor. I'm not seeing her. Tuesday? They know I never go on Tuesdays. I've never been on Tuesday yet. Doctor Thorpe said . . .

    (*It comes to her that she is alone in the room. Putting down the handbag she rises and crosses slowly and flatfooted to the sideboard. She attempts to open the right-hand cupboard but, discovering it is locked, returns to the couch and again takes up her handbag.*)

He's as bad. And she encourages him. He lives in that bed. (*Noting the appointment card on the couch she picks it up*) And where's that crêpe bandage they were going to get me? (*She puts down the card*) What's he always keep it locked up for, anyroad? There's neither sense nor reason in that. And she never tells you anything.

    (ALICE FISHER, *Geoffrey's wife, enters from the kitchen. She is a woman in her middle forties. Both* ALICE *and her husband have had working class upbringings, but Geoffrey's success as a garage owner has moved them up into this new stratum of society. At the moment* ALICE *is caught up in the normal day-to-day rush of breakfast-time. She is speaking to her husband who is in the kitchen.*)

ALICE: Well, you do what you think fit, Geoffrey. Do what you like – it's no good me saying anything. But I know what I'd do. He still owes you for that last job you did for him . . .

    (ALICE *crosses the room towards the hall, ignoring*

her mother who speaks to her as she passes.)

FLORENCE: Who's Doctor Blakemore? Which one is that, then? Is that the one you went to?

ALICE (*entering the hall she calls up the stairs*): It's time we were having you down, my lad. That bedroom clock's not fast, you know. It's half-past nine turned.

(ALICE *turns and re-enters the living-room.*)

FLORENCE: I'll bet it's that blackie, isn't it? I'll bet it's him.

ALICE: Who? Blakemore? Yes, I think it is.

FLORENCE: I'm not seeing him. I shan't go. I shall stop at home.

ALICE: If they say you've got to see him — you've got to see him, Mother. It's no good arguing. That's all there is to it.

(GEOFFREY FISHER *enters from the kitchen. He is a tall man in his early fifties. He is carrying a few invoices and, crossing and seating himself in an armchair, he begins to go through them.*)

FLORENCE: They caused all that bother on the buses in Birmingham. And Egypt. Mau-Mau. I make no wonder Eden's always so badly. And him upstairs. He's just as bad. I think it's time his father talked to him. I don't know why he puts up with it. I can't understand why he lets him carry on like that.

GEOFFREY (*looking up from the invoices he speaks to* ALICE. *In his speech he uses the adjective 'bloody' so frequently that it becomes completely meaningless*): It's all right you talking, Alice, you don't understand. I've got no bloody choice. I can't turn work away.

ALICE: I've said what I've got to say. I'm not saying anything. I'm keeping out of it.

FLORENCE: They let him carry on just as he likes. I wouldn't. I'd see to him.

GEOFFREY: Where's his bloody lordship, then?

FLORENCE: I'd tell her. She lets him lead her on. She wants to go up to him with a wet dish-cloth and wring it over his face. That'll get him up.

GEOFFREY: He wants a bloody good hiding.

FLORENCE: . . . that'd move him . . .

ALICE: I've shouted him three times.

FLORENCE: . . . that'd shift him . . .

GEOFFREY: It's every morning alike.

FLORENCE: . . . he'd have to get up then.

GEOFFREY: You let him do just as he likes!

ALICE (*taking up the poker and a small shovel from the fireplace she crosses into the hall and calls up the stairs*): Billy! . . . Billy! (*She bangs the poker against the shovel*) I shan't tell you again. If I come up there you'll know about it! I suppose you know what time it is! Your boiled egg's stone cold and I'm not cooking another.

FLORENCE: She let's him do just as he likes.

GEOFFREY: Go up to him. Go up and kick him out. He's bloody idle!

(ALICE *returns into the living-room and places the poker and shovel back in the fireplace.*)

ALICE: It's all right you sitting there. You don't stand need to talk. You haven't emptied them ashes yet.

FLORENCE: She wants to go up to him. I would. (*She is now returning the objects to her handbag and pauses when she comes to the appointment card*) It's a mystery to me about that crêpe bandage. I know I had it. It's in this house somewhere.

GEOFFREY: You can't put anything down in this house. Not without somebody bloody shifting it. And who keeps taking my invoices out of that vase? Somebody bloody does.

FLORENCE: He ought to see that window's properly locked every night. He never bolts that back door properly. It wants doing. There's some more blackies moved in where Whitakers used to live.

(BILLY FISHER *begins to come down the bedroom stairs. He is nineteen years old and slightly built. He is wearing an old raincoat over his pyjamas. He is smoking a cigarette.*)

ALICE: Is that him? He's stirred himself at last, then.

I'll see what his breakfast is doing.

(ALICE *exits to the kitchen as* BILLY *reaches the foot of the stairs.* BILLY *takes the morning paper from behind the door and enters the living-room.*)

FLORENCE: She lets him do just as he likes.

BILLY (*reading aloud from the paper*): Cabinet Changes Imminent.

GEOFFREY: Yes, and you'll be bloody imminent if you don't start getting up on a morning.

BILLY: Good morning, Father.

GEOFFREY: Never mind bloody good mornings. It's bloody afternoon more like. If you think your mother's got nothing better to do than go round cooking six breakfasts every morning you've got another think coming.

FLORENCE: She lets him do what he wants.

BILLY (*ignoring his father he turns and bows, acting out the situation to his grandmother*): Your servant, ma'am.

GEOFFREY: And you stop that bloody game. I'm talking to you. You're bloody hopeless. And you can start getting bloody well dressed before you come down in the morning.

FLORENCE: He wants to burn that raincoat. He wants to burn it. Sling it on the fire-back. Then he'll have to get dressed whether or no.

BILLY: I gather that he who would burn the raincoat is Father and he who should get dressed of a morning is my good self. Why do you always address all your remarks to the sideboard, Grandmother?

GEOFFREY (*almost rising from his chair*): Here, here, here! Who do you think you're bloody talking to? You're not out with your daft mates now. And what time did you get in last night? If it was night. This bloody morning, more like.

(ALICE *enters from the kitchen.*)

BILLY: I really couldn't say. 'Bout half-past eleven, quarter to twelve. Good morning, Mother.

GEOFFREY: More like one o'clock, with your bloody half-past eleven! Well, you can bloody well start coming in of a night-time. I'm not having you gallivanting round at all hours, not at your bloody age.

BILLY: Who are you having gallivanting around, then?

GEOFFREY: And I'm not having any of your bloody lip. I'll tell you that, for a start.

ALICE: What were you doing down at Foley Bottoms at nine o'clock last night?

BILLY: Who says I was down at Foley Bottoms?

ALICE: Never mind who says, or who doesn't say. That's got nothing to do with it. You were there – somebody saw you. And it wasn't that Barbara you were with, either.

FLORENCE: He wants to make up his mind who he is going with.

GEOFFREY: He knocks about with too many lasses. He's out with a different one every night. He's like a bloody lass himself.

BILLY: Well, you want to tell whoever saw me to mind their own fizzing business.

ALICE: It is our business – and don't you be so cheeky. You're not old enough for that.

FLORENCE: If she's coming for her tea this afternoon she wants to tell her. If she doesn't I will.

BILLY: I suppose that she who's coming for her tea is Barbara and she who wants to tell her is Mother and . . .

ALICE: I've told you – shut up. I'm going to tell her, don't you fret yourself. You've never played fair with that girl. Carrying on. I'm surprised she bothers with you. You shouldn't mess her about like that. One and then the other. That's no way to carry on. I know where you'll finish up – you'll finish up with none of them – that's where you'll finish up.

GEOFFREY: He'll finish up on his bloody ear-hole. I'm not having him staying out half the night. Not at his age. He's not old enough. He'll wait till he's twenty-one before he starts them bloody tricks. I've told him before, he can start coming in of a night or else go and live somewhere else.

BILLY: Perhaps I will do.

ALICE (*ignoring him*): I can't understand that Barbara — why she does bother with you. Are you supposed to be getting engaged to her or aren't you?

GEOFFREY: He doesn't know who he's bloody getting engaged to.

FLORENCE: He wants to make his mind up.

ALICE (*ignoring* GEOFFREY *and* FLORENCE): Because she's not like these others, you know. That time I saw you in the arcade with her she looked respectable to me. Not like that Liz or whatever her name is. That scruffy one you reckoned to be going about with. Her in that mucky skirt. Do you ever see anything of her still?

GEOFFREY: He sees so many bloody lasses he doesn't know who he does see.

FLORENCE: He wants to make his mind up — once and for all. He wants to make his mind up who he is going with.

BILLY: I haven't seen Liz for three months.

ALICE: Well, who were you with then? Down at Foley Bottoms? Last night?

BILLY: Rita.

GEOFFREY: Who the bloody hell's Rita?

FLORENCE: She wants to see that he makes his mind up.

ALICE: I shall tell Barbara this afternoon — I shall tell her, make no mistake about that.

GEOFFREY: He's never satisfied with what he has got — that's his bloody trouble. He never has been. It's ever since he left school. It's ever since he took that job—clerking. Clerking for that undertaker — what kind of a bloody job's that?

BILLY: Perhaps I might not be doing it much longer.

GEOFFREY: You what?

ALICE: What do you mean?

BILLY: I've been offered a job in London.

GEOFFREY (*turning away in disgust*): Don't talk bloody wet.

ALICE: How do you mean? A job in London? What job in London?

BILLY (*taking a crumpled envelope from his raincoat*

pocket): What I say, I've been offered a job in London. Script-writing.

GEOFFREY: Bloody script-writing.

ALICE: What script-writing?

GEOFFREY: Script-writing! He can't write his bloody name so he can read it. Who set him up?

BILLY (*proudly*): Danny Boon.

ALICE: Danny who?

BILLY (*going into a slow, exasperated explanation*): I told you before. Boon. Danny Boon. I told you. He was on at the Empire the week before last. When he was there I told you. I went to see him. I went to his dressing-room. I took him some of my scripts. Well, he's read them. He's read them and he likes them. And he's sent me this letter. He's offered me a job in London. Script-writing. Danny Boon. The comedian. He's been on television.

FLORENCE (*addressing the television*): It's always boxing; boxing and horse shows.

ALICE (*ignoring her*): Danny Boon? I don't remember ever seeing him.

GEOFFREY: No, and neither does anybody else. It's another of his tales. Danny Boon! He's made him up.

ALICE: What kind of a job?

BILLY: I've told you. Script-writing.

GEOFFREY: It's like all these other tales he comes home with. He can't say two words to anybody without it's a bloody lie. And what's he been telling that woman in the fish shop about me having my leg off? Do I look as though I've had my leg off?

BILLY: It wasn't you. It was Barbara's uncle. She gets everything wrong – that woman in the fish shop.

ALICE: You'll have to stop all this making things up, Billy. There's no sense in it at your age. We never know where we are with you. I mean, you're too old for things like that now.

BILLY (*displaying the letter*): Look – all right then. I've got the letter – here. He wants me to go down to see him.

In London. To fix things up. I'm going to ring up this morning and give them my notice.

ALICE: You can't do things like that, Billy. You can't just go dashing off to London on spec.

GEOFFREY (*disparagingly*): He's not going to no bloody London. It's them that'll be ringing him up, more like. You'll get the sack — I'll tell you what you'll get. What time are you supposed to be going in there this morning, anyroad?

BILLY: I'm not. It's my Saturday off this week.

GEOFFREY: You said that last bloody week. That's three bloody weeks in a row.

BILLY: I got mixed up.

GEOFFREY: I've no patience with you. (*He places the invoices in his pocket and rises from his chair*) Anyway, I've got some work to do if you haven't.

ALICE: Are you going in towards town, Geoffrey?

GEOFFREY: I'm going in that direction.

ALICE: You can drop me off. I'm going down as far as the shops.

GEOFFREY: I can if you're not going to be all bloody day getting ready. I'm late now.

ALICE (*crossing towards the hall*): I'm ready now. I've only to slip my coat on.

(ALICE *goes out into the hall and puts on a coat which is hanging on the rack.* GEOFFREY *turns to* BILLY.)

GEOFFREY: And you can get your mucky self washed — and get bloody dressed. And keep your bloody hands off my razor else you'll know about it.

FLORENCE (*raising her voice*): Is she going past Driver's? 'Cause there's that pork pie to pick up for this afternoon's tea.

ALICE (*re-entering the living-room*): I'm ready. I'll call in for that pie. (*To* BILLY) Your breakfast's on the kitchen table. It'll be clap-cold by now.

GEOFFREY (*crossing towards the door. He turns for a final sally at* BILLY): And you can wash them pots up when you've finished. Don't leave it all for your mother.

ALICE: I shan't be above an hour, Mother.

(ALICE *and* GEOFFREY *go out through the hall and into the garden.* BILLY *exits into the kitchen.*)

FLORENCE: I shouldn't be left on my own. She's not said anything now about the insurance man. I don't know what to give him if he comes.

(ALICE *and* GEOFFREY *are moving down the garden.*)

GEOFFREY: I'm only going as far as the lane, you know. I don't know why you can't get the bloody bus . . .

(ALICE *and* GEOFFREY *exit.* BILLY *re-enters from the kitchen. He is carrying a cup and a teapot.*)

BILLY: I can't eat that egg. It's stone cold.

FLORENCE: There's too much waste in this house. It's all goodness just thrown down the sink. We had it to eat. When I was his age we couldn't leave nothing. If we didn't eat it then it was put out the next meal. When we had eggs, that was. We were lucky to get them. You had to make do with what there was. Bread and dripping.

BILLY (*sitting down he pours himself a cup of tea*): Do you want a cup of tea?

FLORENCE: And if you weren't down at six o'clock of a morning you didn't get that.

BILLY (*he drinks and grimaces*): They don't drink tea in London at this time of a morning. It's all coffee. That's what I'll be doing this time next week.

FLORENCE: Sundays was just the same. No lying-in then.

(BILLY *and his grandmother are now in their own separate dream-worlds.*)

BILLY: Sitting in a coffee-bar. Espresso. With a girl. Art student. Duffel-coat and dirty toe-nails. I discovered her the night before. Contemplating suicide.

FLORENCE: If you had a job in them days you had to stick to it. You couldn't get another.

BILLY (*addressing his imaginary companion*): Nothing is as bad as it seems, my dear. Less than a week ago my father felt the same as you. Suicidal. He came round after the operation and looked down where his legs should have been. Nothing.

220

FLORENCE: We couldn't go traipsing off to London or anywhere else. If we got as far as Scarborough we were lucky.

BILLY: Just an empty space in the bed. Well, he'll never be World Champion now. A broken man on two tin legs.

(BILLY *slowly levers himself out of his chair and limps slowly and painfully around the room leaning heavily against the furniture.*)

FLORENCE (*addressing* BILLY *in the third person*): He's not right in the head.

(BILLY *realizes he is being watched and comes out of his fantasy.*)

I wouldn't care, but it makes me poorly watching him.

BILLY (*rubbing his leg and by way of explanation*): Cramp.

FLORENCE: He wants to get his-self dressed.

(ARTHUR CRABTREE *enters the garden and approaches the front door. He is about the same age as* BILLY. *He is wearing flannels, a sports coat and a loud checked shirt. He pushes the door-bell which rings out in two tones in the hall.*)

FLORENCE (*as* BILLY *crosses to answer the bell*): He shouldn't be going to the door dressed like that.

(BILLY *opens the door and, together with* ARTHUR, *goes into a routine — their usual way of greeting each other.* ARTHUR *holds up an imaginary lantern and peers into an imaginary darkness.*)

ARTHUR (*in a thick north country accent*): There's trouble up at the mill.

BILLY (*also in a thick north country accent*): What's afoot, Ned Leather? Is Willy Arkwright smashing up my looms again?

ARTHUR: It's the men. They'll not stand for that lad of yours down from Oxford and Cambridge.

BILLY: They'll stand for him and lump it. There's allus been an Oldroyd at Oldroyd's mill and there allus will be.

ARTHUR: Nay, Josiah! He's upsetting them with his fancy

college ways and they'll have none of it. They're on the march! They're coming up the drive!

BILLY: Into the house, Ned, and bar the door! We've got to remember our Sal's condition.

(*They enter together and march into the living-room where they both dissolve into laughter.*)

FLORENCE: Carrying on and making a commotion. It's worse than Bedlam. Carrying on and all that noise. They want to make less noise, the pair of them.

ARTHUR: Good morning, Mrs Boothroyd.

FLORENCE: He wants to make less noise and get his-self dressed.

BILLY: Do you want a cup of tea, Arthur? I'm just having my breakfast.

ARTHUR: You rotten idle crow! Some of us have done a day's work already, you lazy get.

BILLY: Why aren't you at work now?

ARTHUR: Why aren't you at rotten work, that's why I'm not at work. Come to see where you are. They're going bonkers at the office. You never turned in last Saturday either.

BILLY: Isn't it my Saturday off this week?

ARTHUR: You know rotten well it isn't.

FLORENCE (*getting up from the couch*): They're all idle. They're all the same. They make me badly.

(FLORENCE *crosses the room and exits up the stairs to the bedroom.*)

BILLY: I could say I forgot and thought it was.

ARTHUR: You can hellers like. You said that last week.

BILLY: Tell them my grandad's had his leg cut off.

ARTHUR: You haven't got a rotten grandad. Anyroad, I can't tell them anything. I'm not supposed to have seen you. I've come up in my break. I'm supposed to be having my coffee. I'm not telling them anything. I'm having enough bother as it is with our old lady. What with you and your lousy stories. Telling everybody she was in the family way. She's heard about it. She says she's going to come up here and see your father.

BILLY: Cripes, she can't do that! It was only last night I told him she'd just had a miscarriage. She's not supposed to be up yet.

ARTHUR: What the hell did you tell him that for?

BILLY: I hadn't any choice. My mother was going to send a present round for the baby.

ARTHUR: The trouble with you, cocker, is you're just a rotten pathological liar. Anyway, you've done it this time. You've dropped yourself right in with not coming in this morning.

BILLY: I can get out of that. I'll think of some excuse.

ARTHUR: There's more to it than that, matey. Shadrack's been going through your postage book.

BILLY: When?

ARTHUR: This morning, when do you think? There's nearly three rotten quid short. All there is in the book is one stinking lousy rotten threepenny stamp and he says he gave you two pound ten stamp money on Wednesday.

BILLY: Fizzing hell! Has he been through the petty cash as well?

ARTHUR: Not when I left. No. Why, have you been fiddling that as well?

BILLY: No, no . . . I haven't filled the book up, though.

ARTHUR: And he was going on about some calendars — I don't know what he meant.

BILLY (crossing to the sideboard): I do.

(BILLY takes a small key from his raincoat pocket and opens the right-hand cupboard. As he does so a pile of large envelopes fall out on to the carpet followed by a few odds and ends.)

There you are, Tosh, two hundred and sixty of the bastards.

ARTHUR: What?

BILLY: Maring calendars.

ARTHUR (crosses and picks up an envelope from the floor): What do you want with two rotten hundred and sixty calendars? (He reads the address on the front of the enve-

lope) 'The Mother Superior, The Convent of the Sacred
Heart!'

> (*He tears open the envelope and takes out a large
> wall calendar illustrated with a colourful painting of a
> kitten and a dog. He reads the inscription.*)

'Shadrack and Duxbury, Funeral Furnishers.' These are the
firm's! 'Taste, Tact and Economy.' You skiving nit! You
should have posted these last Christmas.

BILLY: Yes.

ARTHUR: Well, what are they doing in your sideboard
cupboard?

BILLY: I never had enough stamps in the postage book.

ARTHUR: You think that postage money's part of your
bloody wages, don't you?

> (*He bends down and sorts through the pile of papers
> on the floor.*)

Why do you keep them in there?

BILLY: It's where I keep all my private things.

ARTHUR (*picking up a small package*): Private things! A
naffing crêpe bandage!

> (*He throws down the package and picks up a piece of
> blue notepaper.*)

What's this then?

BILLY (*making a grab for the letter*): Gerroff, man! Give
us that here! That's personal!

ARTHUR (*evading* BILLY's *hand*): What the hell are you
writing to Godfrey Winn for?

BILLY: It's not me. It's my mother.

ARTHUR (*reading the letter*): 'Dear Sir, Just a few lines to
let you know how much I enjoy Housewives' Choice every
day, I always listen no matter what I am doing, could you
play JUST A SONG AT TWILIGHT for me.' That's a turn-up for
the top ten! She isn't half with it, your old lady! (*Reading*)
'I don't suppose you get time to play everyone that writes to
you, but this is my favourite song. You see my husband often
used to sing it when we were a bit younger than we are now.
I will quite understand if you cannot play. Your respectfully

Mrs A. Fisher.' So why didn't you post this then?

BILLY: I couldn't be bothered. (*He makes a further attempt to grab the letter*) Give us it here!

ARTHUR (*holding him off*): 'P.S. My son also writes songs, but I suppose there is not much chance for him as he has not had the training. We are just ordinary folk.'

BILLY (*snatches the letter and tosses it into the cupboard*): I'm not ordinary folk even if she is. (*He crams the envelopes containing the calendars back into the cupboard*) I keep trying to get rid of them. It was bad enough getting them out of the office.

ARTHUR: How long have they been here?

BILLY: Not long. I used to keep them in that coffin in the basement at work. You can't get rid of the fizzing things! It's like a bloody nightmare. They won't burn. I've tried tearing them up and pushing them down the lavatory – all they do is float.

ARTHUR: Makes no difference what you do with them. Duxbury's on to you. He knows about them.

BILLY (*stuffing the last of the calendars into the cupboard he locks the door*): Oh well . . . so what. He knows what he can do with his calendars. I don't give a monkey's. I'm leaving. I've got another job.

ARTHUR: Leaving?

BILLY: I'm going to ring him up this morning and give him my notice.

ARTHUR: Yes, and we've heard that one before.

BILLY: No, straight up. I'm going to London.

ARTHUR: What as – road-sweeper?

BILLY (*grandiloquently*): Ay road sweepah on the road – to fame! (*He returns to his normal voice*) I've got that job with Danny Boon.

ARTHUR: You haven't!

BILLY: Yes – Script-writer. Start next week.

ARTHUR: You jammy burk! Have you though, honest?

BILLY: Yeh – course I have. It's all fixed up. He sent me a letter. Asking me to work for him.

ARTHUR: What's he paying you?

BILLY: A cowing sight more than I get from Shadrack and flaming Duxbury's.

ARTHUR: What? Counting the postage?

BILLY: What's it to you? This is it for me, boy! Success! Saturday Night Spectacular! Sunday Night at the Palladium! Script by!

ARTHUR: Ta-ra-ra-raaa!

BILLY: Billy Fisher! Directed by!

ARTHUR: Ta-ra-ra-raaa!

BILLY: William Fisher! Produced by!

ARTHUR: Ta-ra-ra-raaa!

BILLY: William S. Fisher!

ARTHUR: Ta-ra-ra-raaa!

BILLY: A W. S. Fisher Presentation! 'Mr Fisher, on behalf of the British Television Industry, serving the needs of twenty million viewers, it gives me great pleasure to present you with this award, this evening, in recognition of the fact that you have been voted Television Script-writer of the Year – for the seventh year running.'

ARTHUR (*picking up a vase from the sideboard he places it in* BILLY's *hands*): Big-head.

BILLY (*returning the vase to the sideboard*): Rot off. You wait and see.

ARTHUR (*taking a small bottle of tablets from his trouser pocket*): So you won't be needing these now, then, will you?

BILLY: What's them?

ARTHUR: Passion pills. What I said I'd get for you.

BILLY (*taking the bottle incredulously*): Let's have a look, mate. (*He opens the bottle and is about to swallow one of the tablets*) What do they taste like?

ARTHUR: Here, go steady on, man! They'll give you the screaming ad-dabs.

BILLY (*returning the tablet to the bottle*): How did you get hold of them?

ARTHUR: From a mate of mine who got demobbed. He brought them back from Singapore.

BILLY: I'll bet they're bloody aspirins.

ARTHUR: Do you want to bet? You want to ask this bloke, tosher.

BILLY: How many do you give them?

ARTHUR: Just one. Two two-and-nines at the Regal, a bag of chips and one of these and you're away. Who's it for anyway?

BILLY: Barbara . . . Bloody hell!

ARTHUR: What's up?

BILLY: She's supposed to be coming round this morning.

ARTHUR: I thought it was this afternoon? For her tea?

BILLY (*placing the bottle of tablets on the sideboard*): No, I've got to see her first. Our old man'll go bald if he sees her before I've had a word with her. She thinks he's in the Merchant Navy.

ARTHUR: You what?

BILLY (*crossing hurriedly towards the hall*): On petrol tankers. (*He indicates the tea-things*) Shift them into the kitchen for me. Shan't be a tick.

> (BILLY *runs up the stairs in the hall and into his bedroom.* ARTHUR *picks up the teapot and exits into the kitchen.* ARTHUR *re-enters and crosses to the sideboard where he picks up the bottle of tablets.* BILLY *appears at the top of the stairs with his clothes in his hands.* BILLY *moves down the stairs and enters the living-room.* ARTHUR *replaces the tablets on the sideboard.*)

ARTHUR: What time's she supposed to be coming?

BILLY (*dressing hastily*): Quarter of an hour since. Where's them passion pills?

ARTHUR: On the sideboard. You're not going to slip her one this morning are you?

BILLY: Why not? I'm pressed for time, man. I'm going out with Rita tonight.

ARTHUR: Well, what about your grandmother?

BILLY: Oh, she's spark out till dinner-time.

ARTHUR: I've lost track of your rotten sex life. Which one are you supposed to be engaged to, anyway?

BILLY: That's what they call an academic question.

ARTHUR: Well, you can't be engaged to both of them at once, for God's sake.

BILLY: Do you want to bet?

ARTHUR: Crikey! Well, which one of them's got the naffing engagement ring?

BILLY: Well, that's the trouble. That's partly the reason why Barbara's coming round this morning – if she did but know it. She's got it. I've got to get it off her. For Rita.

ARTHUR: What for?

BILLY: Ah, well . . . You see, she had it first – Rita. Only I got it from her to give to Barbara. Now she wants it back. I told her it was at the jeweller's – getting the stone fixed. There'll be hell to pay if she doesn't get it.

ARTHUR: The sooner you get to London the better.

BILLY (*tucking his shirt in his trousers and slipping on his jacket*): Are you sure them passion pills'll work on Barbara? She's dead from the neck down.

ARTHUR: You haven't tried.

BILLY: Tried! Who hasn't tried! If you want to try you're welcome. All she does is sit and eat stinking oranges.

ARTHUR: What I can't work out is why you got engaged to her in the first place. What's wrong with Liz?

BILLY: Don't talk to me about Liz. I've not seen her for months. She tooled off to Bradford or somewhere.

ARTHUR: Well, she's tooled back again then. I saw her this morning.

BILLY: What? Liz?

ARTHUR: Yeh – scruffy Lizzie. I bumped into her in Sheepgate. Mucky as ever. It's about time somebody bought her a new skirt.

> (BARBARA *approaches the house. She is about nineteen years old, a large well-built girl in a tweed suit and flat-heeled shoes. She is carrying a large handbag.*)

BILLY: Did she say anything about me?

ARTHUR: I didn't stop. Just said 'Hello.' I wouldn't be seen stood standing talking to that scruffy-looking bird.

(BARBARA *rings the bell*.)

BILLY: That's Barbara! Where's them passion pills!

(BILLY *crosses and taking the bottle from the sideboard he places it in his breast pocket.* ARTHUR *crosses towards the door*.)

ARTHUR: I'll have to get going anyway. I'll get shot when I get back to work. I've been gone nearly half an hour now.

BILLY (*crossing towards the door*): Hang on a couple of minutes, man. Don't make it look too obvious! If she sees you going out and leaving her with me she'll be out of that door like a whippet.

ARTHUR: I'm late now!

BILLY: You can chat her up for a minute.

(BILLY *crosses into the hall and opens the door to admit* BARBARA.)

BILLY: Hallo, darling!

BARBARA (*who uses endearments coldly and flatly*): Hallo, pet.

BILLY (*leading the way*): Come through into the lounge.

BARBARA (*following* BILLY *into the living-room*): Hallo, Arthur.

(ARTHUR *winks at her.* BARBARA *looks round the room*.) What a nice room! (*She crosses to examine the cocktail cabinet*) What a beautiful cocktail cabinet!

BILLY: I made it.

(ARTHUR *reacts to this statement*.)

BARBARA: How clever of you, sweet. I didn't know you could do woodwork.

BILLY: Oh yes, I made all the furniture. (*A pause and then, wildly*) And the garage.

(BARBARA *looks around the room doubtfully*.)

ARTHUR (*coughs*): It's time I was making a move, mate.

BARBARA: You're not going because of me, Arthur?

ARTHUR: No, I'm supposed to be at work. (*To* BILLY) So long, Tosh!

BILLY: So long . . .

BARBARA: 'Bye! . . . Isn't your sister in, Billy?

ARTHUR (*stops short on his way to the door and turns*):
What bloody sister?

(BILLY *unnoticed by* BARBARA *gesticulates to* ARTHUR
to leave. ARTHUR *does so – hastily.*)

BILLY: Barbara, I'm glad you asked me that question.
About my sister.

BARBARA: What is it?

BILLY: Sit down, darling. (BARBARA *sits on the couch*)
Darling, are you still coming to tea this afternoon?

BARBARA: Of course.

BILLY: Because there are some things I want to tell you.

BARBARA: What things, Billy?

BILLY: You know what you said the other night – about
loving me? Even if I were a criminal.

BARBARA: Well?

BILLY: You said you'd still love me even if I'd murdered
your mother.

BARBARA (*suspiciously*): Well?

BILLY: I wonder if you'll still love me when you hear what
I've got to say. You see – well, you know that I've got a
fairly vivid imagination, don't you?

BARBARA: Well, you have to have if you're going to be a
script-writer, don't you?

BILLY: Well, being a script-writer, I'm perhaps – at times
– a bit inclined to let my imagination run away with me.
As you know. (BARBARA *is even more aloof than usual*) You
see, the thing is, if we're going to have our life together –
and that cottage – and little Billy and little Barbara and the
lily pond and all that . . . Well, there's some things we've
got to get cleared up.

BARBARA: What things?

BILLY: Some of the things I'm afraid I've been telling you.

BARBARA: Do you mean you've been telling me lies?

BILLY: Well, not lies exactly . . . But I suppose I've been,
well, exaggerating some things. Being a script-writer . . .
For instance, there's that business about my father. Him
being a sea captain. On a petrol tanker.

BARBARA: You mean he's not on a petrol tanker?

BILLY: He's not even in the navy.

BARBARA: Well, what is he?

BILLY: He's in the removal business.

BARBARA: And what about him being a prisoner-of-war? And that tunnel? And the medal? Don't say that was all lies?

BILLY: Yes. (BARBARA *turns away abruptly*) Are you cross?

BARBARA: No – not cross. Just disappointed. It sounds as though you were ashamed of your father.

BILLY: I'm not ashamed. I'm not – I'm not!

BARBARA: Otherwise why say he was a prisoner-of-war? What was he?

BILLY: A conscientious ob . . . (*He checks himself*) He wasn't anything. He wasn't fit. He has trouble with his knee.

BARBARA: The knee he's supposed to have been shot in, I suppose.

BILLY: Yes. Another thing, we haven't got a budgie, or a cat. And I didn't make the furniture . . . Not all of it, anyway.

BARBARA: How many other lies have you been telling me?

BILLY: My sister.

BARBARA: Don't tell me you haven't got a sister.

BILLY: I did have. But she's dead. If you're still coming for your tea this afternoon they never talk about her.

(BARBARA *remains silent, her head still turned away.*) You remind me of her . . . If you're not coming, I'll understand . . . I'm just not good enough for you, Barbara . . . if you want to give me the engagement ring back – I'll understand.

BARBARA (*turning towards him*): Don't be cross with yourself, Billy. I forgive you.

BILLY (*moving to kiss her*): Darling . . .

BARBARA (*moving away*): But promise me one thing.

BILLY: That I'll never lie to you again? (BARBARA *nods*) I'll never lie to you again. Never. I promise . . . Darling, there is one thing. I have got a grannie.

BARBARA: I believe you.

BILLY: Only she's not blind. She's not very well, though. She's upstairs. Sleeping. She might have to have her leg off.

BARBARA (*kissing him*): Poor darling . . .

BILLY (*moving quickly towards the cocktail cabinet*): Would you like a drink?

BARBARA: Not now, pet.

BILLY (*opening the cabinet*): Port. To celebrate.

BARBARA: All right. Well, just a tiny one.

BILLY: I'm turning over a new leaf.

> (*Unnoticed to* BARBARA *he pours the drinks and taking a tablet from the 'passion pill' bottle, places it in her glass. He crosses with the glasses and sits beside her on the couch.*)

That's yours, darling.

BARBARA (*sitting on the edge of the couch she sips the port*): Let's talk about something nice.

BILLY: Let's talk about our cottage.

BARBARA: Oh, I've seen the most marvellous material to make curtains for the living-room. Honestly, you'll love it. It's a sort of turquoise with lovely little squiggles like wine glasses.

BILLY: Will it go with the yellow carpet?

BARBARA: No, but it will go with the grey rugs.

BILLY (*taking her in his arms*): I love you, darling . . .

BARBARA (*moving away*): I love you.

BILLY: Do you? Really and truly?

BARBARA: Of course I do.

BILLY: Are you looking forward to getting married?

> (BARBARA *takes an orange from her handbag and peels it and eats it during the following dialogue.*)

BARBARA: I think about it every minute of the day.

BILLY: Darling . . . (*He again attempts unsuccessfully to kiss her*) Don't ever fall in love with anybody else.

BARBARA: Let's talk about our cottage.

BILLY (*simulating a dreamy voice*): What about our cottage?

BARBARA: About the garden. Tell me about the garden.

BILLY: We'll have a lovely garden. We'll have roses in it

and daffodils and a lovely lawn with a swing for little Billy and little Barbara to play on. And we'll have our meals down by the lily pond in summer.

BARBARA: Do you think a lily pond is safe? What if the kiddies wandered too near and fell in?

BILLY: We'll build a wall round it. No – no, we won't. We won't have a pond at all. We'll have an old well. An old brick well where we draw the water. We'll make it our wishing well. Do you know what I'll wish?

BARBARA (*shaking her head*): No.

BILLY: Tell me what you'll wish first.

BARBARA: Oh, I'll wish that we'll always be happy. And always love each other. What will you wish?

BILLY: Better not tell you.

BARBARA: Why not, pet?

BILLY: You might be cross.

BARBARA: Why would I be cross?

BILLY: Oh, I don't know . . . You might think me too . . . well, forward. (*He glances at her face but can see no reaction*) Barbara . . . ? Do you think it's wrong for people to have – you know, feelings?

BARBARA: Not if they're genuinely in love with each other.

BILLY: Like we are.

BARBARA (*uncertainly*): Yes.

BILLY: Would you think it wrong of me to have – feelings?

BARBARA (*briskly and firmly*): I think we ought to be married first.

BILLY (*placing his hand on* BARBARA's *knee*): Darling . . .

BARBARA: Are you feeling all right?

BILLY: Of course, darling. Why?

BARBARA: Look where your hand is.

BILLY: Darling, don't you want me to touch you?

BARBARA (*struggling*): It seems . . . indecent, somehow.

BILLY: Are you feeling all right?

BARBARA: Yes, of course.

BILLY: How do you feel?

BARBARA: Contented.

BILLY: You don't feel . . . you know – restless?

BARBARA: No.

BILLY: Finish your drink.

BARBARA: In a minute. (*She opens her handbag and offers it towards him*) Have an orange.

> (BILLY, *snatching the bag from her, throws it down and oranges spill out across the floor.*)

BILLY: You and your bloody oranges!

BARBARA (*remonstratively*): Billy! . . . Darling!

BILLY (*placing his head on her shoulder*): I'm sorry, darling. I've had a terrible morning.

BARBARA: Why? What's happened?

BILLY: Oh, nothing. The usual. Family and things. Just that I've got a headache.

BARBARA: I'm sorry, pet. You know, you ought to see a doctor.

BILLY: I've seen doctors – specialists – I've seen them all. All they could give me was a crêpe bandage. (BARBARA, *unimpressed, licks her fingers*) You know, my darling, I think you have feelings too. Deep down.

BARBARA (*examining her hands distastefully*): Oooh, sticky paws!

BILLY: Wipe them on the cushion. (*He rises as a thought strikes him*) You can go upstairs if you want. Use our bathroom.

BARBARA: Thank you.

> (BARBARA, *picking up her handbag, crosses into the hall and goes upstairs. BILLY picks up her glass and crosses to the cocktail cabinet, where he pours out two more drinks. Taking the 'passion pills' from his pocket he adds two pills to Barbara's glass and then, on impulse, he adds the entire contents of the bottle into her glass. He is standing admiring the glass and its contents as the telephone rings in the hall. He places the glass on the table and crosses into the hall where he picks up the phone.*)

BILLY: The Fisher residence. Can I help you? (*His manner changes*) Oh, hullo, Mr Duxbury. No, well, I'm sorry but I've had an accident. I was just leaving for work and I spilt this hot water down my arm. I had to get it bandaged. . . . Oh, well, I think there's a very simple explanation for that, Mr Duxbury. You see, there's a lot of those figures that haven't been carried forward . . . I use my own individual system . . . No. No, not me, Mr Duxbury. Well, I'm sure you'll find that there's a very simple explanation . . . What? Monday morning? Yes, of course I'll be there. Prompt. Thank you, Mr Duxbury. Thank you for ringing. Good-bye, then . . . (BILLY *puts down the telephone for a moment and is lost in depression. He brightens as, in his imagination, he addresses his employer*) Well, look, Duxbury – we're not going to argue over trivialities. As soon as I've finalized my arrangements with Mr Boon I'll get in touch with you. (*He picks up the telephone*) Hello, Duxbury? . . . I'm afraid the answer is 'no'. I fully agree that a partnership sounds very attractive – but frankly my interests lie in other directions. I'm quite willing to invest in your business, but I just have not the time to take over the administrative side . . . Oh, I agree that you have a sound proposition there . . . Granted! I take your point, Mr Duxbury. What's that little saying of yours? 'You've got to come down to earth.' It's not a question of coming down to earth, old man. Some of us belong in the stars. The best of luck, Mr Duxbury, and keep writing . . . (BILLY *breaks off as* BARBARA *approaches down the stairs and, for her benefit, he goes into another fantasy as she passes him and enters the living-room*) Well, doctor, if the leg's got to come off – it's got to come off . . . (BILLY *replaces the telephone and looks speculatively at the living-room door*) It's not a question of coming down to earth, Mr Duxbury. (*He pauses*) Some of us, Mr Duxbury, belong in the stars.

(BILLY, *who has now regained his self-confidence, enters the living-room and crosses towards* BARBARA *with her glass of port.*)

THE CURTAIN FALLS
END OF ACT I

ACT II

Afternoon of the same day.
It is late afternoon and just after tea-time in the FISHER
household. ALICE *is moving in and out of the kitchen
clearing the tea-things from the living-room table. The
best tea-service has been brought out for* BARBARA's
benefit, although FLORENCE *has insisted upon having
her usual pint-pot. A strange silence has fallen upon the
living-room caused partly by* BARBARA's *disclosure that
she has recently become engaged to* BILLY — *and partly
by* FLORENCE's *insistence on taking her time over her
tea.* FLORENCE, *in fact, is the only one remaining at the
table.* GEOFFREY *has moved away to a chair and* BARBARA
is seated on the couch. BILLY *is in the hall engaged in a
phone conversation and has closed the door to the living-
room.*

BILLY: . . . Rita, will you listen for a minute! . . . No,
listen to what I'm telling you! The ring's still at the
jeweller's! Of course it's all right . . . Well, what's the sense
in coming round here now! It isn't here — I've just told you,
it's at the jeweller's . . . Rita! . . . (*He puts down the phone*)
Oh blimey! . . . (*He takes up the phone and dials a number*)

BARBARA (*in an attempt to break the silence*): Of course,
we haven't fixed the date or anything. (*There is a pause*)
We won't be thinking of getting married for quite a while
yet.

GEOFFREY (*a slight pause*): Well, what you going to live
on? The pair of you? He'll never have a bloody penny.

FLORENCE: And there was none of this hire purchase in
them days. What you couldn't pay for you didn't have. I
don't agree with it. He didn't either. It's only muck and
rubbish when it's there. (ALICE *returns from the kitchen and*

236

fills a tray with used tea-things. She picks up FLORENCE's
pint-pot) I haven't finished with that yet. (ALICE *replaces
the pot.*)

(BILLY *puts down the phone in exasperation. He picks
it up and dials another number.* ALICE *returns into the
kitchen with the tray.*)

BARBARA: We had thought of a cottage in Devon.

GEOFFREY: Bloody Devon! He'll never get past the end
of our street.

FLORENCE: She needn't have opened that tin of salmon –
it's not been touched hardly.

BARBARA: I don't believe in long engagements – but I
don't mind waiting.

GEOFFREY: You'll wait till bloody Domesday if you wait
for that sackless article. He's not had a shave yet.

ALICE (*putting her head round the kitchen door*): Come
on, Mother! It's only you we're waiting for.

FLORENCE (*mumbling to herself*): She knows I haven't got
to be rushed. I don't know what she does it for . . .

(*An awkward silence falls upon the living-room.* BILLY
speaks into the telephone.)

BILLY: Arthur? . . . Look, you've got to do something for
me. Stop Rita coming round here . . . Well, go round to
their house! She's after the ring and Barbara's still got it . . .
No, did she heckerslike! I told you they were aspirins. Don't
stand there yattering, get your skates on!

(*He slams down the receiver.*)

FLORENCE (*who has been mumbling quietly to herself
throughout the above now raises her voice to address the
sideboard*): It's every tea-time alike. Rush, rush, rush.
They've got no consideration. She knows I'm not well.

BARBARA (*politely*): Billy was saying you'd not been well.

GEOFFREY: Take no notice of what he says – he'll have
you as bloody daft as his-self. (BILLY *opens the door and
enters the living-room*) You'll stand talking on that phone
till you look like a bloody telephone. Who was it, then?

BILLY: Only Arthur.

GEOFFREY: What's he bloody want?

BILLY: Oh – nothing.

GEOFFREY: He takes his time asking for it.

ALICE (*enters from the kitchen*): How's his mother?

BILLY (*crossing to the fireplace*): All right – considering.

BARBARA: Arthur's mother? Has she been ill?

GEOFFREY: That's the bloody tale he's come home with.

BILLY (*shuffling awkwardly in front of the fire*): She's been off-colour, but she's all right.

GEOFFREY: By, if I don't knock some sense into you! Stand up straight and get your hands out of your pockets! You want to get married, you do!

FLORENCE: She wants to sew them up. With a needle and cotton. She should sew them up.

GEOFFREY: You'll have to brighten your ideas up, then!

FLORENCE: A needle and a bit of black cotton. That'd stop him. Then he couldn't put them in his pockets.

ALICE: Mother, haven't you finished that tea yet! Why don't you finish it by the fire. I've got to get cleared up.

FLORENCE (*rising and crossing slowly to sit by the fire*): I can't be up and down – up and down – every five minutes. She knows it doesn't do me any good. And that fire's too hot. He banks it up till it's like a furnace in here. I can't be putting up with it . . .

ALICE (*clearing the remains off the table*): Well, it's all very well, Mother, I like to get things done. Then it's finished with.

BARBARA: Can I be giving you a hand, Mrs Fisher?

ALICE: It's all right, Barbara. I don't know why our Billy doesn't wash up once in a while.

GEOFFREY: He can't wash his bloody self, never mind the pots.

BARBARA (*rising and crossing towards the kitchen*): I don't mind . . .

(BARBARA *and* ALICE *exit into the kitchen.* BILLY *crosses to sit on the couch and* GEOFFREY *rises. There is an embarrassed silence. There is a first attempt at 'con-*

tact' between BILLY *and his father*.)

GEOFFREY: She doesn't have much to say for herself . . . Where do you say she works, then?

BILLY: Turnbull and Mason's.

GEOFFREY: Who?

BILLY: Solicitors. Up Sheepgate.

GEOFFREY: Oh aye?

BILLY: Shorthand-typist.

GEOFFREY: She likes her food, doesn't she? She'll take some keeping. By bloody hell! She had her share of that pork pie, didn't she?

BILLY: She lives up Cragside. On that new estate.

GEOFFREY: She'll need to live up Cragside the way she eats. She can shift them tinned oranges when she starts, can't she? Mind you, she needs it. She's a big lass, isn't she? Big-boned.

BILLY: Yes.

GEOFFREY (*after a pause*): You're reckoning on getting married then?

BILLY: Thinking about it.

GEOFFREY: You've got your bloody self engaged, anyroad.

BILLY: Yes.

GEOFFREY: So she was saying. You never told us.

BILLY: No. I was meaning to.

GEOFFREY: That was a bit of a daft trick to do, wasn't it?

BILLY: Oh, I don't know.

GEOFFREY: I mean, at your age like. You're only young yet. You're not old enough to start thinking about getting married.

BILLY: There's no hurry.

GEOFFREY: No. But you'll have to put your mind to it sometime.

BILLY: Yes.

GEOFFREY: I mean, you can't go carrying-on the way you've been carrying-on — now, you know. Messing about with different lasses.

BILLY: No — I know. I realize that.

GEOFFREY: You've not only yourself to consider. I don't see why you couldn't have waited a bit. I don't see why you couldn't have told us — your mother and me.

BILLY: I've said — I was meaning to.

GEOFFREY: She's not — you haven't got her into trouble — I mean, there's nothing like that about it, is there?

BILLY: No . . . No — 'course not.

(BILLY *looks across at his father and we feel, for a moment, that they are about to make some point of contact.*)

GEOFFREY: Well, that's something, anyroad. I suppose she's all right. Just with you not saying anything, that's all.

BILLY: Yes.

GEOFFREY: Only you'll have to start thinking about getting married. Saving up and that.

BILLY: There's plenty of time yet.

FLORENCE: Well, she didn't touch none of that salmon. I know that. Nobody did. She puts too much out. There's some folk would be glad of that. I tell her . . .

(BILLY *shows some impatience.*)

GEOFFREY: 'Course, I don't believe in interfering. You've made your mind up. I don't want you to come to me and say that I stopped you doing it.

BILLY: Well, Dad, it's not that simple. I've not really decided what we'll be doing yet.

GEOFFREY: You couldn't do no worse than us when we started. Me and your mother. We'd nothing — I hadn't two ha'pennies to scratch my backside with. We had to manage.

BILLY: I'm not bothered about managing, Dad. It's just that I hadn't made my mind up.

GEOFFREY (*almost reverting back to his normal antagonism*): Well, you want to get your bloody mind made up, lad. Right sharp. Before she does it for you.

BILLY: You see . . .

FLORENCE (*interrupting*): I told her. I had my say. I told her, you don't get married till you're twenty-one.

BILLY: Just a minute, Grandma . . .

FLORENCE (*ignoring him*): You can do as you like then,
I said. Only, I said, don't come running back to me when
you can't manage. I said you'll have it to put up with . . .

BILLY (*completely exasperated*): For Christ's sake belt up!

GEOFFREY (*losing his temper completely*): You what! (*He
moves across and grabs* BILLY *by his shirt*) You what did
you say? What was that? What did you say?

BILLY (*frightened but unrepentant*): I merely remarked . . .

GEOFFREY (*shouting*): Talk bloody properly when you talk
to me! You were talking different a minute ago, weren't
you? What did you just say to your grandma? What did
you just say?

ALICE (*enters from the kitchen*): Hey, what's all this
row? (*She indicates the kitchen*) Don't you know we've got
somebody here?

GEOFFREY: I can't help who's here! She might as well
know what he is! Because I'll tell her! (*Shaking him*) He's
ignorant! That's what you are, isn't it? Ignorant! Ignorant!
Ignorant! Isn't it?

ALICE: Well, don't pull him round. That shirt's clean on.

GEOFFREY (*releasing his hold on* BILLY): I'll clean shirt
him before I've finished!

ALICE: Well, what's he done?

GEOFFREY: I'll clean shirt him round his bloody ear-hole.
With his bloody fountain pens and his bloody suède shoes!
Well, he doesn't go out tonight, I know where he gets it
from. He stops in tonight and tomorrow night as well.

BILLY: Look . . .

GEOFFREY: Don't 'look' me! With your look this and look
that! And you get all that bloody books and rubbish or
whatever it is cleared out of that sideboard cupboard as
well! Before I chuck 'em out — and you with 'em!

BILLY: What's up? They're not hurting you are they?

(BARBARA *enters and stands in the kitchen doorway
uncertainly*.)

GEOFFREY: No, and they're not bloody hurting you either!

ALICE (*quietly*): Well, I don't know what you've done now.

GEOFFREY: Answering back at his grandmother. If that's what they learned him at Grammar School I'm glad I'm bloody uneducated! Anyroad, I've finished with him! He knows where there's a suitcase. If he wants to go to London he can bloody well go.

ALICE (*sharply*): Oh, but he's not.

GEOFFREY: I've finished with him. He can go.

ALICE: Oh, but he's not.

GEOFFREY: He's going! He can get his bloody things together! He's going out!

ALICE: Oh, but he's not. Oh, but he's not. Oh, but he is not!

BILLY (*trying to get a word in*): Look, can I settle this . . .

GEOFFREY (*interrupting*): It's ever since he started work. Complaining about this and that and the other. If it isn't his boiled eggs it's something else. You have to get special bloody wheat flakes for him because there's a bloody plastic bloody submarine in the packet. Splashing about in the kitchen at his age. He wants putting away. Well, I've had enough – he can go.

ALICE: Oh, but he's not. Now, you just listen to me, Geoffrey. He's not old enough to go to London or anywhere else.

GEOFFREY: He's old enough to get himself engaged. He thinks he is. He's old enough and bloody daft enough.

ALICE: Well, you said yourself. He doesn't think. He gets ideas in his head.

GEOFFREY: He can go. I've finished with him.

ALICE: Oh, but he is not. Not while I'm here.

BARBARA (*who has been staring at* FLORENCE): Mrs Fisher . . .

GEOFFREY (*ignoring her*): He wants to get into the bloody Army, that's what he wants to do.

ALICE (*spiritedly*): Yes, and you want to get into the bloody Army as well.

BARBARA: Mrs Fisher. I don't think Billy's grandma's very well.

(ALICE, GEOFFREY *and* BILLY *turn and look at* FLORENCE *who is sitting slumped in her chair.*)

ALICE (*rushing across to her mother*): Now look what you've done!

GEOFFREY (*to* BILLY): I hope you're bloody satisfied now. She's had another do.

ALICE: It's no use blaming him, Geoffrey. You're both as bad as each other. Well, don't just stand there – get me the smelling salts.

BARBARA (*coming forward*): Can I be doing anything, Mrs Fisher?

ALICE: No . . . no, it's all right. She's getting old, that's all. He'll see to it.

GEOFFREY (*crossing to the sideboard he searches through the drawers*): It's happening too bloody often is this. We can't be having this game every fortnight – neither sense nor reason in it.

ALICE: Well, she can't help it, Geoffrey. It's not her fault.

GEOFFREY: She'll have to see that bloody doctor. If I've to take time off and take her myself – she'll have to see him.

ALICE: She won't see him.

GEOFFREY: It's getting past a joke is this. It's not his bloody fault he's a nigger. (*Rifling through a second drawer*) I wish you'd keep them salts in the same place. Never here when you want them.

ALICE (*patting her mother's wrists*): Hurry up, Geoffrey!

FLORENCE (*who has been slowly coming round during the above begins to mumble*): I told her about that fire. Banking it up. I get too hot and then I go off. They don't think. Rushing me with my tea . . .

ALICE: It's all right, Mother. You'll be all right . . .

GEOFFREY (*he locates the bottle of smelling salts and crosses and hands them to* ALICE): Does she want these bloody salts or not?

ALICE (*taking the bottle from* GEOFFREY): She'd better

have them. (*She opens the bottle and holds it under* FLORENCE's *nose.*)

FLORENCE: Feathers.

GEOFFREY: She's off. She's bloody rambling.

FLORENCE: She wants to burn some feathers. Never mind salts. I can't be doing with salts. They make me bilious.

ALICE: It's all right, Mother. (*To* GEOFFREY) We'd better get her upstairs. She's too hot in here anyway.

GEOFFREY: She'll be too bloody cold if she doesn't see that doctor. It's not fair on us. It's us that has it to put up with.

BARBARA: Shall I fetch you a glass of water?

ALICE: No – she doesn't have water. She'll be all right in a minute.

GEOFFREY: It's happening too regular is this. It's every week alike. And it's always on bloody Saturdays. We can't even sit down to us tea in peace.

ALICE: Don't go on at her – you'll only make her worse. Just help me get her off to bed.

GEOFFREY (*putting his arm round* FLORENCE *and raising her to her feet. He is gruffly compassionate*): Come on then, Mother. Let's be having you. She's a bloody ton weight. She puts some weight on for somebody who never eats nothing. (*To* FLORENCE) You're putting weight on.

ALICE: Don't stand there, Billy. Help your father.

GEOFFREY (*piloting* FLORENCE *towards the door*): By bloody hell – don't ask him to do nothing. He'll drop her down the bedroom stairs.

ALICE (*crossing to help him*): You never give him a chance.

> (ALICE *and* GEOFFREY *support* FLORENCE *and move off through the hall and up the stairs.*)

FLORENCE: They ought to put a bed down here . . . Them stairs is too steep . . . They could have got the bungalow . . .

GEOFFREY: Now steady . . . Steady on, lass . . . Plenty of time . . .

FLORENCE (*continues to mumble to herself as they go upstairs. We cannot hear what she is saying but one sentence comes out plainly as they exit into the bedroom*): It's all these blackies. . . .

(*In the living-room there is an embarrassed silence between* BILLY *and* BARBARA. BILLY *absent-mindedly picks up* FLORENCE's *handbag and looks inside it. He goes through the contents idly and takes out an obsolete ration book.*)

BILLY: Do you know, she still keeps her old ration book.

BARBARA: I noticed she didn't look very well. Even at tea-time. I noticed but I didn't like to say anything.

BILLY (*after a pause*): You wouldn't think she'd been all over the world, would you? Paris – Cairo – Vienna . . .

BARBARA (*incredulously*): Who? Your grandma?

BILLY: My grandad was in the Diplomatic Corps. Before he had his leg off. He could speak seven languages, you know. They went all over.

BARBARA (*completely disbelieving him she decides to ignore this statement*): Do you think your mother's going to like me, pet?

BILLY: He was in the French Foreign Legion for nine years.

BARBARA: I think we should get on with each other. It's better when you do – really. When families stick together. Why didn't you tell them we'd got engaged?

BILLY: I was going to. Did you show them the ring?

BARBARA (*examining the ring*): Of course. I show it to everybody. It's lovely. I won't be completely happy until I've got the other one to go with it.

BILLY: Darling . . . (*Taking her hand*) You will always love me, won't you?

BARBARA: You know I will.

BILLY (*his fingers on the engagement ring*): I still say this ring's too big. Why won't you let me get it altered?

BARBARA (*pulling her hand away*): I don't think it's too big. Anyway, I want everybody to see it first.

BILLY: Well, don't blame me if you lose it. My mother was saying it was nearly coming off while you were washing up. It'll only take a couple of days. And then it'll be there for ever. (*Romantically*) For ever and ever . . .

BARBARA: Sweet . . .

BILLY: So go on, then. Give me it. You can have it back on Wednesday.

BARBARA: No, I'll never take it off. Never – never.

BILLY: Give me the cowing ring!

BARBARA: Billy!

BILLY (*moving away from her in disgust*): Oh, please yourself, then. Don't say I didn't warn you.

> (RITA *approaches the house through the garden. She is a small girl with blonde hair – seventeen years old but she dresses to look much older. She is common and hard and works in a snack bar.*)

BARBARA: Now you're cross. Don't be, pet. I'll take care of it. And I'll never lose it.

> (RITA *rings the bell.*)

BILLY: Just a minute. (*He crosses into the hall and opens the front door*) Rita!

RITA (*moving forward menacingly*): Right, I suppose you . . .

BILLY (*interrupting her*): Just a minute! (*He slams the door on* RITA *and moves across the hall to speak to* BARBARA) Just a minute! (*He closes the living-room door.*)

ALICE (*appearing at the top of the staircase*): Who is it, Billy?

BILLY: Just a minute!

> (BILLY *opens the front door and enters the garden, closing the door behind him.*
>
> BARBARA *takes an orange from her handbag and is peeling it as the lights fade down on the living-room and the lights fade up on the garden set.*)

BILLY: Hello, Rita.

RITA (*her conversation consists mainly of clichés and expressions picked up on amorous evenings spent with friendly American airmen*): Ooh! Look what's crawled out of the cheese!

BILLY: Hello, Rita – sorry I can't ask you in.

RITA: Get back in the knife-box, big-head.

BILLY: We're flooded. The pipes have burst.

RITA: Are you kidding? Here, pull the other one – it's got bells on it.

BILLY: What's the matter, darling? Is anything wrong?

RITA: Hark at Lord Muck. Don't come the innocent with me, you know what's wrong. I thought you were going to your uncle's on Wednesday night.

BILLY: I did go to my uncle's. My Uncle Herbert's

RITA: Well, you didn't then – because somebody saw you. Sitting in the Gaumont. With your arm round a lass eating oranges.

BILLY: They didn't see me. I was at my Uncle Ernest's playing Monopoly.

RITA (imitating him): At my Uncle Ernest's playing Monopoly. You rotten liar! You're just muck. You're rotten, that's what you are. And where's my engagement ring?

BILLY: I'm glad you asked me that question. Because I called into the shop this morning and the man said it might be another week.

RITA (again imitating him): The man said it might be another week. You're worse than muck. You're rotten.

BILLY: No, because they can't do it up here. They've got to send it to Bradford. They've got three people off ill.

RITA (again imitating him): Three people off ill. Yes, I suppose they're all having their legs off. To hear you talk everybody's having their leg off. And another thing, I thought I was coming round for my tea this afternoon. To meet your rotten mother.

BILLY: Yes, darling, but something happened. My grandma was taken ill. Last Thursday. They've got her in bed.

RITA: Well, I am going to see your rotten mother – I'll tell you that. My name's not 'Silly,' you know. Either you get me that rotten ring back or I'm going to see your rotten mother.

BILLY (attempting to quieten her): Ssh, darling!

RITA (*raising her voice*): And your rotten father! And your rotten grandmother! (*In a wild attempt to quieten* RITA, BILLY *takes her in his arms and kisses her. She responds with an automatic animal passion. They break away*) You are rotten to me, Billy. I'm not kidding, you know. I still want that ring back. (*Her voice rises again*) And my dad wants to know where it is as well. We're supposed to be engaged, you know.

BILLY: You once said you didn't want to marry me.

RITA: Don't come that tale with me. I said I didn't want to live in a rotten cottage in rotten Devon — that's all.

BILLY: We'll live wherever you like, darling. Nothing matters as long as we're together.

RITA: Well, can you get it back tonight, then?

BILLY: Of course I can, darling. If that's what you want. (*He kisses her again*) Darling, darling, darling . . .

RITA (*pushing* BILLY *away as his hand creeps round her back*): Hey, Bolton Wanderer! Keep your mucky hands to yourself.

BILLY: Tell me you're not cross with me, darling.

RITA (*imitating him*): Tell me you're not cross . . . Put another record on, we've heard that one. And get that ring back.

BILLY: I will. I promise, darling. I'll go down to the shop. I'll give it to you tonight — at the dance.

RITA: You'd better do — or else there'll be bother. I wouldn't like to be in your shoes if my father comes round. And he will, you know. And he won't stand arguing in the garden. (BILLY *kisses her again*) Go on, then. Go in and get your coat on — and get off for that ring.

BILLY: See you tonight, darling.

RITA: Never mind see you tonight, shops'll be shut in half an hour. You'll get off now. Go on, then, get your coat. You can walk me down as far as the bus-stop. Go on, Dateless, don't stand there catching flies.

BILLY: I can't go yet.

RITA: Why not? What's stopping you?

BILLY: I'm waiting to go to the lavatory. My mam's on.

RITA: I'll be walking on. You catch me up.

(RITA *walks off, slowly, down the garden and exits.*
BILLY *enters the house. As he crosses through the hall the*
lights fade down in the garden and up in the living-
room. BARBARA *is just finishing eating the orange.*)

BILLY: Hey, listen! I've just had my fortune told by a gipsy.

BARBARA: I've eaten a whole orange while I've been
waiting.

BILLY: She says there's a curse on me.

BARBARA: Your mother's not come down yet. Neither has
your father.

BILLY: I'm going to experience sorrow and misfortune but
after a long journey things will start to go right. Hey, she
had a baby on her back like a Red Indian.

BARBARA: Do you think she'll be all right – your grandmother?

(BILLY *crosses and sits in the armchair.*)

BILLY: Who? Oh, my grandma! Yes, she'll be all right.
It's just that she's got this rare disease – they're trying a new
drug out on her.

BARBARA: She looked as though she was having some
kind of fit at first. I noticed when you were having that row
with your father.

BILLY: They've only tried it out three times – this drug.
Once on President Eisenhower, then the Duke of Windsor
and then my grandma.

BARBARA: Honestly! No wonder your father gets cross
with you.

BILLY: How do you mean?

BARBARA: Well, all these stories you keep on telling – no
wonder he keeps losing his temper.

BILLY: Oh, you don't take any notice of him.

BARBARA: Billy . . . ?

BILLY: What?

BARBARA: What was your father saying? About you going
to London?

BILLY: Did he? When? I never heard him.

BARBARA: When he was talking about answering back at your grandmother. When he got hold of your shirt. He said, 'If you want to go to London you can "B" well go.' He swore.

BILLY: I know. He's been summonsed twice for using bad language.

BARBARA: Yes, but what did he mean?

BILLY: What? About going to London?

BARBARA: Yes.

BILLY: Ah, well – there's a very interesting story behind that . . .

BARBARA: No, Billy, this is important – to us. You've got to think about me now.

BILLY (*he rises and crosses towards her*): It's for you I'm doing it, my darling.

BARBARA: What do you mean?

BILLY (*sitting down beside her and taking her hand he goes off into a fantasy*): Isn't it obvious? How can we go on living like this?

BARBARA (*automatically freeing her hand she takes an orange from her handbag*): What do you mean, pet? Like what?

BILLY: In this – this atmosphere. Do you honestly think that we could ever be happy – I mean really happy – here?

BARBARA: Where?

BILLY: In this house. There's the shadow of my father across this house. He's a bitter man, Barbara.

BARBARA (*she settles down and begins to peel the orange*): Why? What for? What about?

BILLY: He's jealous. Every time he looks at me he sees his own hopes and the failure of his own ambitions.

BARBARA: Your father?

BILLY: He had his dreams once. He can't bear it – seeing me on the brink of success. He was going to be a writer too.

BARBARA: Billy, if this is going to be another of your stories . . .

BILLY: You don't have to believe me. The evidence is here – in this house.

BARBARA: Evidence? How do you mean – evidence?

BILLY (*pointing to the sideboard*): It's all in there.

BARBARA: What is?

BILLY: Go and look for yourself. In that cupboard.

(BARBARA *rises and crosses to the sideboard. She tugs at the handle on* BILLY's *cupboard.*)

BARBARA: It's locked.

BILLY (*meaningly*): Yes.

BARBARA: Where's the key?

BILLY: God knows. I was four years old when that was locked, Barbara. It's never been opened since.

BARBARA (*crossing towards* BILLY): Well, what's supposed to be in it?

BILLY: Hopes! Dreams! Ambitions! The life work of a disillusioned man. Barbara, there must be forty or fifty unpublished novels in that cupboard. All on the same bitter theme.

BARBARA (*in half-belief*): Well, we can't all be geniuses.

BILLY: Perhaps not. But he crucified himself in the attempt. Sitting night after night at that table. Chewing at his pen. And when the words wouldn't come he'd take it out on us.

BARBARA: But what about going to London? What about our cottage in Devon?

(ALICE *enters from the bedroom and crosses down the stairs.*)

BILLY: Well, it's all down South, Barbara. We could live in the New Forest. We could have a cottage there – a woodman's cottage – in a clearing.

BARBARA: I think I'd be frightened. Living in a forest.

BILLY (*he puts his arm round her*): Not with me to look after you, you wouldn't.

(BILLY *rises awkwardly as* ALICE *enters the room. ALICE is faintly preoccupied. She crosses towards the kitchen and speaks almost to herself.*)

ALICE: Well, she seems to be resting.

(ALICE *exits into the kitchen. There is a slight feeling of embarrassment between* BILLY *and* BARBARA *and then* BARBARA *speaks to break the silence.*)

BARBARA: Are we going out dancing tonight?

BILLY: If you like . . . (*He claps his hand to his forehead in an over-dramatic gesture*) Oh, no! Just remembered!

BARBARA (*suspiciously*): What?

BILLY: I promised to go round to my Uncle Herbert's tonight. To play Monopoly. It's his birthday.

BARBARA: Funny you never told me before. You're always having to go round to your Uncle Herbert's. Anyway, I thought it was your Uncle Ernest who played Monopoly?

BILLY: Ah, well . . . I'm glad you asked me that question. You see, my Uncle Herbert . . .

BARBARA (*interrupting*): Oh, don't bother. You and your relatives. If I didn't know you better I'd think you had another girl.

BILLY: Darling! What a thing to say!

BARBARA: You know that Liz is back in town, don't you?

BILLY: Liz who?

BARBARA: You know who. That dirty girl. I'm surprised you weren't ashamed to be seen with her.

BILLY: Oh, her . . . I haven't seen her for donkeys' years.

(ALICE *enters from the kitchen. She is carrying a tumbler containing a white liquid which she is stirring with a spoon.*)

ALICE: Her breathing's all right – she's still awake, though. I think she'd be better if we could get her off to sleep.

BARBARA: She was looking tired this afternoon.

ALICE (*gently reprimanding*): Well, I blame you as much as anybody. You set your father off and then it sets her off. I've told you time and time again.

BILLY (*half-ashamed*): She's all right now is she, then?

ALICE: Is she ever all right?

BARBARA: Are you quite sure there's nothing I can do?

Could she eat an orange?

ALICE: I'm going to get the doctor in to her – be on the safe side. Whether she wants him or not. Your father's sitting with her. (*She hands him the tumbler*) Can you take this up without spilling it?

BILLY (*taking the tumbler reluctantly*): Who? Me?

ALICE: Either that or ring the doctor up for me. (*Rather impatiently*) But do something, lad, don't just stand there.

> (ALICE *turns away from him and walks briskly into the hall where she picks up the phone.* BILLY *stands indecisively for a moment and then crosses through into the hall and up the stairs as* ALICE *dials the number. She waits for a reply and glances up at* BILLY *who has, for no reason at all, developed a limp. She calls up to him.*)

ALICE: Now, what are you playing at!

> (BILLY *stops limping and quickens his pace and exits into the bedroom as* ALICE *turns back to the phone.*)

Hello, is that the surgery? . . . Well, it's Mrs Fisher, forty-two Park Drive . . . Yes, that's right. Only it's my mother again. Mrs Boothroyd. Do you think the doctor could call round? . . , Oh, dear. Only we've got her in bed again . . . I've given her her tablets – and the mixture . . . Well, will you ask him to come round as soon as he can . . . Yes. Yes, I will, I will – thank you very much. Goodbye.

> (ALICE *replaces the phone and crosses into the living-room.*)

ALICE: You don't like to bother them on a Saturday but what else can you do?

BARBARA: Is the doctor coming, Mrs Fisher?

ALICE: He's coming sometime – when he's ready. It'll be nine o'clock again, I suppose. He's already out on his calls.

BARBARA: I shouldn't worry. He'll be round as soon as he can.

ALICE (*sitting*): You can't help worrying sometimes. If I don't worry nobody else will. It's just getting me down, is this. It's just one thing after another.

BARBARA (*returns to her seat on the couch and takes up*

the orange): Would you like a piece of orange, Mrs Fisher?

ALICE (*she looks up and, for the first time, realizes that* BARBARA *is trying to help*): No. No, thank you. Not just at this minute, love. Thank you.

BARBARA: Would it be better if I went? (*Half-rising*) I mean, if I'm in the way . . .

ALICE: No, don't be silly. You sit yourself down. I'm only sorry it's happened while you were here.

BARBARA (*returning to her seat*): You can't arrange illnesses, can you?

ALICE: You can't. I only wish you could. Only she has these turns and all you can do is put her to bed. But she always seems to pick the most awkward times. Still, you can't blame her. It's not her fault. You might think it is to hear him talk. You'd think she does it on purpose, to listen to him.

BARBARA: She might be better before the doctor comes.

ALICE: It wears me out, I know that. And if it isn't her it's our Billy. I don't know what we're going to do with him.

BARBARA: I think he wants to help – but he doesn't like to offer.

ALICE: He didn't used to be like this. He's got to grow up sometime. I don't know, it might be better if he did go to London. It might put some sense into him if he had to look after himself.

BARBARA: Well, that's what I don't understand, Mrs Fisher. Is he going to London?

ALICE: Well, he reckons he is. Hasn't he said anything to you?

BARBARA: Well, not really. I only heard what his father said. I tried to ask him.

ALICE: What did he say to you?

BARBARA: Nothing, really. (*She indicates the sideboard*) He just started talking about that cupboard.

ALICE: Oh, don't talk to me about that cupboard. I don't know what he keeps in there. I'm frightened to ask, to tell you the honest truth.

BARBARA: He said it had been locked since he was four years old.

ALICE: I don't know why he says these things. I mean, what good does it do him? It's not as if he gets anything out of it.

BARBARA: I'm sure I don't know. He told me Mr Fisher was a captain on a petrol ship.

ALICE: Don't let his father hear you say that – else there'll be trouble. He'll murder him one of these days. If he knew all I know he'd have murdered him long ago. I could do it myself sometimes. And he says things we can find out about, that's what I don't understand. He told me that young lad who works in the fruit shop had gassed himself – and he knows I go in there every Tuesday.

BARBARA: I know. He says all kinds of things.

ALICE: I don't know where he'll end up – it's not our fault, I do know that. We've done our best for him. His father says it's since he started work – but I know different. It's ever since he went to that grammar school. He wanted to go, so we let him – he'd not been there five minutes before he wanted to leave. And we had it all to pay for, you know – he never appreciated it. School uniform, he loses his cap first week. Cricketing trousers, he never wore them. We bought him a satchel and he let a lad run away with it. Then there was his books to pay for – well, he never reads them. It's just been a waste of time and money. You'd think he'd been dragged up. He's not cleaned his shoes for six months.

BARBARA: I tell him about his shoes. He takes no notice. And his hair – he won't have a haircut, will he?

ALICE: Well, he doesn't take after me – or his father. And it's us that's got to clean up after him. He got them suède shoes so he wouldn't have to bother cleaning them – but you can't just not touch them. He trod in some dog-dirt on Tuesday and, do you know, he walked it round this house for three days. I had to get a knife and scrape it off myself, in the finish. (*Distastefully, recalling the incident*)

Pooh! You could smell it all over the house.

BARBARA: My mother won't have a dog. And she hates cats.

ALICE: You can't keep on telling him — it just goes in one ear and out the other. He wants watching all the time, that's his trouble. You see, if he'd gone into the business with his father, like we wanted him to, we could have kept an eye on him more. But he won't listen. He went after all kinds of daft jobs. That lady in the Juvenile Employment Bureau, she lost patience with him. He wouldn't have this and he wouldn't have that. And she offered him some lovely jobs to begin with. He could have gone as a Junior Trainee at the Co-op Bank if he'd wanted to. She offered him that.

BARBARA: I know somebody who works there, she likes it. They've got their own Social Club.

ALICE: She just stopped bothering. She couldn't get any sense out of him. She asked him what he did want in the end and he told her he wanted to be either a merchant seaman or a concert pianist. Grammar School! You'd think he'd been to the Silly School. He shows me up.

BARBARA: How did he come to work for Shadrack and Duxbury's?

ALICE: Don't ask me. He'd been left school a fortnight and he was still no nearer a job — he wanted to work in the museum by this time. We were sick and tired of having him lounging about the house. His father comes home one morning at twelve o'clock and finds him playing with some plasticine. He went mad. He told him straight out. He says, you get out of this house and get yourself a job, my lad, he says. And, he says, don't you dare come back without one — or I'll knock your blooming head right off your shoulders, only he didn't say blooming.

BARBARA: No, I can imagine.

ALICE: So, of course, our Billy goes out and waltzes back two hours later and says he's working for an undertaker — start on Monday. He's been there ever since.

BARBARA: I don't think he likes it, though, does he?

ALICE: Like it or lump it, he's got to work for his living. Never mind going to London. He's got no mind of his own, that's his trouble. He listens to these pals he's got. What they do he's got to do. I'm only glad he's found himself a sensible lass, for once.

(BILLY *enters from the bedroom and crosses down the stairs.*)

BARBARA: I think it was that girl he used to go about with before he met me, Mrs Fisher. That funny girl. That Liz. She used to put a lot of ideas into his head.

(BILLY *pauses at the foot of the stairs and listens to their conversation.*)

ALICE: Oh, that one. I've seen him with her. She looked as though a good bath wouldn't do her any harm. I don't know what kind of a family she comes from. I'm only glad she's gone.

BARBARA: She's come back again, didn't you know? She goes off all over, all the time. By herself. I don't think she's got any family. Do you know what I don't like about her, Mrs Fisher? She smokes and she keeps her cigarette in her mouth when she's talking. I could never do that. It looks common.

ALICE: You could always tell when he'd been out with her. The ideas he used to come home with. He comes home one night and says he wants to go off on holiday with her. To the Norfolk Broads, if you like. I told him — straight. I said, that's not the way we do things in this house. I said, if you want to go on holiday you can come to Morecambe with us — and if you don't you can stop at home.

BARBARA: I don't believe in mixed holidays — not before you're married.

ALICE: I'm sure you don't, love. You wouldn't be sitting here if you did, I can tell you.

BARBARA: He was saying you wouldn't mind if I went to Blackpool with him for a week — but I wouldn't. I don't believe in anything like that.

ALICE: He was saying what?

BILLY (*entering hastily and changing the subject*): Hey, listen!

> (ALICE *and* BARBARA *turn to* BILLY *who is trying to think of something to say next. He tries to joke in desperation.*)

Fifteen men under one umbrella and not one of them got wet. (*He evokes no reaction*) It wasn't raining.

ALICE (*to* BARBARA): Well, you can't say you don't know what you're letting yourself in for. (*To* BILLY) Stop acting so daft with people poorly. We've got enough on our plates without you.

BARBARA: How's your grandma, Billy? Is she any better?

ALICE: Has she gone off to sleep yet?

BILLY: She looks all right to me.

ALICE: Is your father all right with her? Would he like me to go up? Does he want anything?

BILLY: I don't know.

ALICE: No, and I don't suppose you care. (*Losing her temper*) Have you had a wash since you got up this morning?

BILLY: 'Course I have.

ALICE: Yes, a cat-lick. I bet you didn't take your shirt off, did you? You'll have to smarten your ideas up, you know, if you want to go script-writing. They don't have them on the BBC with mucky necks. You'll start washing your own shirts in future, I can't get them clean.

BILLY (*acutely embarrassed but, for* BARBARA's *benefit, he pretends to be amused and winds an imaginary gramophone handle*): Crikey Moses, she's off!

BARBARA: Well, you can't say you've had a shave this morning, Billy, because you haven't.

BILLY: I'm growing a beard, if you want to know.

ALICE: Oh no, you're not. We're having no beards in this house.

BARBARA: I don't think I'd like you with a beard, Billy.

ALICE: He's not having a beard.

BILLY: I'm having a bloody beard.

ALICE: Hey, hey, hey! Language! Don't you start coming

out with that talk! Else you'll get a shock coming, big as you are! We get enough of that from your father.

BILLY: Well, I'm still having a beard. I can grow one in six weeks.

BARBARA: I don't think you should, Billy. Not if your mother doesn't want you to.

ALICE: He's got no say in the matter. If I say he doesn't grow a beard, he doesn't grow one.

BILLY: What's up with you? It's my stinking face!

ALICE: I'll not tell you again about that language! You can start to alter yourself, that's what you can do, my lad. We're not going on like this for much longer. Either brighten your ideas up or do as your father says — and get off to London or where you like. Because we're not going on like this, day in and day out! It's not fair on nobody!

BILLY: Oh, shut up!

ALICE: And you can start watching what you say to people, as well. What did you say to me about that lad in the fruit shop? Gassing himself? And what have you been telling Barbara about that cupboard?

BILLY: What cupboard?

ALICE: You know very well what cupboard!

BILLY: I don't know what cupboard. How do you mean — cupboard?

BARBARA: Your sideboard cupboard.

BILLY: What about it?

BARBARA: That evidence you were talking about. In the cupboard. When you were four years old. All these unpublished novels. Where your father was chewing his pen up.

BILLY: Oh, that! Oh, you should have said. No, you're getting mixed up. I was talking about his invoices that he writes out. He keeps them in that vase — I didn't say anything about any cupboard.

BARBARA (shocked): Billy Fisher! I don't know how you can stand there! He'll be struck down dead one of these days.

BILLY (*with a pretence at innocence*): What's up?

ALICE: He can stand there as if butter wouldn't melt in his mouth.

BILLY: I don't know what you're all on about.

BARBARA: Oh yes, you do. Don't try and make it out as if it's me, Billy.

BILLY: It is you. Look – Barbara – you were sitting over there, weren't you? On that couch. Because you were eating an orange. And I was standing over there. Right? It is right, isn't it? You were sitting there and I was standing there.

BARBARA: Yes, but then you said your father . . .

ALICE: Never mind what he said, love, I know what he is.

(RITA *enters the garden and stands, for a moment, hesitantly outside the front door.*)

BILLY: Yes, you'll believe her, won't you?

ALICE: I'd believe anybody before you, Billy. I'm very sorry, but there it is. I'd believe Hitler before I'd believe you.

BILLY: Why don't you come straight out and call me a liar, then!

ALICE: Well, you are one. I don't care who knows it.

BILLY: Well, that's a nice thing for a mother to say, isn't it?

ALICE: Yes, and you're a nice son for a mother to have, aren't you? You don't think what you're doing to me, do you? You never consider anybody except yourself.

BILLY: I suppose you do, don't you?

ALICE: Yes, I do. I worry about you, I know that.

BILLY: Well, what about me? Don't you think I worry? I worry about the H-bomb. You didn't know I nearly went on the Aldermaston march last Easter, did you? I don't want another war, you know. And what about all them refugees? From Hungary and that? You never stop to consider them, do you? Or South Africa. (*At which point* RITA *makes up her mind, and, without knocking, marches into the house and into the living-room*) Do you know, Barbara, if you were a blackie and we lived in South Africa I'd be in gaol by now. Doing fifteen years. (*At which point he breaks off as* RITA *makes her entrance*) Hallo, Rita . . .

RITA (*to* BILLY, *indicating* ALICE): It takes her some time to come out of the lavatory, doesn't it? What's she been doing? Writing her will out?

ALICE (*outraged*): Do you usually come into people's houses without knocking?

RITA: I do when people have got my private property. (*To* BILLY) Come on – give.

BILLY: Rita, I don't think you've ever met my mother, have you?

RITA: No, but she'll know me again, won't she. Come on, you and your stinking rotten jewellers. I'm not daft, you know.

ALICE (*shocked*): We're not having this! Where does she think she is?

BILLY (*attempting to guide* RITA *towards the door he takes her elbow*): I'll just take Rita as far as the bus stop, mother.

RITA (*shrugging him away*): Take your mucky hands off me, you rotten toffee-nosed get. You didn't think I'd come in, did you?

ALICE: No, but I think you'll go out, young lady. And if you've anything to say to my son you'd better just remember where you are.

BILLY: Well, I'm very glad you have come, Rita, because I feel I owe you a word of explanation.

RITA (*imitating him*): Oooh, I feel I owe you a word of explanation. Get back in the cheese, with the other maggots.

ALICE: I'm not putting up with this – I shall bring his father down.

RITA: You can bring his rotten father down. I hope you do. And his rotten grandma.

BARBARA: Billy's grandma, for your information, happens to be ill in bed.

RITA (*turning to* BARBARA *for the first time*): Oooh, look what the cat's brought in. Get Madam Fancy-knickers. I suppose this is your rotten sister. I thought she was supposed to be in a rotten iron lung.

BARBARA: For your information, I happen to be Billy's fiancée.

RITA (*imitating* BARBARA): Oooh, for your information. Well, for your information, he happens to be engaged to me. In front of a witness.

BILLY: How do you mean? What's witnesses got to do with it?

BARBARA: Billy, will you kindly tell me who this girl is?

RITA (*imitating her*): Oooh, Billy, will you kindly tell me. Aw, go take a long walk on a short pier, you squint-eyed sow, you're nothing else.

ALICE: Barbara, would you kindly go upstairs and ask Mr Fisher to come down for a minute.

RITA: You can fetch him down. Fetch all the rotten lot down. You can fetch the cowing iron lung down as well, for all I care.

ALICE: I've never been spoken to like this in all my days.

BARBARA: Shall I go up, Mrs Fisher?

RITA (*imitating her*): Oooh, shall I go up, Mrs Fisher? If you can get up the stairs with them bow legs, you can.

ALICE: It's all right, Barbara. I'll deal with this young madam. I've met her type before.

BILLY: I think I can explain all this.

BARBARA: Yes, I think you've got some explaining to do, Billy.

RITA: He can explain until he's blue in the rotten face. It makes no difference to me.

ALICE: If I knew your mother, young lady, wouldn't I have something to say to her.

RITA: You can keep out of this. It's between me and him. (*To* BILLY) Where's my ring? Has she got it? (BARBARA's *right hand instinctively goes to her left.*) She has, hasn't she? You've given it to her, haven't you?

BILLY: Ah, well – yes, but you see . . . Only there's been a bit of a mix-up. You see, I thought Barbara had broken the engagement off . . .

BARBARA: Billy!

RITA: Yeh, well you've got another think coming if you think I'm as daft as she is. You gave that ring to me. And don't think you can go crawling out of it, 'cause you can't. You seem to forget I've got a witness, you know. I've got two. 'Cause Shirley Mitchem saw you giving me it, as well – so you needn't think she didn't. I can go down to the Town Hall, you know.

ALICE: Now, don't you come running in here with them tales, my girl. You know as well as I do he's under age.

RITA: Ask him if he was under age down at Foley Bottoms last night. 'Cause I'm not carrying the can back for nobody. He wasn't under-age then. He was over-age more like.

ALICE: Get out! Get out of my house!

BARBARA: Have you been untrue to me, Billy? I've got to know.

RITA (*imitating her*): Oooh, have you been untrue to me, Billy! Get out of your push-chair, babyface. (*To* BILLY) You're just rotten, aren't you? You are – you're rotten, all through. I've met some people in my time, but of all the lying, scheming . . . anyway, you gave that ring to me.

BILLY: Yes, but, look, Rita . . .

RITA (*interrupting*): Don't talk to me, you rotten get. Well, she can have you – if she knows what to do with you, which I very much doubt. You rotten lying get. Gar – you think you're somebody, don't you? But you're nobody. You miserable lying rotten stinking get.

BILLY: Does this mean you're breaking off our engagement?

RITA: You don't get out of it like that. I want that ring.

BARBARA (*finding the right word at last*): Billy, have you been – having relations with this girl?

RITA (*swinging round on* BARBARA): What do you think he's been doing? Knitting a pullover? You know what you can do, don't you? You can give me that ring. Because it's mine.

ALICE: If you don't stop it this minute! (*To* BILLY) As for you, I hope you know what you've done, because I don't.

RITA: Are you going to give me that ring?

BARBARA: I shall give the ring back to Billy – if and when I break off the engagement.

BILLY (*moving towards her*): Barbara . . .

RITA: Yes, you can go to her. She can have you. And she knows what she can do, the squint-eyed, bow-legged, spotty, snotty-nosed streak of nothing.

BARBARA: And you know what you can do as well. You can wash your mouth out with soap and water.

RITA (*imitating*): Oooh, you can wash your mouth out with soap and water. You could do with some soap in your ears, you've got carrots growing out of them. Well, you can give me that ring. Before I come over there and get it.

ALICE: You can get out of this house. I won't tell you again.

RITA: Save your breath for blowing out candles. I want my ring. (*Crossing towards* BARBARA) Yes, and I'm going to get it.

ALICE: Get out of my house! Get out! Get out!
    (GEOFFREY FISHER *enters from the bedroom and crosses slowly down the stairs.*)

RITA (*moving right up to* BARBARA): Are you going to give me that ring, or aren't you?

GEOFFREY (*half-way down the stairs*): Mother! . . . Mother! . . .

RITA: Because you'll be in Emergency Ward Ten if I don't get it – right sharpish.

BARBARA: Don't you threaten me . . .

RITA: I won't threaten you – I'll flatten you! Give me that cowing ring back! (*She makes a grab for* BARBARA's *hand.*)

BARBARA (*pushing her away*): I won't . . . I won't . . .

ALICE: Will you stop it, the pair of you!

GEOFFREY (*enters the room and stands in the doorway. He appears not to comprehend what is happening*): Mother!
    (GEOFFREY's *word silences* ALICE, BILLY *and* BARBARA *who turn and look at him.*)

RITA (*unconcerned*): Give me the ring!

GEOFFREY: You'd better come upstairs. Come now. I think she's dead.

THE CURTAIN FALLS
END OF ACT II

ACT III

Later the same evening.

It is about half-past nine and quite dark in the garden outside the FISHERS' *house. When the action of the play takes place in the garden, however, a street lamp fades up from the road beyond the garden and off-stage. There is also a small light in the porch of the house. As the curtain rises* GEOFFREY FISHER *is going through the contents of* BILLY'S *cupboard which are, at the moment, spread across the floor of the living-room by the sideboard.* ALICE FISHER *is sitting in a chair by the fire. She is obviously distraught by the death of her mother.* GEOFFREY *rummages through the envelopes and papers and then rises, shaking his head.*

GEOFFREY: Well, I can't bloody find it. It's not in here, anyway. He hasn't got it. It's about the only bloody thing he hasn't got.

ALICE: She might not have had one, Geoffrey – you know what she was like.

GEOFFREY (*although he hasn't changed his vocabulary there is a more tender note than usual in his voice*): Don't talk so bloody wet, lass. Everybody's got a Birth Certificate.

ALICE: Well, you don't know, Geoffrey, they might not have had them in those days. She was getting on.

GEOFFREY: Everybody's got a bloody Birth Certificate. They've had them since the year dot. If he's got it squat somewhere I'll bloody mark him for life.

ALICE: You can't blame our Billy for everything, Geoffrey. What would he want with it?

GEOFFREY (*indicating the papers on the floor*): What's he want with this bloody lot? There's neither sense nor bloody reason in him. And where is he, anyway? Where's he taken himself off to?

ALICE: I don't know, Geoffrey. I've given up caring.

GEOFFREY: You'd think he could stay in one bloody night of the year. He ought to be in tonight. He ought to be in looking after his mother. He's got no sense of bloody responsibility, that's his trouble.

ALICE: Well, she liked her cup of tea. We'll have that pint-pot to put away now. She's used that pint-pot for as long as I can remember.

GEOFFREY: She liked her bloody tea, there's no getting away from it. (*He half-jokes in an attempt to lift* ALICE *out of her depression*) If I had a shilling for every pot of tea she's supped I'd be a rich man today. Well, there's one good thing to be said for it, when does the dustbin man come around? 'Cause he can take all them tins of condensed milk out of her bedroom.

ALICE: We can't throw them away. Somebody might be glad of them. We could send them round to the Old People's Home, or something.

GEOFFREY: Get away with you, you'd poison the bloody lot of them. That stuff doesn't keep for ever you know. They'll be green mouldy.

ALICE: I thought it was supposed to keep—condensed milk.

GEOFFREY: It won't keep twenty bloody years, I'm sure. She's had that pile of tins stacked up there since nineteen thirty-nine. And there's not one of them been opened — not one.

ALICE: Well, they went scarce, Geoffrey, when the war started, you know. That's why she started saving them.

GEOFFREY: Went scarce? Too bloody true they went scarce, she had them all. She hoarded them — she was like a squirrel with them. If Lord Woolton had heard about her in nineteen forty-one she'd have got fifteen years. By bloody hell, she would. (*He reminisces gently*) Hey! I say! Do you remember how I used to pull her leg about it. How I used to tell her the Food Office was ringing up for her? You couldn't get her near that bloody telephone. She used to let it ring when we were out – she must have lost me pounds.

ALICE (*not cheered by* GEOFFREY's *attempt at humour*): Well, I only hope you manage as well when you're as old as she was. She's not had an easy life – I wish I could have made it easier for her. She had all us to bring up, you know. And that took some doing.

GEOFFREY: No – she didn't do too bad, to say. What was she? Eighty-what?

ALICE: She'd have been eighty-three in August. Either eighty-three or eighty-two. She didn't seem to know herself.

GEOFFREY: Well, I shan't grumble if I last as long – she had a fair old crack of the whip.

ALICE: She didn't suffer, that's something to be grateful for. Some of them hang on for months and months. What did you say she was talking about? Before she went?

GEOFFREY: Don't ask me. I couldn't hear for that bloody shambles that was going on down here. I've never heard anything like it in all my born days.

ALICE: Well, you can blame our Billy for that, because I do. I've not finished with that Rita-whatever-her-name-is. I shall find out where she lives. I shall go round and I shall find out.

GEOFFREY: I know her. She works in that milk-bar in Sheepgate. I know her and I know her bloody father as well. You know him. Him that's always racing that whippet on the moor. Him with them tattoos all up his arms. Supposed to work in the market, when he does work. They live in them terrace-houses. Down Mill Lane.

ALICE: Well, I shall go round. I shall go round and see her mother.

GEOFFREY: You'll go bloody nowhere. You keep away. We've got enough to cope with without getting mixed up with that lot.

ALICE: I only wish she could have been spared it. If you can't die in peace, what can you do.

GEOFFREY: You don't want to go fretting yourself about

that. She heard nothing about it. She was miles away.

ALICE: And what do you say she said. Did she know you?

GEOFFREY: Well, she did at first. She was all right after you went down. And she was all right when our Billy came up with her medicine. She took that all right and kept it down. She was just ramblin' on – like she does. She was chuntering on about a tin of salmon going to waste. Then something about getting her pension book changed at the post office next week. She never knew, you see. It was just this last five minutes when she started to slaver. I was holding her up in bed and she just slumped forward. I thought she was having a bloody fit. But no – she just gave a little jerk with her head – like that. Then she started to slaver. She was just like a baby, Alice. Just like a baby, slavering and gasping for breath. She wet my handkerchief through, I know that. Then she sits straight up – by herself – and says, 'Where's my Jack.' I had to think who she was talking about. Then I remember she must have meant your father. Only she always used to call him John, didn't she?

ALICE (*half to herself*): She hardly ever called him Jack.

GEOFFREY: Then she said, 'I love you, Jack.' Oh, and before that she said, 'What are you thinking about?' – she must have been talking to your father, she couldn't have been talking to anyone else. But you had to listen close to, to hear what she was saying. She could hardly speak. By the time she went she couldn't speak at all. She was just slavering.

(*There is a pause.*)

ALICE: You should have called me.

GEOFFREY (*suddenly compassionate*): She wouldn't have known you. And you wouldn't have liked to have seen her like that. You couldn't have done anything for her – nobody could.

ALICE: You should have called me, Geoffrey.

GEOFFREY: I didn't think it would have done you any good to see her, that's all. (*Reverting to his normal tones*) And, listen! If he thinks he's going to the funeral in them bloody suède shoes, he's got another think coming. There'll be all them Masonics coming – I'm not having him showing me up. He'll get some bloody black ones or stop at home.

ALICE: He's got some black ones but he won't wear them.

GEOFFREY: Well, make him. And think on and see that he gets a bloody good wash on Tuesday morning. When did he have a bath last?

ALICE: Well, there'll be no baths on Tuesday, 'cause I'm not lighting any fires – I shall be too busy. And I still know nothing about the funeral. I wish I'd have seen Mr Duxbury.

GEOFFREY: You only just missed him. If you'd have gone to your Emily's five minutes later you would have seen him. Anyway, they're doing everything, Shadrack and Duxbury's. He says they'll fix the tea for us – the lot.

ALICE: And you still haven't told me what Mr Duxbury said about our Billy – about him getting into bother at work.

GEOFFREY: Don't talk to me about our Billy. I'm going to start putting him in the coal cellar when people come. Duxbury comes to the door – I take him straight upstairs. He starts measuring her up so I left him to it. Come down here and walk into the living-room and there's bloody Dopey sat in here. He's let the fire go out. Kettle boiling its bloody head off. He's sitting with his shoes and socks off and all muck between his toes watching bloody Noddy on television. (*Losing his temper*) His grandmother bloody dead upstairs and all he can do is watch Noddy.

ALICE: I can't understand him. He doesn't seem to have any feeling for anybody.

GEOFFREY: I told him. I said to him, 'What are you bloody doing? Do you know Mr Duxbury's upstairs?' He was out of that chair and through that door like a shot. I watched him out of our bedroom window – putting his shoes and socks on in the street. I'll bloody swing for him before I've finished, I will.

ALICE: Well, what did Mr Duxbury say about him?

GEOFFREY: He wasn't going to say anything. Not today. Until I asked him if our Billy had rung up and asked for his cards, like he said he was. Then the lot came out. (*He indicates the calendars*) There's all these calendars he's supposed to have posted, for one. Then there's his petty cash – that doesn't add up. Then there's his postage book. Two pound ten postage money he's had. And he's supposed to have pinched a brass plate off a coffin. What does he want to do a bloody trick like that for?

ALICE: You didn't say anything about postage money before – you just said petty cash.

GEOFFREY: I don't know. Don't ask me. The whole bloody lot's wrong from start to finish. He can't keep his hands off nothing.

ALICE: But what did he say about not taking him to court?

GEOFFREY: How many more bloody times? He says if he stays on – and does his work right, and pays this money back – and stops giving back-chat every five minutes – he'll hear no more about it.

ALICE: But what about him going to London?

GEOFFREY: How the bloody hell can he go to London? He'll go to Dartmoor if he's not careful. He's to stop on there until he's paid this money back – and I know I'm not paying it, if he goes down on his bended knees I'm not paying it.

ALICE: It's a mystery to me why he wanted to take that money in the first place. He never buys anything – and if he does go short he knows he's only to come to me.

GEOFFREY: You've been too soft with him, that's been the bloody trouble, all along. Anyway, you know what he's spent it on, don't you? That bloody engagement ring. That's where the money's gone. Well, he can get that back to the shop for a start. And he can get engaged when he's twenty-one and not before. And he brings no more bloody lasses round here. And he comes in at nine o'clock in future – never mind half-past eleven. There's going to be some changes in this house.

ALICE: Yes, and you've said that before and it's made no difference. He used to get on her nerves.

GEOFFREY: Well, she's not got him to put up with any more. He used to lead her a dog's life. I've seen him — mocking her. And where is he? He's got no bloody right to be out.

ALICE: I don't know where he's got to.

GEOFFREY: He'll know where he's got to when he rolls in here. He'll go straight out again — through the bloody window.

ALICE: We don't want any more rows tonight, Geoffrey. My nerves won't stand it. You've had one row today and you saw what happened. She was all right till you started on our Billy.

GEOFFREY: Don't start bloody blaming me for it. For God's sake. I told her often enough to go to see that doctor.

ALICE: You know very well why she wouldn't go.

GEOFFREY: It was your bloody job to see that she did. I'm not on tap twenty-four hours a bloody day. I've got work to do.

(*They are building up to an argument.*)

ALICE: And I've got my work to do as well. I did my best. I tried to make her go. You know why it was. It was because he was a blackie.

GEOFFREY: I don't care if he was sky-blue bloody pink with yellow dots on. You should have gone with her.

ALICE (*almost in tears*): It was only this afternoon she was sitting in that chair with a pot of tea. You can say what you like, she was all right till you started on to our Billy.

GEOFFREY: She was never all right. She hadn't been all right for bloody months.

ALICE: It's tomorrow morning I'm thinking about. When I should be taking her up her pot of tea and a Marie Louise biscuit.

GEOFFREY: Will you shut up about bloody pots of tea! You won't fetch her back with pots of bloody tea. She'll get no pots of tea where she's gone.

ALICE: Well, I like to think she will! (*She rises and crosses towards the kitchen.*)

GEOFFREY: Where are you going now?

ALICE: I'm going to make myself one.

GEOFFREY: Sit you down. I'll see to it.

ALICE: No. No. I'm better when I'm doing something. I'd rather be occupied.

> (ALICE *exits into the kitchen and* GEOFFREY *crosses to join her.*)

GEOFFREY: I'll give you a hand, anyway.

> (GEOFFREY *exits into the kitchen as the lights fade down in the living-room. The lights fade up in the garden – both from the porch and the street lamp. We discover* BILLY *sitting on the garden seat, rather cold and his hands dug deep in his pockets. He lights a cigarette, then rises and crosses to the front door where he listens for a moment through the letter-box. Hearing nothing he returns towards the garden seat and sits disconsolately.*
>
> BILLY *hums to himself and then turns on the seat and takes up a garden cane. He toys with the cane for a moment, attempting to balance it on his finger. His humming grows louder and he stands and conducts an imaginary orchestra using the cane as a baton. He is humming a military march and he suddenly breaks off as the garden cane becomes, in his imagination, a rifle. He shoulders the cane and marches briskly up and down the garden path.*)

BILLY (*marching*): Lef', Ri', lef', ri', lef'-ri'-lef'! Halt! (*He halts*) Order arms! (*He brings the cane down to the 'Order' position.*)

> (*He pauses for a moment and the garden cane becomes, in his imagination, an officer's baton which he tucks under his arm and then he marches smartly off to an imaginary saluting base a few paces away. He has become, in his imagination, a major-general.*)

Dearly beloved Officers and Gentlemen of the Desert Shock Troops. We are assembled at the grave-side here this evening to pay our respects to a great lady. There are many of us here tonight who would not be alive now but for her tender mercies although in her later years she was limbless from the waist down. She struggled valiantly to combat ignorance and disease. Although she will be remembered by the world as the inventor of penicillin and radium we, of this proud regiment, will remember her as our friend – the Lady of the Lamp. I call upon you all to join with me in observing two minutes' silence.

(BILLY *removes an imaginary hat which he places under his arm. He lowers his head respectfully and stands in silence. Imitating a bugle he hums the 'Last Post'. He is still standing, his head lowered, as* ARTHUR *and* LIZ *enter the garden. Although* LIZ *is about the same age as* BARBARA *and* RITA *she has more maturity and self-possession. Although she is dressed casually and is, in fact, wearing the black skirt we have heard so much about, she is not as scruffy as we have been led to believe. She is also wearing a white blouse and a green suède jacket. She is not particularly pretty but is obviously a girl of strong personality.* LIZ *is the only girl for whom* BILLY *has any real feelings.* LIZ *and* ARTHUR *stand for a moment looking at* BILLY, *who has not noticed them.*)

ARTHUR: What's up with him, then?

BILLY (*startled and embarrassed*): I didn't hear you coming . . . (*He sees* LIZ *for the first time and is even more embarrassed*) Liz . . .

LIZ: Hallo, Billy . . .

ARTHUR: What are you on, then? He's saying his prayers.

BILLY (*he scratches the ground with the cane with an assumed casualness*): No, I was just standing. Just thinking to myself. (*To* LIZ) Arthur told me you were back.

ARTHUR: You looked like one of them stinking gnomes we've got in our garden. With a maring fishing rod. (BILLY *tosses the garden cane into the garden*) What are you standing out here for? Won't they let you in?

BILLY (*irritated*): Can't I stand in my own rotten garden now? (*To* LIZ) When did you get back?

LIZ: Last week . . .

ARTHUR (*before she can continue*): Hey, is it right your grandma's snuffed it?

BILLY: You what? Yes. This afternoon. Funeral's on Tuesday.

ARTHUR: Fizzing hell! I was only talking to her this morning.

BILLY (*to* LIZ): Why didn't you ring up?

ARTHUR (*before she can reply*): You don't half drop me in it! I thought you'd made it up. I told our old lady you'd made it up! She'll go stinking bald.

BILLY (*to* LIZ): You've got the number. You could have rung me up.

LIZ: I was going to, Billy.

ARTHUR (*again before she can continue*): Do you know what I was going to do? If I'd had enough money. I was going to send a wreath round. With a little card saying in capital letters: 'YOU STINKING LOUSE-BOUND CROWING LIAR.' I was sure you'd made it up.

BILLY (*annoyed*): What are you talking about? What would I want to make up a thing like that for?

ARTHUR: Oh, get George Washington. (*In a mimicking falsetto*) Please, sir, I cannot tell a lie. I chopped up Grandma.

BILLY (*turning to* ARTHUR): Look, why don't you just jack it in. Eh?

ARTHUR: All right, all right. Keep your shirt on. Don't go biting my head off.

BILLY: Well, you want to grow up.

ARTHUR: You what! Listen who's talking. You're a right one to talk. Grow up? Blimey! (*He turns to* LIZ) Do you know what he once did? He saves up these plastic boats you get out of corn-flake packets. He does! He saves them all. He keeps them in his desk. Well, do you know what he once did? He filled up a baby's coffin with water – down in the basement – and started playing at naval battles. He thinks I don't know.

BILLY: Aw, shut up. Anyway, I don't sit in the lavatory

all morning. Reading mucky books.

ARTHUR: No, and I don't go around playing at Winston Churchills when I think nobody's looking.

BILLY: Aw, belt up, man!

ARTHUR (*tapping* BILLY *on the chest*): You just want to stop telling people to belt up. You want to go careful, man. Or else somebody's going to belt you.

BILLY: Yeh – you and whose army?

ARTHUR: I'm not talking about me. I'm talking about somebody else.

BILLY: Who?

ARTHUR: Somebody's brother.

BILLY: Whose naffing brother? What are you talking about?

ARTHUR: Rita's naffing brother. Who do you think? That's what I came up to tell you – thanks very much for asking. It's the last favour I'll do you, I know that. I've just seen him down at the dance hall. Screaming blue murder. I wouldn't like to be in your shoes, man, when he gets you.

BILLY (*uneasily*): I'm not frightened of him.

ARTHUR: You what! He'll bloody slaughter you. He will, you know, he's not kidding.

BILLY: So what?

ARTHUR: So what, he says. I knew you should never have given her that ring in the first place. I told you, didn't I? Well, she still wants it back, you know. You've had your chips.

BILLY: Aaahh – who cares.

ARTHUR: You'll bloody care when you're in the infirmary getting stitched up. Well, you've had it coming, matey, let's face it. You and your rotten lying. Well, I know what I'd do if I was you – and I didn't want to get crippled. I'd get off to that job in London, dead smartish – that's if there is a job in London.

BILLY: What do you mean – if there is a job in London?

ARTHUR: I mean, if it isn't another of your stinking lies!

BILLY: I'll go – don't you worry.

ARTHUR: I'm not worrying, Tosh. I've got more to do with my time. But I'll tell you this much, you can stop going round giving out the patter about our old lady. Because if I hear – once more – about her being in the family way, I'll be round here myself. Never mind Rita's brother.

BILLY: Aw – dry up . . .

ARTHUR (*going off*): Well, I've told you, man. (*He turns to* BILLY) And don't think I'm covering up for you any more – 'cause I'm not.

BILLY (*softly*): Aw – get knotted. (ARTHUR *exits.* BILLY *turns to* LIZ) He talks too much. (*There is a slight pause as they stand and look at each other.*) . . . Hallo, Liz.

LIZ: Hallo, Billy.

BILLY: When did you get back?

LIZ: Last week.

BILLY: Why didn't you ring me up?

LIZ: I was going to.

BILLY: Thank you very much.

LIZ: No – really. I was going to. I thought I'd see you at the dance tonight. I went to the dance. I thought you'd be there.

BILLY: I couldn't go.

LIZ: No. No – I know. I heard about your grandma. I'm sorry.

BILLY. Yes. (*Changing the subject*) I haven't seen you for months.

LIZ: Five weeks. You didn't waste much time, did you?

BILLY: Why? What do you mean?

LIZ: Getting engaged. To everybody.

BILLY: Oh – that.

LIZ: You're mad.

BILLY (*he shrugs his shoulders*): Where have you been?

LIZ: Oh – here and there.

BILLY: Why didn't you write?

LIZ: I did – once. I tore it up.

BILLY: You're always tearing it up.

LIZ (*changing the subject*): How's everything with you?

How's the script-writing? How's the book coming along?

BILLY (*enthusiastically*): Oh, I've finished it. It's going to be published next Christmas. (*She gives him a long, steady look*) I haven't started writing it yet.

LIZ: You are mad.

BILLY: Yes. (LIZ *sits on the garden seat*) Liz . . . ?

LIZ: Mmmm . . . ?

BILLY (*sitting beside her*): Do you find life complicated?

LIZ: Mmmm. So-so.

BILLY: I wish it was something you could tear up and start again. Life – I mean. You know – like starting a new page in an exercise book.

LIZ: Well, it's been done. Turning over a new leaf.

BILLY: I turn over a new leaf every day – but the blots show through.

LIZ: What's all this about London?

BILLY: I've been offered a job down there.

LIZ: Honestly?

BILLY: Honestly. A sort of job.

LIZ: Good. I'm glad. Perhaps it's your new leaf.

BILLY (*proud of the phrase*): I turn over a new leaf every day – but the blots show through the page.

LIZ: Well, perhaps a new leaf isn't good enough. Perhaps you need to turn over a new volume.

BILLY: Yes.

LIZ: Are you going to take that job?

BILLY: I think so.

LIZ: You only think so?

BILLY: I don't know.

LIZ: You know, my lad, the trouble with you is that you're – what's the word? – introspective. You're like a child at the edge of a paddling pool. You want very much to go in, but you think so much about whether the water's cold, and whether you'll drown, and what your mother will say if you get your feet wet . . .

BILLY (*interrupting*): All I'm doing is wondering whether to dive or swim.

Liz: Perhaps you need a coach.

Billy: Do you know why I'm so fascinated by London?

Liz: No. Why?

Billy: A man can lose himself in London. London is a big place. It has big streets – and big people . . .

Liz (*giving him another look*): Mad.

Billy: Perhaps I need to turn over a new paddling pool.
    (*There is a pause as they look at each other.*)

Liz: Who do you love?

Billy (*adopting his thick North Country accent*): Thee, lass.

Liz: Yes, it sounds like it, doesn't it?

Billy: I do, lass.

Liz: Say it properly, then.

Billy: I do, Liz. I do.

Liz: What about Barbara?

Billy: Well, what about her?

Liz: Well, *what* about her?

Billy: All over.

Liz: You've said that before.

Billy: I know. This time it is all over.

Liz: And what about the other one? Rita-whatever-her-name-is.

Billy: That's all over, too.
    (*There is a pause.* Billy *takes out a packet of cigarettes, lights two and gives one to* Liz.)

Liz: I want to marry you, you know, Billy.

Billy: I know, Liz – I know. We will – one day.

Liz: Not one day. Now.

Billy: Do you?

Liz: Next week will do. Before you go to London. Or when you get there. Whichever you prefer.

Billy: I think I get engaged a bit too often.

Liz: I don't want to get engaged. I want to get married.

Billy: Is that why you keep sloping off every few weeks? Because you want to get married?

Liz: I want to get married.

BILLY: All right. All right.

LIZ: How do you mean – all right? I've just proposed to you and you say 'all right'. Aren't you supposed to say 'this is so sudden' or 'yes' or something?

BILLY: I don't know.

LIZ (*she puts her arms round him and kisses him. He responds. They break away*): Billy . . .

BILLY: Yes?

LIZ: You know what you wanted me to do? That night? When we walked through the park? And I said 'another night'?

BILLY: I remember.

LIZ: Well, it's another night tonight, isn't it?

BILLY (*afraid but excited*): Are you sure?

LIZ: Yes.

BILLY: Where could we go?

LIZ: I've got a room. There's no one there.

BILLY: What do you think we ought to do about – you know, babies.

LIZ: Have them. Lots and lots of them.

BILLY: No, I mean tonight.

LIZ: It's all right. (*After a pause*) Billy . . . ?

BILLY: Yes?

LIZ: Ask you something?

BILLY: What?

LIZ: Do you know what *virgo intacta* means?

BILLY: Yes.

LIZ: Well, I'm not.

BILLY: No. I somehow didn't think you were.

LIZ: Want me to tell you about it?

BILLY: No. (*He kisses her*) All right, yes. Tell me about it.

LIZ: No – not now.

BILLY: Tell me about it.

LIZ: You think that's why I'm always going away, don't you?

BILLY: I don't know.

LIZ: Ask me where I've been for the past five weeks.

BILLY: What difference does it make?

LIZ: None – I suppose. It's just that every so often I want to go away. It's not you, Billy. I want to be here with you. It's the town. It's the people we know. I don't like knowing everybody – or becoming a part of things. Do you see what I mean?

BILLY: Yes . . . yes.

LIZ: What I'd like is to be invisible. You know, to be able to move around without people knowing, and not having to worry about them. Not having to explain all the time.

BILLY: Liz . . . Liz! Listen! Listen! Liz, do you know what I do? When I want to feel invisible. I've never told anybody. I have a sort of – well, it's an imaginary country. Where I go. It has its own people . . .

LIZ (*interrupting*): Do you do that? I knew you would. Why are we so alike, Billy? I can read your thoughts. A town like this. Only somewhere over by the sea. And we used to spend the whole day on the beach. That's what I used to think about.

BILLY: This is more than a town – it's a whole country. (*He is getting excited*) I'm supposed to be the Prime Minister. You're supposed to be the Foreign Secretary – or something.

LIZ (*with mock obedience*): Yes, sir.

BILLY: I think about it for hours. Sometimes I think, if we were married, with a house of our own, we could just sit and imagine ourselves there.

LIZ: Yes, we could.

BILLY: I want a room, in the house, with a green baize door. It will be a big room, and when we go into it, through the door, that's it, that's our country. No one else would be allowed in. No one else will have keys. They won't know where the room is. Only we'll know. And we'll make models of the principal cities. You know, out of cardboard. And we could use toy soldiers. Painted. For the people. We could draw maps. It would be a place to go on a rainy afternoon. We could go there. No one would find us. I thought we could have a big sloping shelf running all the way down one wall, you know, like a big desk. And we'd have a lot of blank paper on it and design our own newspapers. We could even make uniforms, if we wanted to. It would be our country . . . (*He falters away.*)

LIZ: Let's have a model train that the kids won't be allowed to use.

BILLY: Liz . . . ? Will you marry me?

LIZ: Yes. (*He kisses her*) Billy . . .?

BILLY: Yes?

LIZ: Are you really going to London or just pretending?

BILLY: I'm thinking about it.

LIZ: Only thinking?

BILLY: Well, going. Soon, anyway.

LIZ: When's soon?

BILLY: Well, soon.

LIZ: That's a bit vague. Soon. Why not now?

BILLY: It's difficult.

LIZ: No, it's easy. You just get on a train and four hours later there you are — in London.

BILLY: It's easy for you, you've had the practice.

LIZ: I'll come with you.

BILLY: That'd be marvellous — if we could.

LIZ (*she rises*): But we can, Billy! We can! What is there to stop us?

BILLY (*thinking seriously about it for the first time*): Well, there's . . . I don't know . . . you've got to make all sorts of arrangements, haven't you?

LIZ: You buy a ticket, that's all. You buy a ticket and get on a train. That's all there is to it.

BILLY: I never thought about it like that.

LIZ: Billy, we can! We can go! We can go tonight!

BILLY: But, Liz . . .

LIZ: There's the midnight train. We can catch that. It gets in at King's Cross Station. Breakfast at Lyons Corner House. Then we get a tube — we get a tube from Piccadilly Circus to Earl's Court. I've got friends there, Billy. They'll put us up. They'd give us a room.

BILLY (*almost convinced. He rises*): Tonight, Liz?

LIZ: Yes, tonight! Twelve-five from New Street station. We'll be in London tomorrow. We can go to Hyde Park in the afternoon. We'll go to the pictures tomorrow night – the Odeon, Marble Arch. What time is it now?

BILLY (*glancing at his watch*): Just after ten.

LIZ: I'm going, Billy. Are you coming?

BILLY (*his mind made up*): Yes, Liz. I'm coming.

LIZ: Are you sure?

BILLY: I'm coming with you.

LIZ (*briskly*): Right, then. I'm going home. Now. And I'm going to pack my things. I'll meet you at the station. In that refreshment room. In an hour's time. Eleven o'clock. I'll get the tickets. Two singles to London. You won't let me down, Billy?

BILLY: I'm coming.

LIZ: What will you tell your father and mother?

BILLY: They know already – more or less.

LIZ: You won't let them talk you out of it?

BILLY: I'm coming.

> (*The lights begin to fade up in the living-room. GEOFFREY enters from the kitchen, takes up a newspaper, sits down and begins to read. The lights fade slightly in the garden.*)

LIZ (*she kisses BILLY*): Eleven o'clock.

BILLY: Eleven.

> (*LIZ goes off down the garden. BILLY watches her go and then turns and enters the house. GEOFFREY rises at the sound of the door. BILLY enters the living-room. He registers shock as he sees that his cupboard has been opened.*)

GEOFFREY: What time of bloody night do you call this?

BILLY: It's only ten.

GEOFFREY: I don't care what bloody time it is. Who said you could go out? And where've you been?

BILLY: I've only been out. Why? Did you want some chips bringing in?

GEOFFREY: I'll chip you. I'll chip you round your bloody earhole if I start on you. Have you been out dancing?

BILLY: No, 'course I haven't.

GEOFFREY: If you've been out dancing with your grandma lying dead I'll bloody murder you, I will.

BILLY (*feigning innocence*): What's up?

GEOFFREY: What's up — you know what's up. What have you done with that letter of your mother's?

(BILLY *glances in fear at the envelopes on the floor.*) Do you hear me? I'm talking to you!

BILLY: What letter?

GEOFFREY: What, what, what! Don't keep saying bloody 'what'. You know what letter. That what she gave you to post to Housewives' Choice.

BILLY: I told her once. I posted it.

GEOFFREY (*taking the letter from his pocket*): You posted bloody nothing. You've had it in that cupboard. It was given to you to post. You bloody idle little swine.

BILLY: I did post it. That's just the rough copy.

GEOFFREY: What are you talking about? Rough copy? It's your mother's letter. How could you have posted it?

BILLY: Look — the letter my mother wrote was full of mistakes, that's all. I just thought it would stand a better chance if I wrote it out again — properly. That's all.

(ALICE *enters from the kitchen.*)

GEOFFREY: Well, who told you to write it out again? And who told you to open it? You keep your thieving hands off other people's things! And where did you get all them bloody calendars from, and all?

BILLY: What calendars?

GEOFFREY (*fingering his belt*): By bloody hell! I'll give you 'what' if you don't stop saying 'what, what', my lad! You know what! Don't think I haven't been talking to Mr Duxbury — because I have. I've heard it all. You make me a laughing-stock. You can't keep your hands off nothing. And where's that monkey wrench out of my garage? I suppose you know nothing about that?

BILLY: No, 'course I don't. What do I want with a monkey wrench?

GEOFFREY: What do you want with two hundred bloody calendars! And what have you been doing with their name-plates as well? You're not right in the bloody head.

BILLY (*losing his temper*): I'm not right! I'm not right! I didn't want to work for Shadrack and flaming Duxbury's! You made me take the rotten job! Now you can answer for it.

GEOFFREY: Don't bloody shout at me, you gormless young get – or I'll knock your eyes out.

BILLY: God give me strength.

GEOFFREY: Give you strength, he wants to give you some sense! You're like a bloody Mary-Ann! Well, I hope your mother gets more sense out of you.

ALICE: Well, you've got yourself into a fine mess, lad, haven't you?

BILLY: Have I?

ALICE: I'm only thankful she knows nothing about it. (*She glances up at the ceiling*) Why didn't you post that letter of mine?

BILLY: I did post it. I was telling Dad. I just wrote it out again, that's all. There was some mistakes in it.

ALICE: Yes, well we can't all be Shakespeares, can we? And what's all this about you taking money from work?

BILLY: What money?

GEOFFREY (*warningly*): I've told you.

BILLY: What? I haven't taken any money.

GEOFFREY: There's two pound ten short in your postage book. Never mind petty cash.

BILLY: Oh, that ... I ...

ALICE: What did you do with it, Billy?

GEOFFREY: He's spent it. That's what he's bloody done with it.

ALICE: Well, it's just beyond me. You didn't have to take money, Billy. You could have come to me.

GEOFFREY: You've had things too bloody easy. That's

been your trouble. You can't carry on at work like you do at home, you know.

BILLY: Well, I told you I didn't want to work there when I first started, didn't I?

GEOFFREY: You didn't want to work for nobody, if you ask me aught. You thought you'd live on me, didn't you?

BILLY: No, I didn't. I could have kept myself.

ALICE: Kept yourself – how?

BILLY: Writing scripts.

GEOFFREY: Writing bloody scripts, you want to get a day's work done, never mind writing scripts. Who do you think's going to run this bloody business when I'm gone?

BILLY: You said you didn't want me in the business.

GEOFFREY: Only because you were so bloody idle! Somebody's got to carry on with it! Who's going to keep your mother?

BILLY (*with an attempt at humour*): Why, you're not retiring, are you?

GEOFFREY: Don't try and be funny with me, lad! Or you'll laugh on the other side of your face!

ALICE: And what did you tell me about Arthur's mother? She wasn't having a baby, you know very well she wasn't.

BILLY: It was only a joke.

GEOFFREY: A joke; it sounds like a bloody joke!

ALICE: And why did you tell her I'd broken my leg?

BILLY: I didn't know you knew Arthur's mother.

ALICE: Yes, you don't know who I know and who I don't know, do you? If you want to know, she rang me up. And what did you do with that cardigan she gave you for me, last Christmas?

BILLY (*vaguely*): I think I gave it to the refugees.

ALICE: Well, you've got a new cardigan to find by tomorrow morning. Because she's coming round to see me.

BILLY (*emphatically*): I won't be here tomorrow morning.

GEOFFREY: You won't be here to bloody night if you talk to your mother in that tone of voice!

BILLY: I'm not going to be here tonight. I'm leaving.

ALICE: What are you talking about?

BILLY (*decisively*): I'm getting the midnight train. Tonight. I'm taking that job in London.

ALICE: If you're in any more trouble, Billy, it's not something you can leave behind you. You put it in your suitcase and take it with you.

GEOFFREY: Well, he's not taking that suitcase of mine upstairs. (*Turning to* BILLY) Anyway, you're not going to London or nowhere else — so you can get that idea out of your head, for a kick-off.

BILLY: I mean it, Dad. I'm going.

GEOFFREY: And I bloody mean it, and all. (*Raising his voice*) You stop here till that money's paid back. You can thank your lucky stars Mr Duxbury's not landed you in court.

BILLY: Grateful! Grateful! Grateful for this, grateful for that! That's all I've ever heard! Grateful you let me go to the grammar school! We've been hearing that one since the first day I went there. What am I supposed to do? Say 'thank you very much' three times a day for my marvellous education?

GEOFFREY: Well, it's a chance we never had!

BILLY: Yes, and don't we bloody well know it! I even had to be grateful for winning my own scholarship! And what did you say when I came running home to tell you I'd won it? Don't think I've forgotten! I was eleven years old! I came belting out of those school gates and I ran all the way! Just to tell you! And what did you say? That you'd have to pay for the uniform and I'd have to be grateful! And now I'm supposed to be grateful to Shadrack and stinking Duxbury! Why? What for? For letting me sit at one of their rotten desks all day?

ALICE (*gently reasoning*): Well, you took the job, Billy.

GEOFFREY: Yes, and he's stopping there till that money's paid back.

BILLY: I'm not arguing about it. I'm going! (*He crosses towards the door.*)

GEOFFREY: Go, then! I've finished with you!

(BILLY *enters the hall and moves up the stairs.*
GEOFFREY *crosses to the door and calls after* BILLY *as he
exits into the bedroom.*)

They'll take you to court, you know! I won't stop them!
I'm not paying it back! And don't think you're taking my
suitcase!

(GEOFFREY *crosses back into the living-room and
stands silent.* ALICE *sits in the chair by the fire.*)

ALICE: Oh, dear me . . . Oh, dear me . . .

(BILLY *enters from the bedroom and charges down the
stairs and into the living-room. He is carrying a small
battered suitcase. He crosses to the sideboard and, opening a drawer, begins to pack the case with shirts, socks,
ties and a pullover.* GEOFFREY *watches him in silence.*)

ALICE (*concerned*): What time train do you reckon you're
catching?

BILLY: Midnight.

ALICE: Well, what time does it get in?

BILLY: Tomorrow morning.

ALICE: And where are you going to live when you get
there?

GEOFFREY: He'll finish up in the Salvation Army Hostel.

ALICE (*as* BILLY *packs a pair of socks*): All them socks
need darning, you know. (BILLY *makes no reply*) Well,
you'll want more than one suit . . . And what about your
grandma's funeral on Tuesday?

(BILLY *has now placed all his clothing in the case. He
stoops and begins to pack the calendars.*)

GEOFFREY (*in disbelief*): What the thump are you packing
them bloody calendars for?

BILLY: I thought I'd post them.

ALICE: Well, you'll be expected at the funeral, you know.

GEOFFREY (*disparagingly*): He's not going anywhere.

BILLY (*slamming the case shut he rises*): I'm going.

(He picks up the case and crosses to the door.)

GEOFFREY (*half-relenting*): Don't act so bloody daft.

(BILLY *pauses for a moment, his hand on the door,*

287

caught up in the embarrassment of leaving.)

BILLY: Well, I'll write to you then. Soon as I've got fixed up. (*Acutely embarrassed.*) I'm sorry about my grandma . . .

(*He goes out.*)

ALICE: Oh, dear me . . . Oh, dear me . . .

GEOFFREY: They can summons him. I've finished.

ALICE: You'll have to pay it, Geoffrey. Will he be all right on his own?

GEOFFREY: He won't bloody go – he'll be back in five minutes.

ALICE: We know nothing about where he's going and what he's supposed to be doing. Who's that fellow he says he's going to work for? That comedian?

GEOFFREY: I don't bloody know.

ALICE: It was in that letter he had in his pocket in that old raincoat.

(GEOFFREY *crosses and takes the envelope from the raincoat which is hanging in the hall. He returns into the living-room reading the letter to himself as he walks. He then reads the letter aloud to* ALICE.)

GEOFFREY: 'Dear Mr Fisher, Many thanks for script and gags, I can use some of the gags and pay accordingly. As for my staff job, well, I regret to tell you, I do not have staff beside my agent, but several of the boys do work for me, you might be interested in this. (*He pauses*) Why not call in for a chat next time you are in London? Best of luck and keep writing. Danny Boon.'

ALICE (*after a pause*): Run down to the station and fetch him back.

GEOFFREY: He's off his bloody rocker.

ALICE: You'll have to go stop him, Geoffrey.

GEOFFREY: Nay, he's big enough to look after himself now. He can stand on his own two feet for a change. I've finished. I've done my whack for him.

ALICE: I wonder if he's got any money?

GEOFFREY: That's his look-out. It doesn't belong to him if he has. You can depend on that.

ALICE: Oh, dear me . . . Oh, dear me . . .

GEOFFREY: There's no need for him to starve. He can get a job if he sets his mind to it. And gets up in a morning.

ALICE: Well, what's he going to do?

GEOFFREY: He can go clerking – same as here. There's a lot of offices in London. Well, there's one thing certain. I know what I'm going to bloody do: I'm off to bed. I've enough on my plate without worrying my head over that one. He can go to hell, he can.

ALICE: Do you want a cup of Ovaltine, or anything?

GEOFFREY: No. You want to get off to bed as well, lass.

ALICE (rising): I always used to take her one up at this time. I'll have to get used to it – not having to.

GEOFFREY: Aye, well . . .

ALICE: Is the back door locked, Geoffrey?

GEOFFREY: I've seen to it.

(They cross into the hall. GEOFFREY switches off the light in the living-room and automatically drops the catch on the yale lock. GEOFFREY follows ALICE up the stairs. As they go up the porch light fades up and RITA and ARTHUR enter the garden.)

GEOFFREY (with assumed cheerfulness): Well, he'll come home at holiday times. And happen some week-ends.

(GEOFFREY switches out the hall light from the top of the stairs and follows ALICE into the bedroom.)

ARTHUR (with relief as he sees the hall light go out): There you are! They've gone to bed.

RITA: Have a look through the rotten letter-box.

ARTHUR: You can see! They've gone to bed. You don't think they're sitting there with no lights on, do you?

RITA: Well, he's not getting out of it – 'cause I shall come round in the morning. Our kid'll come round as well. Our kid'll duff him up. He'll get that ring back.

ARTHUR: You and your kid and that louse-bound ring! Come on, let's get down to Foley Bottoms. Get some snogging hours in.

RITA: He needn't think he's got away with it – 'cause he

hasn't. He'll be a stretcher case tomorrow morning. (*She screams up at the bedrooms*) You'll be a stretcher case tomorrow morning! You wait! You rotten yellow-bellied squint-eyed get! You're nothing else! You closet!

(*We hear the sound of a window being flung open and* ALICE *shouting*.)

ALICE: Get away! Don't you know we've got somebody dead in this house!

(*We hear the window slammed shut*.)

RITA (*screaming*): You want to be all rotten dead! You want gassing!

ARTHUR: Shut up, Rita! She knows my mother.

RITA: I don't care.

ARTHUR: They're not worth bothering about. Come on — let's get down to Foley Bottoms. We're just wasting time stuck here.

RITA (*allowing* ARTHUR *to place his arm around her and pilot her out of the garden*): Well, we'll be round here first thing tomorrow morning. (*As they exit*) We get up before they do . . .

(ARTHUR *and* RITA *go off.*

There is a pause and then BILLY *enters and walks slowly and dejectedly to the front door. He puts down his case and, taking a key from his pocket, opens the door and enters. He crosses into the living-room and, closing the door behind him, switches on the light. He stands indecisively for a moment and then crosses and switches on the radio. He crosses to his suitcase and opens it as the sound of a dance-band comes from the radio. He stands for a moment and, as the music continues, he compulsively lifts his hand and begins to conduct. He glances towards the ceiling, wondering if he is making too much noise, then crosses and switches off the radio. He returns to the suitcase which he carries over to the sideboard. He opens his cupboard and is neatly stacking the calendars back into the cupboard.*)

THE CURTAIN FALLS

PLAY WITH A TIGER
By Doris Lessing

This play was first produced at the Comedy Theatre, London, on March 22nd, 1962, by Oscar Lewenstein, with the following cast:

ANNA FREEMAN	Siobhan McKenna
TOM LATTIMER	William Russell
MARY JACKSON	Maureen Pryor
HARRY PAYNE	Godfrey Quigley
JANET STEVENS	Anne Lawson
DAVE MILLER	Alex Viespi

The action takes place in Anna Freeman's room on the first floor of Mary Jackson's house in Earls Court, London, S.W.5.

At the opening of the play the time is about nine in the evening; at its close it is about four in the morning.

Directed by Ted Kotcheff

CHARACTERS

ANNA FREEMAN: A woman of thirty-five, or so, who earns her living on the artistic fringes.

DAVE MILLER: An American, about thirty-three, who is rootless on principle.

MARY JACKSON: About ten years older than Anna: a widow with a grown-up son.

TOM LATTIMER: Who is on the point of taking a job as business manager of a woman's magazine. About thirty-five, a middle-class Englishman.

HARRY PAYNE: Fifty-ish. A journalist.

JANET STEVENS: In her early twenties, the daughter of an insurance agent – American.

AUTHOR'S NOTES ON DIRECTING
THIS PLAY

When I wrote *Play with a Tiger* in 1958 I set myself an artistic problem which resulted from my decision that naturalism, or, if you like, realism, is the greatest enemy of the theatre; and that I never wanted to write a naturalistic play again.

Now this play is about the rootless, declassed people who live in bed-sitting-rooms or small flats or the cheaper hotel rooms, and such people are usually presented on the stage in a detailed squalor of realism which to my mind distracts attention from what is interesting about them.

I wrote *Play with a Tiger* with an apparently conventional opening designed to make the audience expect a naturalistic play so that when the walls vanished towards the end of Act I they would be surprised (and I hope pleasantly shocked) to find they were not going to see this kind of play at all.

But there had to be a bridge between the opening of the play, and the long section where Anna and Dave are alone on the stage, and this bridge is one of style. This is why Anna's room is tall, bare, formal; why it has practically no furniture, save for the bed and the small clutter around it; and why there are no soft chairs or settees where the actors might lounge or sprawl. This stark set forces a certain formality of movement, stance and confrontation so that even when Dave and Anna are not alone on the stage creating their private world, there is a simplicity of style which links the two moods of the play together.

It is my intention that when the curtain comes down at the end, the audience will think: Of course! In this play no one lit cigarettes, drank tea or coffee, read newspapers, squirted soda into Scotch, or indulged in little bits of 'business' which indicated 'character'. They will realize, I hope, that they have been seeing a play which relies upon its style and its language for its effect.

DORIS LESSING, 1963

Postscript, 1972

I have now seen this play done in various countries and in various manners, on stage and on television. There is a bad mistake that can easily be made. This is to cast Dave as a fool, a stud, or a nothing-man, making it 'a woman's play'. Some Women's Liberation groups have done this, turning the thing into a self-righteous aria for the female voice. I have seen a production where all the lines were cut to do with Dave's politics, his commitment to social change, his courage in living as he believes he must live, thus making him into a witless Don Juan. If Dave is not cast and acted so that he has every bit as much weight as Anna, then the play goes to pieces. Ideally Dave should be played by an actor who is a Jew. Better, by an American Jewish actor.

Another thing I have seen done wrong is to make the play relentlessly solemn, and on one note. I am afraid this is the perennial author's complaint: a play may be a comedy and sad, sad and a roaring farce. The undernote, or ground of this particular play, should be that humour which comes from growing older. For this reason, it is not a good thing to let the audience forget that these people are in their thirties and forties: it is not a play about young people.

DORIS LESSING 1972

ACT I

The action of this play takes place in ANNA FREEMAN'S
room on the first floor of MARY JACKSON'S *house, on a
street in London with heavy traffic.* ANNA *has lived here
for some years. There is another room, behind this one,
used by her son, now at school; but* ANNA *sleeps and
lives in this room. It is very large and looks formal
because it is underfurnished. There are double doors at
left-back. When they are open the landing can be seen,
and part of the stairway leading up. The house was
originally built for rich people and still shows signs of
it. The landing and stairs are spacious and carpeted
in dark red; the banisters are elegant and painted white.
The upper part of the doors are of glass, and therefore
the doorway has a dark red curtain, usually drawn back.
The room is painted white, walls and ceilings. There
is a low wide divan, covered in rough black material,
in the right back corner; a window, with dark red
curtains, in the right wall; a large, round, ornate mirror,
on the left wall; a low shelf of books under the window.
The floor is painted black and has in the centre of it a
round crimson carpet. There are two stiff-looking
chairs on either side of the mirror, of dark wood, and
seated in dark red. The life of the room is concentrated
around the divan. A low table by its head has a telephone, and is loaded with books and papers, and a small
reading light. At the foot of the divan is another low
table, with a typewriter, at which* ANNA *works by kneeling, or squatting, on the divan. This table has another
reading light, and a record player. Around the divan
is a surf of books, magazines, newspapers, records,*

cushions. There is a built-in cupboard, hardly noticeable until opened, in the right wall. Two paraffin heaters, of the cheap black cylindrical kind, are both lit. It is winter. The year is 1958. At the opening of the play the time is about nine in the evening, at its close it is four in the morning.

(ANNA *is standing at the window, which is open at the top, her back to the room. She is wearing slacks and a sweater: these are pretty, even fashionable; the reason for the trousers is that it is hard to play Act II in a skirt.*

TOM *is standing behind* ANNA, *waiting, extremely exasperated. This scene between them has been going on for some time. They are both tense, irritated, miserable.*

TOM's *sarcasm and pomposity is his way of protecting himself from his hurt at how he has been treated.*

ANNA's *apparent casualness is how she wards off a hysteria that is only just under control. She is guilty about* TOM, *unhappy about* DAVE — *and this tension in her underlies everything she says or does until that moment towards the end of Act I when* DAVE, *because of his moral ascendancy over her, forces her to relax and smile.*

A moment's silence. Then a scream and a roar of traffic, which sounds as if it is almost in the room. TOM *loses patience, goes past* ANNA *to window, slams it shut, loudly.*)

TOM : Now say: 'I could repeat every word you've said.'

ANNA (*in quotes*): I've scarcely seen you during the last two weeks. You always have some excuse. Mary answers the telephone and says you are out. I was under the impression we were going to be married. If I'm wrong please correct me. I simply cannot account for the change in your attitude ... how's that?

(TOM *looks at her, gives her a small sardonic bow, goes past her to a chair which is set so he is facing half away*

*from her. He sits in it in a pose which he has clearly been
occupying previously — for ANNA looks at him, equally
sardonic. Since the chair is hard and upright, not designed for comfort, he is almost lying in a straight line
from his crossed ankles to his chin, which is upturned
because he is looking with weary patience at the ceiling.
His fingertips are held lightly together.*

*ANNA, having registered the fact that his pose is de-
signed to annoy, goes back to the window and stands
looking down.)*

ANNA: That man is still down there. Do you know, he
comes every night and just stands there, hour after hour
after hour. And it's so cold.

TOM: Yes, it is . . . Anna, I was under the impression that
my attraction for you, such as it is, of course, was that I'm
rather more reliable, more responsible? than the usual run
of your friends?

ANNA: Do you realize that man hasn't so much as moved
a muscle since he arrived at six? There he stands, gazing up
at that window. And the top half of that house is a brothel.
He must have seen one of the girls in the street and fallen
in love. Imagine it, I've been living here all these years and
I never knew that house was a brothel. There are four
Lesbians living together, and that poor sap's in love with one
of them. Well, isn't it frightening?

TOM: When you walked into my flat that evening — if
I may remind you of it — you said you were in search of a
nice solid shoulder to weep on. You said you couldn't stand
another minute of living like this. Well?

ANNA: I asked the policeman at the corner. Why yes,
miss, he said, all fatherly and protective, they've been there
for years and years. But don't you worry your pretty little
head about a thing, we have our eyes on them all the time.

TOM: I suppose what all this amounts to is that your fascinating American is around again.

ANNA: I told you, no. I haven't seen Dave for weeks. Perhaps I should go down and tell that poor moon-struck idiot

— look, you poor sap, all you've got to do is to go upstairs with fifty shillings in your hand and your goddess is yours?

TOM: And while you're about it, you could take him off for a nice cup of tea, listen to his troubles and tell him yours.

ANNA: Yes I could. Why not?

TOM: You're going to go on like this I suppose until the next time Dave or some similarly fascinating character plays you up and you decide that good old Tom will do for a month or so?

ANNA: Tom, it's nine-fifteen. You're expected at the Jeffries at nine-thirty.

TOM: I did accept for you too.

ANNA: Yes you did, and you didn't even ask me first.

TOM: I see.

ANNA: No, you don't see, Tom, until two weeks ago you said you couldn't stand either of the Jeffries, you said, quote, they were boring, phoney and stupid. But now he's going to be your boss it's different?

TOM: No, they're still boring, phoney and stupid, but he is going to be my boss.

ANNA: You said if you took Jeffries' job, you'd be in the rat-race, stuck in the rut, and bound hand and foot to the grindstone.

TOM: I finally took that job because we were going to be married — so I thought.

ANNA: But now we're not going to be married you'll turn down the job? (*As he does not reply*) I thought not. So don't use me to justify yourself.

TOM: You really do rub things in, Anna. All right then. For a number of years I've been seeing myself as a sort of a rolling stone, a fascinating free-lance, a man of infinite possibilities. It turns out that I'm just another good middle-class citizen after all — I'm comfort-loving, conventionally unconventional, I'm not even the Don Juan I thought I was. It turns out that I'm everything I dislike most. I owe this salutary discovery to you, Anna. Thank you very much.

ANNA: Oh, not at all.

TOM (*he now gets up from the chair, and faces her, attacking hard*): Oh my God, you stupid little romantic. Yes, that's what you are, and a prig into the bargain. Very pleased with yourself because you won't soil your hands. Writing a little review here, a little article there, an odd poem or two, a reflection on the aspect of a sidelight on the backwash of some bloody movement or other — reading tuppenny-halfpenny novels for publishers, Mr Bloody Black's new book is or is not an advance on his last. Well, Anna, is it really worth it?

ANNA: Yes it is. I'm free to live as I like. You won't be, ever again.

TOM: And worrying all the time how you're going to find the money for what your kid wants. Do you think he's going to thank you for living like this?

ANNA: That's right. Always stick the knife in, as hard as you can, into a person's weakest spot.

TOM: An art you are not exactly a stranger to? You live here, hand to mouth, never knowing what's going to happen next, surrounding yourself with bums and neurotics and failures. As far as you're concerned anyone who has succeeded at anything at all is corrupt. (*She says nothing*) Nothing to say, Anna? That's not like you.

ANNA: I was thinking, not for the first time, unfortunately, how sad it is that the exquisite understanding and intimacy of the bed doesn't last into the cold light of day.

TOM: So that's all we had in common. Thank you, Anna, you've now defined me.

ANNA: All right, all right, all right. I'm sorry. What else can I say — I'm sorry.

> (*There is a knock on the door.*)

ANNA: Come in.

TOM: Oh my God, Mary.

MARY (*outside the door*): Pussy, pussy, pussy.

> (*A knock on the door.*)

ANNA: Come in.

TOM: She's getting very deaf, isn't she?

ANNA: She doesn't know it. (*As the door opens*) For the Lord's sake don't say . . . (*she imitates him*) . . . I was under the impression we had said come in, if I'm wrong please correct me.

TOM: Just because you've decided to give me the boot, there's no need to knock me down and start jumping on me.

(*Mary comes in, backwards, shutting the door to keep the cat out.*)

MARY: No pussy, you stay there. Anna doesn't really like you, although she pretends she does. (*To* ANNA) That cat is more like a dog, really, he comes when I call. And he waits for me outside a door. (*Peeping around the edge of the door*) No, puss, wait. I won't be a minute. (*To* ANNA) I don't know why I bothered to christen that cat Methuselah, it never gets called anything but puss. (*Sprightly with an exaggerated sigh*) Really, I'm getting quite an old maid, fussing over a cat . . . If you can call a widow with a grown up son an old maid, but who'd have believed I'd have come to fussing over a cat. (*Seeing* TOM) Oh, I didn't know you were here.

TOM: Didn't you see me? I said hullo.

MARY: Sometimes I think I'm getting a bit deaf. Well, what a surprise. You're quite a stranger, aren't you?

TOM: Hardly a stranger, I should have said.

MARY: Dropped in for old times' sake. (TOM *is annoyed.* MARY *says to* ANNA) I thought we might go out to the pub. I'm sick of sitting and brooding. (*As* ANNA *does not respond – quick and defensive*) Oh I see, you and Tom are going out, two's company and three's none.

ANNA: Tom's going to the Jeffries.

MARY (*derisive*): Not the Jeffries – you must be hard up for somewhere to go.

ANNA: And I think I'll stay and work.

TOM: Anna is too good for the Jeffries.

MARY: Who isn't?

(ANNA *has gone back to the window, is looking down into the street.*)

TOM (*angrily*): Perhaps you'd like to come with me, since Anna won't.

MARY (*half aggressive, half coy*): You and me going out together – that'd be a change. Oh, I see, you're joking. (*Genuinely*) Besides, they really are so awful.

TOM: Better than going to the pub with Methuselah, perhaps?

MARY (*with spirit*): No, I prefer Methuselah. You don't want to bore yourself at the Jeffries. Stay and have some coffee with us.

ANNA (*her back still turned*): It's the Royal Command.

MARY: Oh. You mean you've taken that job after all? I told Anna you would, months ago. There, Anna, I told you he would. Anna said when it actually came to the point, you'd never bring yourself to do it.

TOM: I like the idea of you and Anna laying bets as to whether the forces of good or evil would claim my soul.

MARY: Well, I mean, that's what it amounts to, doesn't it? But I always said Anna was wrong about you. Didn't I, Anna? Anna always does this. (*Awkwardly*) I mean, it's not the first time, I mean to say. And I've always been right. Ah, well, as Anna says, don't you, Anna, if a man marries, he marries a woman, but if a woman marries, she marries a way of life.

TOM: Strange, but as it happens I too have been the lucky recipient of that little aphorism.

MARY: Well, you were bound to be, weren't you? (*She sees* TOM *is furious and stops*) Harry telephoned you, Anna.

ANNA: What for?

MARY: Well, I suppose now you're free he thinks he'll have another try.

TOM: May I ask – how did he know Anna was free. After all, I didn't.

MARY: Oh don't be silly. I mean, you and Anna might not have known, but it was quite obvious to everyone else . . . well, I met Harry in the street some days ago, and he said . . .

TOM: I see.

MARY: Well, there's no need to be so stuffy about it, Tom—

(*A bell rings downstairs.*)

MARY: Was that the bell? Are you expecting someone, Anna?

TOM: Of course she's expecting someone.

ANNA: No.

MARY (*who hasn't heard*): Who are you expecting?

ANNA: Nobody.

MARY: Well, I'll go for you, I have to go down anyway. Are you in or out, Anna?

ANNA: I'm out.

MARY: It's often difficult to say, whether you are in or out, because after all, one never knows who it might be.

ANNA (*patiently*): Mary, I really don't mind answering my bell you know.

MARY (*hastily going to the door*): Sometimes I'm running up and down the stairs half the day, answering Anna's bell. (*As she goes out and shuts the door*) Pussy, pussy, where are you, puss, puss, puss.

TOM: She's deteriorating fast, isn't she? (ANNA *patiently says nothing*) That's what you're going to be like in ten years' time if you're not careful.

ANNA: I'd rather be like Mary in ten years' time than what you're going to be like when you're all settled down and respectable.

TOM: A self-pitying old bore.

ANNA: She is also a kind warm-hearted woman with endless time for people in trouble . . . Tom, you're late, the boss waits, and you can't afford to offend him.

TOM: I remember Mary, and not so long ago either – she was quite a dish, wasn't she? If I were you I'd be scared stiff.

ANNA: Sometimes I am scared stiff. (*Seriously*) Tom, her son's getting married next week.

TOM: Oh, so that's it.

ANNA: No, that's not it. She's very pleased he's getting

married. And she's given them half the money she's saved
– not that there's much of it. You surely must see it's going
to make quite a difference to her, her son getting married?

Toм: Well, he was bound to get married some time.

ANNA: Yes he was bound to get married, time marches
on, every dog must have its day, one generation makes way
for another, today's kittens are tomorrow's cats, life's like that.

Toм: I don't know why it is, most people think I'm
quite a harmless sort of man. After ten minutes with you
I feel I ought to crawl into the nearest worm-hole and die.

ANNA: We're just conforming to the well-known rule
that when an affair ends, the amount of violence and un-
pleasantness is in direct ratio to its heat.

(*Loud laughter and voices outside* – HARRY *and*
MARY.)

Toм: I thought you said you were out. Mary really is
quite impossible.

ANNA: It's Harry who's impossible. He always takes it
for granted one doesn't mean him.

Toм (*angry*): And perhaps one doesn't.

ANNA: Perhaps one doesn't.

Toм: Anna! Do let's try and be a bit more . . .

ANNA: Civilized? Is that the word you're looking for?

(HARRY *and* MARY *come in.*)

HARRY (*as he kisses* ANNA): Civilized, she says. There's
our Anna. I knew I'd come in and she'd be saying civilized.
(*Coolly, to* Toм) Oh, hullo.

Toм (*coolly*): Well, Harry.

MARY (*who has been flirted by* HARRY *into an over-respon-
sive state*): Oh, Harry, you are funny sometimes. (*She
laughs*) It's not what you say, when you come to think of
it, it's the way you say it.

HARRY: Surely, it's what I say as well?

ANNA: Harry, I'm not in. I told Mary, I don't want to
see anybody.

HARRY: Don't be silly, darling, of course you do. You
don't want to see anybody, but you want to see me.

Tom (*huffy*): Anna and I were talking.

Harry: Of course you are, you clots. And it's high time you stopped. Look at you both. And now we should all have a drink.

Tom: Oh damn. You and Mary go and have a drink.

Harry: That's not the way at all. Anna will come to the pub with me and weep on my shoulder, and Tom will stay and weep on Mary's.

Tom (*rallying into his smooth sarcasm*): Harry, I yield to no one in my admiration of your tact but I really must say . . .

Harry: Don't be silly. I got a clear picture from Mary here, of you and Anna, snarling and snapping on the verge of tears – it doesn't do at all. When a thing's finished it's finished. I know, for my sins I'm an expert.

Tom: Forgive me if I make an over-obvious point, but this really isn't one of the delightful little affairs you specialize in.

Harry: Of course it was. You two really aren't in a position to judge. Now if you weren't Tom and Anna, you'd take one look at yourselves and laugh your heads off at the idea of your getting married.

Anna (*she goes to the window and looks down*): Harry, come and see me next week and I'll probably laugh my head off.

Harry: Next week's no good at all. You won't need me then, you'll have recovered.

Tom (*immensely sarcastic*): Surely, Harry, if Anna asks you to leave her flat, the least you can do is to . . . (Anna *suddenly giggles.*)

Harry: There, you see? How could you possibly marry such a pompous idiot, Anna. (*To* Tom, *affectionately*) Anna can't possibly marry such an idiot, Tom. Anna doesn't like well-ordered citizens like you, anyway.

Mary: I don't know how you can say well-ordered. He was just another lame duck until now.

Harry: But he's not a lame duck any more. He's going

to work for Jeffries, and he'll be administering to the spiritual needs of the women of the nation through the 'Ladies Own'.

TOM: I'm only going to be on the business side. I won't be responsible for the rubbish they — (*He stops, annoyed with himself.* HARRY *and* MARY *laugh at him.*)

HARRY: There you are, he's a solid respectable citizen already.

TOM (*to* HARRY): It's not any worse than the rag you work for is it?

HARRY (*reacts to* TOM *with a grimace that says touche! and turns to* ANNA): When are you going to get some comfortable furniture into this room?

ANNA (*irritated almost to tears*): Oh sit on the floor, go away, stop nagging.

HARRY: Don't be so touchy. The point I'm trying to make is, Tom'd never put up with a woman like you, he's going to have a house with every modern convenience and everything just so . . . Anna, what've you done with Dave?

ANNA: I haven't seen him for weeks.

HARRY: That's silly, isn't it now?

ANNA: No.

HARRY: Now I'm going to give you a lot of good advice, Anna and . . .

TOM: Fascinating, isn't it? Harry giving people advice.

MARY: Harry may not know how to get his own life into order, but actually he's rather good at other people.

HARRY: What do you mean, my life is in perfect order.

TOM: Indeed? May I ask how your wife is?

HARRY (*in a much used formula*): Helen is wonderful, delightful, she is very happy and she loves me dearly.

TOM (*with a sneer*): How nice.

HARRY: Yes, it is. And that's what I'm going to explain to you, Anna. Look at Helen. She's like you, she likes interesting weak men like me, and . . .

TOM: Weak is not the word I'd have chosen, I must say.

MARY: Surely not weak, Harry?

307

ANNA: Weak is new, Harry. Since when, weak?

HARRY: I'll explain. It came to me in a flash, one night when I was driving home very late – it was dawn, to be precise, you see, weak men like me ...

ANNA (*suddenly serious*): Harry, I'm not in the mood.

HARRY: Of course you are. We are always in the mood to talk about ourselves. I'm talking about you, Anna. You're like Helen. Now what does Helen say? She says, she doesn't mind who I have affairs with provided they are women she'd like herself.

TOM: Charming.

MARY: But Harry, Helen's got to say something ... well, I mean to say.

ANNA: I simply can't stand your damned alibis.

HARRY: Tom must have been bad for you, Anna, if you're going to get all pompous. Helen and I ...

ANNA (*snapping*): Harry, you forget I know Helen very well.

HARRY (*not realizing her mood*): Of course you do. And so do I. And you ought to take on Dave the way Helen's taken me on ...

ANNA: Harry, go away.

HARRY (*still blithe*): No, Anna. I've been thinking. You've got to marry Dave. He needs you.

(MARY *makes a warning gesture at* HARRY, *indicating* ANNA.)

(*To* MARY) Don't be silly, darling. (*To* ANNA *again*) Helen knows I'll always come back to her. Anna, Dave needs you. Have a heart. What'll Dave do?

ANNA (*snapping into hysterical resentment*): I'll tell you what he'll do. He'll do what you did. You married Helen who was very much in love with you. When she had turned into just another boring housewife and mother you began philandering. She had no alternative but to stay put.

HARRY: Anna, Anna, Anna!

ANNA: Oh shut up. I know Helen, I know exactly what sort of hell she's had with you.

HARRY: Tom, you really have been bad for Anna, you've made her all bitchy.

ANNA: Dave will marry some girl who's in love with him. Oh, he'll fight every inch of the way, of course. Then there'll be children and he'll be free to do as he likes. He'll have a succession of girls, and in between each one he'll go back and weep on his wife's shoulder because of his unfortunately weak character. Weak like hell. She'll forgive him all right. He'll even use her compliance as an additional attraction for the little girls, just as you do. My wife understands me, he'll say, with a sloppy look on his wife. She knows what I'm like. She'll always be there to take me back. God almighty, what a man.

HARRY: Anna, you little bitch.

ANNA: That's right. But there's just one thing, Dave shouldn't have picked on me. I'm economically independent. I have no urge for security so I don't have to sell myself out. And I have a child already, so there's no way of making me helpless, is there, dear weak, helpless Harry?

HARRY: Mary, you should have told me Anna was in such a bitchy mood and I wouldn't have come up.

MARY: But I did tell you, and you said 'Well, Anna won't be bitchy with me.'

(*The door bell, downstairs.*)

MARY: I'll go.

ANNA: Mary, I'm out.

MARY: Well, don't blame me for Harry, he insisted. (*As she goes out*) Pussy, pussy, puss, puss.

HARRY: I can't think what Mary would do if Anna did get married.

TOM (*spitefully*): They are rather like an old married couple, aren't they?

(ANNA *pulls down the window with a crash and turns her back on them.*)

HARRY: But so nice to drop in on for aid and comfort when in trouble. (*To* ANNA's *back*) Anna, I'm in trouble.

ANNA: Don't worry, you'll be in love with someone else

in a few weeks.

HARRY (*humorous but serious*): But I won't. This girl, my poppet, she's getting married. (*As* ANNA *shrugs*) For God's sake woman, shut the window, it's freezing. (ANNA *shuts it, but remains looking down*) She met some swine at a party – actually he's very nice. A handsome young swine – he really is nice. She's marrying him – actually, I advised her to. Anna!

ANNA: Did you expect her to hang round for the rest of her life in a state of single blessedness because you didn't want to break up your happy home with Helen? (*She turns, sees his face, which is genuinely miserable*) Oh all right. I'm sorry. I'm very sorry. (*She puts her arms around him.*)

HARRY: There's my Anna. (*To* TOM) I'm sure you've never seen this side of her, but she is a sweet girl, at heart.

TOM: Well, now you've gained your little meed of sympathy from Anna, perhaps I may be permitted to say a word or two?

HARRY: No. You two should just kiss and say goodbye and stop tormenting each other.

TOM: Anna, I know that what goes on in the street is a hundred times more interesting than I am, but . . .

HARRY: Of course it is, she's waiting for Dave.

ANNA: I'm not waiting for Dave.

> (*She comes away from the window. Sits on the bed, her head in her hands.*)

TOM: I want to talk to Anna.

MARY (*from downstairs*): Puss, puss, puss, puss.

TOM (*mocking her*): Puss, puss, puss, puss.

HARRY: Mary should get married. Anna, you should make Mary get married before it's too late.

TOM: Before it's too late!

ANNA: Mary could marry if she wanted.

TOM (*derisively*): Then why doesn't she?

ANNA: Strange as it might seem to you, she doesn't want to get married just for the sake of getting married.

HARRY: Yes, but that's all very well, Anna. It's all right

310

for you — you're such a self-contained little thing. But not for Mary. You should get her married regardless to the first clot who comes along.

ANNA: I — self-contained!

TOM: Yes, it's true — self-contained!

MARY (*from downstairs*): Pussy, pussy, yes come here, puss, puss, puss, puss.

TOM (*to* HARRY): She's getting worse. (*As* ANNA *stiffens up*) Yes, all right, Anna, but it's true. (*To* HARRY) She's man-crazy . . .

HARRY: Oh you silly ass.

TOM: Well she is. She's crazy for a man, wide open, if you so much as smile at her, she responds. And Anna says she doesn't want to marry. Who are you fooling, Anna?

ANNA (*sweetly*): Perhaps she prefers to be sex-starved than to marry an idiot. Which is more than can be said about most men.

HARRY: Now Anna, don't start. Anna, Tom's a nice man, but he's pompous. (*To* TOM) You're a pompous ass, admit it, Tom.

TOM: All I said was, Mary's man-crazy.

ANNA (*on the warpath*): Do you know how Tom was living before he started with me?

HARRY: Yes, of course. Anna, don't make speeches at us!

TOM: Well, how was I living before I started with you?

HARRY: Oh, my God.

ANNA: What is known as a bachelor's life — Tom's own nice inimitable version of it. He sat in his nice little flat, and round about ten at night, if he felt woman-crazy enough, he rang up one of three girls, all of whom were in love with him.

HARRY: Christ knows why.

ANNA: Imagine it, the telephone call at bedtime — are you free tonight, Elspeth, Penelope, Jessica? One of them came over, a drink or a cup of coffee, a couple of hours of bed, and then a radio-taxi home.

HARRY: Anna!

ANNA: Oh from time to time he explained to them that they mustn't think his kind attentions to them meant anything.

HARRY: Anna, you're a bore when you get like this.

TOM: Yes, you are.

ANNA: Then don't call Mary names.

(MARY *comes in.*)

MARY (*suspicious*): You were talking about me?

ANNA: No, about me.

MARY: Oh I thought it was about me. (*To* ANNA) There's a girl wants to see you. She says it's important. She wouldn't give her name.

ANNA (*she is thinking*): I see.

MARY: But she's an American girl. It's the wrong time of the year – summer's for Americans.

ANNA: An American girl.

MARY: One of those nice bright neat clean American girls, how they do it, I don't know, all I know is that you can tell from a hundred yards off they'd rather be seen dead than with their legs or their armpits unshaved, ever so antiseptic, she looked rather sweet really.

HARRY: Tell her to go away and we'll all wait for you. Come on, Tom.

TOM: I'm staying.

HARRY: Come on, Mary, give me a nice cup of coffee.

MARY: It's a long time since you and I had a good gossip.

(HARRY *and* MARY *go out, arm in arm.*)

TOM: Well, who is she?

ANNA: I don't know.

TOM: I don't believe you.

ANNA: You never do.

(MARY'S *voice, and the voice of an American girl, outside on the stairs.*

JANET STEVENS *comes in. She is a neat attractive girl of about 22. She is desperately anxious and trying to hide it.*)

JANET: Are you Anna Freeman?

ANNA: Yes. And this is Tom Lattimer.

JANET: I am Janet Stevens. (*She has expected* ANNA *to know the name*) Janet Stevens.

ANNA: How do you do?

JANET: Janet Stevens from Philadelphia. (*As* ANNA *still does not react*) I hope you will excuse me for calling on you like this.

ANNA: Not at all.

> (JANET *looks at* TOM. ANNA *looks at* TOM. TOM *goes to the window, turns his back.*)

JANET (*still disbelieving* ANNA): I thought you would know my name.

ANNA: No.

TOM: But she has been expecting you all afternoon.

JANET (*at sea*): All afternoon?

ANNA (*angry*): No, it's not true.

JANET: I don't understand, you were expecting me this afternoon?

ANNA: No. But may I ask, how you knew me?

JANET: Well, we have a friend in common. Dave Miller.

TOM (*turning, furious*): You could have said so, couldn't you, Anna?

ANNA: But I didn't know.

TOM: You didn't know. Well, I'm going. You've behaved disgracefully.

ANNA: Very likely. However just regard me as an unfortunate lapse from the straight and narrow on your journey to respectability.

> (TOM *goes out, slamming the door.*)

ANNA (*politely*): That was my – fiancé.

JANET: Oh, Dave didn't say you were engaged.

ANNA: He didn't know. And besides, I'm not 'engaged' any longer.

> (*A silence.* ANNA *looks with enquiry at* JANET, *who tries to speak and fails.*)

ANNA: Please sit down, Miss Stevens.

(JANET *looks around for somewhere to sit, sits on a chair, smiles socially. Being a well brought up young lady, and in a situation she does not understand, she is using her good manners as a last-ditch defence against breaking down.*

ANNA *looks at her, waiting.*)

JANET: It's this way, you see Dave and I . . . (*At* ANNA's *ironical look she stops*) . . . What a pretty room, I do so love these old English houses, they have such . . .

(ANNA *looks at her: do get a move on.*)

JANET: My father gave me a vacation in Europe for passing my college examinations. Yes, even when I was a little girl he used to promise me – if you do well at college I'll give you a vacation in Europe. Well, I've seen France and Italy now, but I really feel more at home in England than anywhere. I do love England. Of course our family was English, way back of course, and I feel that roots are important, don't you?

ANNA: Miss Stevens, what did you come to see me for?

JANET: Dave always says he thinks women should have careers. I suppose that's why he admires you so much. Though of course, you do wear well. But I say to him, Dave, if you *work* at marriage then it *is* a career . . . sometimes he makes fun because I took domestic science and home care and child care as my subjects in college, but I say to him, Dave, marriage is important, Dave, I believe that marriage and the family is the most rewarding career a woman can have, that's why I took home care as my first subject because I believe a healthy and well-adjusted marriage is the basis for a healthy nation.

ANNA: You're making me feel deficient in patriotism.

JANET: Oh, Dave said that too . . . (*She almost breaks down, pulls herself together: Fiercely*) You're patronizing me. I don't think you should patronize me.

ANNA: Miss Stevens, do let's stop this. Listen to me. I haven't seen Dave for weeks. Is that what you came here to find out?

JANET: I know that you are such old friends. He talks about you a great deal.

ANNA: I've no doubt he does. (*She waits for* JANET *to go on, then goes on herself*) There's a hoary psychological joke – if I can use the word joke for a situation like this – about the way the betrayed women of the heartless libertine get together to lick their wounds – have you come here to make common cause with me over Dave? Because forgive me for saying so, but I don't think you and I have anything in common but the fact we've both slept with Dave. And that is not enough for the basis of a beautiful friendship.

JANET: No! It wasn't that at all, I came because . . . (*she stops.*)

ANNA: I see. Then you've come because you're pregnant. Well, how far have you got?

JANET: Five months.

ANNA: I see. And you haven't told him.

JANET: I knew if I told him he'd give me money and . . . well I love him. It would be good for him to have some responsibility wouldn't it?

ANNA: I see.

JANET: Yes, I know how it looks, trapping a man. But when I was pregnant I was so happy, and only afterwards I thought – yes, I know how it looks, trapping a man, but he said he loved me, he said he loved me.

ANNA: But why come and tell me? (*As* JANET *doesn't answer*) He's ditched you, is that it?

JANET: No! Of course he hasn't. (*Cracking*) I haven't seen him in days. I haven't seen him. Where is he, you've got to tell me where he is. I've got to tell him about the baby.

ANNA: But I don't know where he is.

JANET: You have to tell me. When he knows about the baby he'll . . . (*As* ANNA *shrugs*) Ah come on now, who do you think you're kidding. Well, I've got his baby, you haven't. You can't do anything about that, can you. I've got his baby, I've got him.

ANNA: Very likely.

JANET: But what can I do? I want to be married. I'm just an ordinary girl and I want to be married, what's wrong with that?

ANNA: There's nothing wrong with that. But I haven't seen Dave, and I don't know where he is, and so there's nothing I can do. (*Finally*) And you shouldn't have come to me.

(JANET *goes out.*)

ANNA (*almost in tears*): Oh Christ. (*Stopping the tears, angrily*) Damn. Damn.

(*She goes to window. At once* MARY *comes in.*)

MARY: Well, who was she? (ANNA *turns her back to hide her face from* MARY) Was she one of Dave's girls? (ANNA *nods.* MARY *moves so that she can see* ANNA'S *face*) Well, you knew there was one, didn't you? (ANNA *nods*) Well, then? (ANNA *nods.*)

ANNA: All right, Mary.

(MARY *is in a jubilant mood. She has been flirting with* HARRY. *Now, seeing* ANNA *is apparently all right, she says what she came in to say.*)

MARY: Harry and I are going out. There's a place he knows we can get drinks. I told him you wouldn't be interested. (*The telephone starts ringing*) Aren't you going to answer it? (*As* ANNA *shakes her head*) Odd, we've known each other all these years. He's really sweet, Harry. You can say what you like, but it's nice to have a man to talk to for a change – after all, how many men are there you can really talk to? (*The telephone stops*) Anna, what are you in this state for?

ANNA: What I can't stand is, the way he makes use of me. Do you know, Mary, all this time he's been letting her know I'm in the background?

MARY: Well, you are, aren't you?

ANNA: 'But Janet, you must understand this doesn't mean anything, because the woman I really love is Anna.' He's not even married to me, but he uses me as Harry uses Helen.

316

MARY (*not wanting to hear anything against* HARRY *at this moment*): Oh I don't know. After all, perhaps Helen doesn't mind. They've been married so long.

ANNA: It really is remarkable how all Dave's young ladies turn up here sooner or later. He talks about me — oh, quite casually, of course, until they go round the bend with frustration and curiosity, and they just have to come up to see what the enemy looks like. Well, I can't be such a bitch as all that, because I didn't say, 'My dear Miss Stevens, you're the fifth to pay me a social call in three years.'

MARY: But you have been engaged to Tom.

ANNA: Yes. All right.

MARY: It's funny, me and Harry knowing each other for so long and then suddenly . . .

ANNA: Mary! the mood Harry's in somebody's going to get hurt.

MARY: It's better to get hurt than to live shut up.

ANNA: After losing that little poppet of his to matrimony he'll be looking for solace.

MARY (*offended*): Why don't you concern yourself with Tom? Or with Dave? Harry's not your affair. I'm just going out with him. (*As she goes out*) Nice to have a night out for a change, say what you like.

> (*The telephone rings.* ANNA *snatches off the receiver, wraps it in a blanket, throws it on the bed.*)

ANNA: I'm not talking to you, Dave Miller, you can rot first.

> (*She goes to the record player, puts on Mahalia Jackson's 'I'm on my Way', goes to mirror, looks into it. This is a long antagonistic look.*)

ANNA (*to her reflection*): All right then, I do wear well.

> (*She goes deliberately to a drawer, takes out a large piece of black cloth, unfolds it, drapes it over mirror.*)

ANNA (*to the black cloth*): And a fat lot of good that does me.

> (*She now switches out the light. The room is tall, shadowy, with two patterns of light from the paraffin*)

heaters reflected on the ceiling. She goes to the window, flings it up.)

ANNA (*to the man on the pavement*): You poor fool, why don't you go upstairs, the worst that can happen is that the door will be shut in your face.

(*A knock on the door – a confident knock.*)

ANNA: If you come in here, Dave Miller . . .

(*DAVE comes in. He is crew cut, wears a sloppy sweater and jeans. Carries a small duffle-bag. ANNA turns her back and looks out of the window. DAVE stops the record player. He puts the telephone receiver back on the rest. Turns on the light.*)

DAVE: Why didn't you answer the telephone?

ANNA: Because I have nothing to say.

DAVE (*in a parody of an English upper-middle-class voice*): I see no point at all in discussing it.

ANNA (*in the same voice*): I see no point at all in discussing it.

(*DAVE stands beside ANNA at the window.*)

DAVE (*in the easy voice of their intimacy*): I've been in the telephone box around the corner ringing you.

ANNA: Did you see my visitor?

DAVE: No.

ANNA: What a pity.

DAVE: I've been standing in the telephone box ringing you and watching that poor bastard on the pavement.

ANNA: He's there every night. He comes on his great black dangerous motor bike. He wears a black leather jacket and big black boots. He looks like an outrider for death in a Cocteau film – and he has the face of a frightened little boy.

DAVE: It's lurve, it's lurve, it's lurve.

ANNA: It's love.

(*Now they stare at each other, antagonists, and neither gives way. DAVE suddenly grins and does a mocking little dance step. He stands grinning at her. ANNA hits him as hard as she can. He staggers. He goes to the*

318

other side of the carpet, where he sits cross-legged, his
face in his hands.)

DAVE: Jesus, Anna.

ANNA (*mocking*): Oh, quite so.

DAVE: You still love me, that's something.

ANNA: It's lurve, it's lurve, it's lurve.

DAVE: Yes. I had a friend once. He cheated on his wife,
he came in and she laid his cheek open with the flat-iron.

ANNA (*quoting him*): 'That I can understand' – a great
country, America.

DAVE (*in appeal*): Anna.

ANNA: No.

DAVE: I've been so lonely for you.

ANNA: Where have you been the last week?

DAVE (*suspicious*): Why the last *week*?

ANNA: I'm interested.

DAVE: Why the last week? (*A pause*) Ringing you and
getting no reply.

ANNA: Why ringing *me*?

DAVE: Who else? Anna, I will not be treated like this.

ANNA: Then, go away.

DAVE: We've been through this before. Can't we get it
over quickly.

ANNA: No.

DAVE: Come and sit down. And turn out the lights.

ANNA: No.

DAVE: I didn't know it was as bad as that this time.

ANNA: How long did you think you could go on – you
think you can make havoc as you like, and nothing to pay
for it, ever?

DAVE: Pay? What for? You've got it all wrong, as usual.

ANNA: I'm not discussing it then.

DAVE: 'I'm not discussing it.' Well, I'm saying nothing
to you while you've got your bloody middle-class English
act on, it drives me mad.

ANNA: Middle-class English. I'm Australian.

DAVE: You've assimilated so well.

ANNA (*in an Australian accent*): I'll say it like this then —
I'll say it any way you like — I'm not discussing it. I'm discussing nothing with you when you're in your role of tuppence a dozen street corner Romeo. (*In English*) It's the same in any accent.

DAVE (*getting up and doing his blithe dance step*): It's the same in any accent. (*Sitting down again*) Baby, you've got it wrong. (ANNA *laughs*) I tell you, you've got it wrong, baby.

ANNA (*in American*): But baby, it doesn't mean anything, let's have a little fun together, baby, just you and me — just a little fun, baby . . . (*In Australian*) Ah, damn your guts, you stupid, irresponsible little . . . (*In English*) Baby, baby, baby — the anonymous baby. Every woman is baby, for fear you'd whisper the wrong name into the wrong ear in the dark.

DAVE: In the dark with you I use your name, Anna.

ANNA: You *used* my name.

DAVE: Ah, hell, man, well. Anna, beat me up and be done with it and get it over. (*A pause*) O.K., I know it. I don't know what gets into me: O.K. I'm still a twelve-year-old slum kid standing on a street corner in Chicago, watching the expensive broads go by and wishing I had the dough to buy them all. O.K., I know it. You know it. (*A pause*) O.K. and I'm an American God help me, and it's no secret to the world that there's bad man-woman trouble in America. (*A pause*) And everywhere else, if it comes to that. O.K., I do my best. But how any man can be faithful to one woman beats me. O.K., so one day I'll grow up. Maybe.

ANNA: Maybe.

DAVE (*switching to black aggression*): God, how I hate your smug female guts. All of you — there's never anything free — everything to be paid for. Every time, an account rendered. Every time, when you're swinging free there's a moment when the check lies on the table — pay up, pay up, baby.

ANNA: Have you come here to get on to one of your anti-woman kicks?

DAVE: Well, I'm not being any woman's pet, and that's what you all want. (*Leaping up and doing his mocking dance-step*) I've kept out of all the traps so far, and I'm going to keep out.

ANNA: So you've kept out of all the traps.

DAVE: That's right. And I'm not going to stand for you either — mother of the world, the great womb, the eternal conscience. I like women, but I'm going to like them my way and not according to the rules laid down by the incorporated mothers of the universe.

ANNA: Stop it, stop it, stop boasting.

DAVE: But Anna, you're as bad. There's always a moment when you become a sort of flaming sword of retribution.

ANNA: At which moment — have you asked yourself? You and I are so close we know everything about each other — and then suddenly, out of the clear blue sky, you start telling me lies like — lies out of a corner-boy's jest book. I can't stand it.

DAVE (*shouting at her*): Lies — I never tell you lies.

ANNA: Oh hell, Dave.

DAVE: Well, you're not going to be my conscience. I will not let you be my conscience.

ANNA: Amen and hear hear. But why do you make me your conscience?

DAVE (*deflating*): I don't know. (*With grim humour*) I'm an American. I'm in thrall to the great mother.

ANNA: Well, I'm not an American.

DAVE (*shouting*): No, but you're a woman, and at bottom you're the same as the whole lousy lot of . . .

ANNA: Get out of here then. Get out.

DAVE (*he sits cross-legged, on the edge of the carpet, his head in his hands*): Jesus.

ANNA: You're feeling guilty so you beat me up. I won't let you.

DAVE: Come here.

(ANNA *goes to him, kneels opposite him, lays her two*
hands on his diaphragm.)
Yes, like that. (*He suddenly relaxes, head back, eyes closed*)
Anna, when I'm away from you I'm cut off from something – I don't know what it is. When you put your hands
on me, I begin to breathe.

ANNA: Oh. (*She lets her hands drop and stands up.*)

DAVE: Where are you going?

    (ANNA *goes back to the window. A silence. A wolf-*
    whistle from the street. Another.)

ANNA: He's broken his silence. He's calling her. Deep
calls to deep.

    (*Another whistle.* ANNA *winces.*)

DAVE: You've missed me?

ANNA: All the time.

DAVE: What have you been doing?

ANNA: Working a little.

DAVE: What else?

ANNA: I said I'd marry Tom, then I said I wouldn't.

DAVE (*dismissing it*): I should think not.

ANNA (*furious*): O-h-h-h.

DAVE: Seriously, what?

ANNA: I've been coping with Mary – her son's marrying.

DAVE (*heartily*): Good for him. Well, it's about time.

ANNA: Oh quite so.

DAVE (*mimicking her*): Oh quite so.

ANNA (*dead angry*): I've also spent hours of every day
with Helen, Harry's ever-loving wife.

DAVE: Harry's my favourite person in London.

ANNA: And you are his. Strange, isn't it?

DAVE: We understand each other.

ANNA: And Helen and I understand each other.

DAVE (*hastily*): Now, Anna.

ANNA: Helen's cracking up. Do you know what Harry
did? He came to her, because he knew this girl of his was
thinking of getting married, and he said: Helen, you know
I love you, but I can't live without her. He suggested they

should all live together in the same house — he, Helen and his girl. Regularizing things, he called it.

DAVE (*deliberately provocative*): Yeah? Sounds very attractive to me.

ANNA: Yes, I thought it might. Helen said to him — who's going to share your bed? Harry said, well, obviously they couldn't all sleep in the same bed, but . . .

DAVE: Anna, stop it.

ANNA: Helen said it was just possible that the children might be upset by the arrangement.

DAVE: I was waiting for that — the trump card — you can't do that, it might upset the kiddies. Well, not for me, I'm out.

ANNA (*laughing*): Oh are you?

DAVE: Yes. (ANNA *laughs*) Have you finished?

ANNA: No. Harry and Helen. Helen said she was going to leave him. Harry said: 'But darling, you're too old to get another man now and . . .'

DAVE (*mocking*): 'Women always have to pay' — and may it long remain that way.

ANNA: Admittedly there's one advantage to men like you and Harry. You are honest.

DAVE: Anna, listen, whenever I cheat on you it takes you about two weeks to settle into a good temper again. Couldn't we just speed it up and get it over with?

ANNA: Get it over with. (*She laughs.*)

DAVE: The laugh is new. What's so funny?

(*A wolf-whistle from the street. Then a sound like a wolf howling.* ANNA *slams the window up.*)

DAVE: Open that window.

ANNA: No, I can't stand it.

DAVE: Anna, I will not have you shutting yourself up. I won't have you spitting out venom and getting all bitter and vengeful. Open that window.

(ANNA *opens it. Stands by it, passive.*)
Come and sit down. And turn the lights out.

(*As she does not move, he turns out the light. The*

room as before: two patterned circles of light on the ceiling from the paraffin lamps.)

ANNA: Dave, it's no point starting all over again.

DAVE: But baby, you and I will always be together, one way or another.

ANNA: You're crazy.

DAVE: In a good cause. (*He sits cross-legged on the edge of the carpet and waits*) Come and sit. (ANNA *slowly sits opposite him. He smiles at her. She slowly smiles back. As she smiles, the walls fade out. They are two small people in the city, the big, ugly, baleful city all around them, over-shadowing them.*)

DAVE: There baby, that's better.

ANNA: O.K.

DAVE: I don't care what you do – you can crack up if you like, or you can turn Lesbian. You can take to drink. You can even get married. But I won't have you shutting yourself up.

(*A lorry roars. A long wolf whistle. Shrill female voices from the street.*)

ANNA: Those girls opposite quarrel. I hate it. Last night they were rolling in the street and pulling each other's hair and screaming.

DAVE: O.K. But you're not to shut it out. You're not to shut anything out.

ANNA: I'll try.

(*She very slowly gets to her feet, stands concentrating.*)

DAVE: That's right. Now, who are you?

END OF ACT I

ACT II

ANNA *and* DAVE, *in the same positions as at the end of Act I. No time has passed. The lights are out. The walls seem to have vanished, so that the room seems part of the street. There is a silence. A lorry roars.*

DAVE: Who are you?

ANNA (*in English*): Anna Freeman.

DAVE: O.K. Go, then.

(*A silence.*)

ANNA: I can't. I'm all in pieces.

DAVE: Then go back. Who are you now?

ANNA (*she slowly stands up, at the edge of the carpet*): Anna.

DAVE: Anna who?

ANNA (*in Australian*): Anna MacClure from Brisbane. (*In English*) The trouble is, she gets further and further away. She's someone else. I know if she goes altogether then I'm done for. (*A pause. In Australian*) The smell of petrol. In a broken-down old jalopy – six of us. It's night. There's a great shining moon. We've been dancing. I'm with Jack. We've stopped at the edge of the road by a petrol pump. All the others are singing and shouting and the petrol pump attendant's angry as a cross cat. Jack says, 'Anna, let's get married.' (*Speaking to* JACK) 'No, Jack, what's all this about getting married. I want to live, Jack, I want to travel, I want to see the world. . . . Yes, I know, but I don't want kids yet. I don't want . . .' (*To* DAVE) He says, 'Anna, you'll be unhappy. I feel it in my bones, you'll be unhappy.' (*She talks back to* JACK) 'I don't care, I tell you. I know if I marry you, you'll be for the rest of my life. You aren't the world, Jack . . . All right, then I'll be un-

happy. But I want a choice. Don't you see, I want a choice.'
(*She crouches down, her hands over her face*) Let's have
the lights, Dave.

DAVE: Wait. Go back some more – that's not Anna Mac-
Clure the Australian. That's Anna MacClure who's already half in Europe.

ANNA: But it's so hard.

DAVE: Breathe slowly and go. Who are you?

ANNA (*slowly standing. In a child's voice, Australian*):
Anna MacClure.

DAVE: Where?

ANNA: On the porch of our house. I've quarrelled with
my mother. (*She stands talking to her mother*) I'm not
going to be like you, ma, I'm not, I'm not. You're stuck
here, you never think of anything but me and my brother
and the house. You're old, ma, you're stupid. (*Listening
while her mother lectures her*) Yah, I don't care. When I
grow up I'm never going to be married, I'm not going to
get old and dull. I'm going to live with my brother on an
island and swim and catch fish and . . . (*She sings*) The
moon is in my windowpane, the moon is in my bed, I'll race
the moon across the sky and eat it for my bread. I don't care,
ma, I don't care . . . (*She dances a blithe, defiant dance. In
English*) Dave, Dave, did you see? That was just like you.

(DAVE *gets up and does his blithe defiant dance beside
her on the carpet. He mocks her.* ANNA, *furious, leaps
over and smacks him.*)

ANNA: 'There, stupid child, you're wicked and stupid,
you're not going to defy me, so you think you'll defy
me . . .'

(*They both at the same moment crouch down in
their former positions on either side of the carpet.*)

ANNA: Let me have the light on now, please Dave.

(DAVE *switches it on, the room becomes the room
again.* DAVE *returns to where he was.*)

DAVE (*patting the carpet beside him*): Anna.

ANNA: No.

DAVE: Let me love you.

ANNA: No.

DAVE (*laughing and confident*): You will, Anna, so why not now.

ANNA: You'll never love me again, never, never, never.

DAVE (*suddenly scared*): Why not? Why not?

ANNA: You know why.

DAVE: I swear I don't.

ANNA: What am I going to be without you, what shall I do?

DAVE: But Baby, I'm here.

ANNA: And what are you going to do with Janet?

DAVE: Janet?

ANNA: Janet Stevens, from Philadelphia.

DAVE: What about her?

ANNA: You don't know her, of course.

DAVE: She's a friend of mine, that's all.

ANNA: Do you know, Dave, if I walked into your room and found you in bed with a girl and said Dave, who is that girl, you'd say what girl? I don't see any girl, it's just your sordid imagination.

DAVE: Some time you've got to learn to trust me.

ANNA: What you mean by trust is, you tell me some bloody silly lie and I just nod my head and smile.

DAVE (*inside the wild man*): That's right, baby, you should just nod your head and smile.

ANNA: You mean, it's got nothing to do with me.

DAVE: That's right, it's got nothing to do with you.

(ANNA *withdraws from him into herself*.)

DAVE: Ah, hell, Anna, she means nothing to me.

ANNA: Then it's terrible.

(*A pause.*)

DAVE: I don't understand why I do the things I do. I go moseying along, paying my way and liking myself pretty well, then I'm sounding off like something, and people start looking at me in a certain way, and I think, Hey, man is that you? Is that you there, Dave Miller? He's taken over again, the wild man, the mad man. And I even stand on one side and watch, pretty awed when you come to think of it. Yes, awed, that's the word. You should be awed too, Anna, instead of getting scared. I can't stand it when you're scared of me.

ANNA: I simply want to run out of the way.

DAVE: The way of what? Go on, tell, I want to know.

ANNA: I want to hide from the flick-knives, from the tomahawks.

DAVE (*with a loud, cruel laugh – he is momentarily inside the wild man*): Jesus. Bloody Englishwoman, middle-class lady, that's what you are. (*Mimicking her*) Flick-knives and tomahawks – how refined.

ANNA (*in the voice of* ANNA MacCLURE): Dave, man, stand up and let it go, let it go.

> (DAVE *slowly stands. He switches off the light – the walls vanish, the city comes up. Back on the carpet, stands relaxed.*)

ANNA: Who are you?

DAVE: Dave Miller, the boss of the gang, South Street, Al Capone's territory . . . Chicago.

ANNA: What's your name?

DAVE: Dave Miller.

ANNA: No, in your fantasy.

DAVE: Baby Face Nelson. No, but the way I dreamed him up, he was a sort of Robin Hood, stealing from the rich to give to the poor.

ANNA: Oh, don't be so childish.

DAVE: That was the point of this exercise I thought.

ANNA: Sorry. Go ahead.

DAVE: I'm fifteen years old. I'm wearing a sharp hat, such a sweet sharp hat – pork-pie, cleft in the middle, set on one side. The hat is in dark green. My jacket is two yards wide across the shoulders, nipped in at the waist, and skirted. In a fine, sweet cinnamon brown. Trousers in forest green, very fancy. My shirt is the finest money can buy, one dollar fifty, at Holy Moses Cut Price Emporium. In deciduous mauve. My

tie is orange and black in lightning stripes. I wear vel-
veteen spats, buttoned sweetly up the side, in hearth-rug
white. I have a key-chain with a key on it, probably about
six feet long, which could sweep the pavement if it hung
free, but it never does, because we stand, lounging on the
street corner, our home, men of the world, twirling the
chain between our fingers, hour after hour through the
afternoons and evenings. That year I'm a shoe-shine boy, a
news-boy and a drug-store assistant. But my life, my real
sweet life is on the pavement. (*Speaking to someone*) Jedd,
see that broad? (*Waits for an answer*) Gee, some dish, bet
she's hot. (*Waits again*) See that dame there, Jesus Christ.
(*He wolf-whistles*.)

> (ANNA *swanks, bottom wagging in front of him. DAVE
> whistles after her. He is echoed by a wolf-whistle from
> the street. ANNA wheels at the window to shut it*.)

DAVE: I told you, keep it open.

> (ANNA *returns, squatting on the edge of the carpet*.)

DAVE: Jesus, Anna, when I think of that kid, of all us
kids, it makes me want to cry.

ANNA: Then cry.

DAVE: The year of our Lord, 1936, all our parents out of
work, and World War II on top of us and we didn't know it.

ANNA: Did you carry a knife?

DAVE: We all did.

ANNA: Ever use it?

DAVE: Hell no, I told you, we were fine idealistic kids.
That was my anarchist period. We stood twirling our key-
chains on the corner of the street, eyeing the broads and I
quoted great chunks of Kropotkin to the guys. Anyone who
joined my gang had to be an anarchist. When I had my
socialist period, they had to be socialists.

ANNA: Go on.

DAVE: Isn't it enough?

ANNA: I'm waiting for the tomahawk. You're seven
years old and you scalp all the nasty adults who don't understand you.

DAVE: O.K. I was a red Indian nine-tenths of my child-hood. O.K. (*In his parody of an English upper-class accent*) There is no point whatever in discussing it . . . O.K. Some-where in my psyche is a tomahawk-twirling Red Indian . . . Anna? Do you know what's wrong with America?

ANNA: Yes.

DAVE: At the street corners now the kids are not prepared to fight the world. They fight each other. Everyone of us, we were prepared to take on the whole world single-handed. Not any longer, they know better, they're scared. A healthy country has kids, every John Doe of them knowing he can lick the whole world, single-handed. Not any more.

ANNA: I know.

DAVE: You know. But you're scared to talk. Everyone knows but they're scared to talk. There's a great dream dead in America. You look at us and see prosperity — and loneliness. Prosperity and men and women in trouble with each other. Prosperity and people wondering what life is for. Prosperity — and conformity. You look at us and you know it's your turn now. We've pioneered the golden road for you . . .

ANNA: Who are you lecturing, Anna MacClure?

DAVE: O.K., O.K., O.K. (*He flops face down on the carpet.*)

(ANNA *puts her arms around his shoulders.*)

DAVE: If you think I'm any safer to touch when I'm flat than when I'm mobile you're wrong. (*He tries to pull her down. She pulls away*) O.K. (*Pause*) Did I tell you I went to a psycho-analyst? Yeah, I'm a good American after all, I went to a psycho-analyst.

ANNA (*mocking him*): Do tell me about your psycho-analysis.

DAVE: Yeah, now I refer, throwing it away, to 'when I was under psycho-analysis'.

ANNA: The way you refer, throwing it away, to 'when I was a car salesman', which you were for a week.

DAVE: Why do you always have to cut me down to size?

ANNA : So, how many times did you go?

DAVE : Twice.

(ANNA *laughs*.)

The first interview was already not a success. Now, doc, I said, I have no wish to discuss my childhood. There is no point whatever in discussing it. I want to know how to live my life, doc. I don't want you to sit there, nodding while I talk. I want your advice, I said. After all, doc, I said, you're an educated man, Eton and Oxford, so you told me – throwing it away, of course. So pass on the message, doc, pass it on.

(ANNA *rolls on the carpet, laughing*.)

It was no laughing matter. I talked for one hour by the clock, begging and pleading for the favour of one constructive word from him. But he merely sat like this, and then he said: 'I'll see you next Thursday, at five o'clock precisely.' I said, it was no laughing matter – For a whole week I was in a trance, waiting for the ultimate revelation – you know how we all live, waiting for that revelation? Then I danced up to his room and lay on to his couch and lay waiting. He said not a word. Finally I said don't think I'm resisting you, doc, please don't think it. Talk doc, I said. Give. Let yourself go. Then the hour was nearly up. I may say, I'd given him a thumbnail sketch of my life previously. He spoke at last: 'Tell me, Mr Miller, how many jobs did you say you had had?' My God, doc, I said, nearly falling over myself in my eagerness to oblige, if I knew, I'd tell you. 'You would admit,' he said at last, 'that the pattern of your life shows, ho, hum, ha, a certain instability?' My God, yes, doc, I said, panting at his feet, that's it, you're on to it, hold fast to it doc, that's the word, instability. Now give, doc, give. Tell me, why is it that a fine upstanding American boy like me, with all the advantages our rich country gives its citizens, why should I be in such trouble. And why should so many of us be in such trouble – I'm not an American for nothing, I'm socially minded, doc. Why are there so many of us in such trouble. Tell me, doc. Give. And why should you, Dr Melville Cooper-Anstey, citizen of England, be sitting in that chair, in a position to dish out advice and comfort? Of course I know that you got all wrapped up in this thing because you, uh, kind of like people, doc, but after all, to kinda like people, doc, puts you in a pretty privileged class for a start — so few citizens can afford to really kinda like people. So tell me doc, tell me . . .

ANNA: Well, don't shout at me, I'm not Doctor Melville Cooper-Anstey.

DAVE: You listen just like him — judging. In possession of some truth that's denied to me.

ANNA: I've always got to be the enemy. You've got to have an enemy . . .

DAVE: You're right. I've got to have an enemy. Why not? I'm not going to love my brother as myself if he's not worth it. Nor my sister, if it comes to that — where was I?

ANNA: Kinda liking people.

DAVE: There was a sort of thoughtful pause. I waited, biting my nails. Then he said, or drawled, 'Tell me, just at random now, is there any thing or event or happening that has seemed to you significant. Just to give us something to get our teeth into, Mr Miller?' Well, doc, I said, just at random, and picking a significant moment from a life full of significant moments, and on principle at that — latch on to that, doc, it's important in our case, that my life has been uninterruptedly full of significant moments . . . but has yours, doc? I want to know? We should talk as equals, doc, has your life been as full as mine of significant moments?

ANNA: Dave, stop boasting.

DAVE: Hell, Anna. If you love me, it's because I lived that way. Well? And so. But to pull just one little cat or kitten out of the bag, doc, I would say it was the moment I woke beside a waitress in Minnesota, and she said to me in her sweet measured voice: 'Honey, you're nuts. Did you know that?' . . . Well, to tell the truth no, I hadn't known it. Light flooded in on me. I've been living with it ever since. And so. I was all fixed up to see one of your opposite numbers in the States, my great country, that was in L.A., Cali-

fornia, where I happened to be at the time, writing scripts
for our film industry. Then I heard he was a stool pigeon
for the FBI. No, don't look like that, doc, don't — very
distasteful, I'll admit, but the world's a rough place. Half
his patients were int-ell-ectuals, and Reds and Pinks, since
intellectuals so often tend to be, and after every couch session,
he was moseying off to the FBI with information. Now,
doc, here's an American and essentially socially-minded, I
want an answer, in this great country, England, I can come
to you with perfect confidence that you won't go trotting
off to MI5, to inform them that during my communist
period I was a communist. That is, before I was expelled
from that institution for hinting that Stalin had his weak
moments. I tend to shoot off my mouth, doc. A weakness, I
know, but I know that you won't, and that gives me a
profound feeling of security.

ANNA: Dave, you're nuts.

DAVE: So said the waitress in Minnesota. Say it often
enough and I'll believe it.

ANNA: So what did Doctor Cooper-Anstey say?

DAVE: He lightly, oh so lightly, touched his fingertips
together, and he drawled: 'Tell me, Mr Miller, how many
women have you had?'

(ANNA *laughs*.)

DAVE: Hey doc, I said, I was talking seriously. I was talking about the comparative states of liberty in my country
and in yours. He said: 'Mr Miller, don't evade my question.'

(ANNA *laughs*.)

DAVE: O.K. doc, if you're going to be a small-minded . . .
but let's leave the statistics, doc. I'm pretty well schooled in
this psycho-analysis bit, I said, all my fine stable well integrated friends have been through your mill. And so I know
that if I pulled out a notebook full of statistics, you'd think
I was pretty sick — you may think it careless of me, doc, but
I don't know how many women I've had. 'But Mr Miller,'
he drawled, 'you must have some idea?' Well, at this point
I see that this particular morale-builder is not for me. Tell

me, Dr Melville Cooper-Anstey, I said, how many women have *you* had?

(ANNA *rolls, laughing.*)

DAVE: Hey, Anna, this is serious, girl. A serious matter . . . hey, ho, was he mad, was Dr Melville Cooper-Anstey sore. He sat himself up to his full height, and he told me in tones of severe displeasure, that I was an adolescent. Yeah, doc, I said, we Americans are all children, we're all adolescent, we know that. But I wanted to know — how many women have you had, doc? Because we have to talk man to man, doc, adolescent or not. There's got to be some sort of equality around this place, I said. After all, I said, one woman is not like another, doc, believe me, if you've slept with one woman you've not slept with them all and don't you think it. And besides, doc, I said, you're an Englishman. That is not without relevance. Because, judging from my researches into this field, Englishmen don't like women very much. So Englishwomen complain. So they murmur in the dark night watches with their arms gratefully around the stranger's neck. Now I like women, doc, I like them. The point is, do you? He laughed. Like this: (DAVE *gives a high whinnying laugh*) But I persisted. I said, doc, do you like your wife? And what is more important, does she like you? Does she, doc? And so.

ANNA: And so?

DAVE: And so he kicked me out, with all the dignity an upper-class Englishman brings to such matters. In tones frozen with good taste, he said, 'Mr Miller, you know how to find your own way out, I think.'

ANNA: It's all very well.

DAVE (*mimicking her*): It's all very well, don't freeze up on me, Anna, I won't have it. (*A pause*) Anna, he did vouchsafe me with two little bits of information from the heights of integration. One. He said I couldn't go on like this. I said, that's right, that's why I've come to you. And two. He said I should get married, have two well-spaced children and a settled job. Ah, doc, now you're at the hub of the thing. What job, I said? Because I'll let you into a secret. What's wrong with all of us is not that our mummies and daddies weren't nice to us it's that we don't believe the work we do is important. Oh, I know I'm earnest, doc, I'm pompous and earnest – but I need work that makes me feel I'm contributing. So doc, give – I'm a man of a hundred talents, none of them outstanding. But I have one thing, doc, just one important thing – if I spend eight hours a day working, I need to know that men, women and children are benefiting by my work. So . . . What job shall I do? Tell me.

ANNA: So?

DAVE: He said I should get any job that would enable me to keep a wife and two children, and in this way I would be integrated into society. (*He flings himself down on the carpet*) Anna, for God's sake, Anna.

ANNA: Don't ask me.

DAVE: Why not? I can't ask Dr Anstey. Because the significant moment I keep coming back to he wouldn't see at all. I drove right across the States, looking up all my friends, the kids who'd been world-challengers with me. They were all married. Some of them were divorced, of course, but that's merely an incident in the process of being married. They all had houses, cars, jobs, families. They were not pleased to see me – they knew I was still unintegrated. I asked each one a simple question. Hey, man, I said, this great country of ours, it's in no too healthy a state. What are we going to do about it? And do you know what they said?

ANNA: Don't rock the boat.

DAVE: You've got it in one, kid. But I had one ace up my sleeve. There was my old buddy, Jedd. He'll still be right in there, fighting. So I walked into his apartment where he was sitting with his brand new second wife. There was a nervous silence. Then he said: 'Are you successful yet, Dave?' And so I took the first boat over.

ANNA: And the wife and the two well-spaced kids?

DAVE: You know I can't get married. You know that if I

335

could I'd marry you. And perhaps I should marry you. How about it?

ANNA: No. The wedding would be the last I'd see of you – you'd be off across the world like a dog with a firecracker tied to its tail.

DAVE: I know. So I can't get married. (*A pause*) Why don't you just trap me into it? Perhaps I need simply to be tied down?

ANNA: No.

DAVE: Why not?

ANNA: Any man I have stays with me, voluntarily, because he wants to, without ties.

DAVE: Your bloody pride is more important to you than what I need.

ANNA: Don't beat me up.

DAVE: I will if I want. You're my woman so if I feel like beating you up I will. And you can fight back . . . Anna, what are you being enigmatic about? All the time, there's something in the air, that's not being said. What is it?

ANNA: Not being said, I keep trying. Don't you really know?

DAVE (*in a panic*): No. What?

ANNA: If I told you, you'd say I was just imagining it. All right, I'll try again, Janet Stevens.

DAVE (*furious*): You're a monomaniac. Janet Stevens. Do you imagine that a nice little middle-class girl, whose poppa's sort of sub-manager for an insurance company, do you imagine she can mean anything to me?

ANNA: Oh my God, Dave.

DAVE: You're crazy. It's you that's crazy.

ANNA: Dave, while you're banging and crashing about the world, playing this role and that role, filling your life full of significant moments—there are other people in the world . . . hell, what's the use of talking to you. (*A pause*) As a matter of interest, and this is a purely abstract question, suppose you married Janet Stevens, what would you have to do?

DAVE: Anna, are you crazy? Can you see me? God help me, I'm a member of that ever-increasing and honourable company, the world's ex-patriates. Like you, Anna.

ANNA: Oh, all right.

DAVE: How the hell could I marry her? She wouldn't understand a word I ever said, for a start.

ANNA: Oh, all *right*.

DAVE: 'There's no point at all in discussing it.'

ANNA: None at all.

DAVE: I said to Dr Melville Cooper-Anstey: This society you want me to be integrated with, do you approve of it? If you don't, what are you doing, sitting there with those big black scissors cutting people into shapes to fit it? Well, doc, I'll tell you something, I don't approve of society, it stinks. I don't want to fit into it, I want society to fit itself to me— I'll make a deal with you, doc, I'll come and lie on this comfortable couch of yours, Tuesdays and Fridays from 2 to 3 for seven years, on condition that at the end of that time society is a place fit for Dave Miller to live in. How's that for a proposition, doc? Because of course that means you'll have to join the Dave Miller fraternity for changing the world. You join my organization and I'll join yours. (*He turns on* ANNA) Hey, Anna, don't just lie there, reserving judgment.

ANNA: I didn't say a word.

DAVE: You never have to. You're like Doctor Melville Cooper-Anstey – you put your spiritual finger-tips together and purse your lips.

ANNA (*furious*): Dave, do you know something—when you need an enemy, you turn me into a kind of – lady welfare worker. Who was the great enemy of your childhood? The lady welfare worker. (*Jumping up – in Australian*) I'm Anna MacClure the daughter of a second-hand car dealer. My grand-father was a horse-doctor. My great-grand-father was a stock farmer. And my great-great-grand-father was a convict, shipped from this our mother country God bless her to populate the outback. I'm the great-great-grand-daughter of a convict, I'm the aristocracy so don't get at me, Dave

Miller, corner-boy, street-gang-leader – I'm as good as you are, any day. (*He pulls her down on to the carpet, she pushes his hands away*) No. I told you, no.

DAVE (*swinging her round to sit by him. His arms round her*): O.K. then baby, we don't have to make love. Like hell we don't. O.K. sit quiet and hold my hand. Do you love me, Anna?

ANNA: Love you? You are me. (*Mocking*) You are the flame, the promise and the enchantment. You are for me – what Janet Stevens is for you. (*She laughs*) Imagine it, Dave Miller, for you the flame is embodied in a succession of well-conducted young ladies, each one more banal than the last. For me – it's you. (*Suddenly serious*) You are my soul.

DAVE (*holding her down beside him*): If I'm your soul, then surely it's in order to sit beside me?

(*They sit, arms round each other,* ANNA's *head on his shoulder.*)

ANNA: I only breathe freely when I'm with you.

DAVE (*complacent*): I know.

ANNA (*furious*): What do you mean? I was on the point of getting married.

DAVE: Don't be absurd.

ANNA: What's going to become of us?

DAVE: Perhaps I shall go back to Doctor Melville Cooper-Anstey – like hell.

ANNA: It's not fair to take it out of Dr Melville Cooper-Anstey just because he isn't God.

DAVE: Of course it's fair. If God wasn't dead I wouldn't be going to Dr Melville Cooper-Anstey. Perhaps I should wrestle with him – after all, these people have what's the word?

ANNA: Stability.

DAVE: You were born with one skin more than I have.

ANNA (*mocking*): But *I* come from a stable home.

DAVE: Doctor Melville Cooper-Anstey said to me: 'Mr Miller, your trouble is, you come from a broken home.' But doc, I said, my home wasn't broken – my parents were both

338

union organizers. He winced. A look of distaste settled around his long sensitive nose. He fought for the right comment. At last it came: 'Really?' he said. Yeah, really, I said. My parents were professional union organizers.

ANNA (*being* DOCTOR MELVILLE COOPER-ANSTEY): Union organizers, Mr Miller.

DAVE: That's right, doc, it's true that my childhood was spent hither and thither as you might say, but it was in a good cause. My mother was usually organizing a picket line in Detroit while my father was organizing a strike in Pittsburgh.

ANNA: Really, Mr Miller.

DAVE: But doc, it was the late 'twenties and early 'thirties – people were hungry, they were out of work.

ANNA: You must stick to the point, Mr Miller.

DAVE: But if I spent my time hither and thither it was not because my parents quarrelled. They loved each other.

ANNA: Were you, or were you not, a disturbed child, Mr Miller?

DAVE: The truth compels me to state, I was a disturbed child. But in a good cause. My parents thought the state of the world was more important than me, and they were right, I am on their side. But I never really saw either of them. We scarcely met. So my mother was whichever lady welfare worker that happened to be dealing with the local delinquents at the time, and my father was, the anarchists, the Jewish socialist youth, the communists and the Trotskyists. In a word, the radical tradition—oh, don't laugh, doc. I don't expect they'll have taught you about the radical tradition in Oxford, England, but it stood for something. And it will again – it stood for the great dream – that life can be noble and beautiful and dignified.

ANNA: And what did he say?

DAVE: He said I was an adolescent. Doc, I said, my childhood was disturbed – by the great dream – and if yours was not, perhaps after all you had the worst of it.

ANNA: You are evading the issue, Mr Miller.

DAVE: But you're all right, you have stability – Anna, you didn't come from a broken home.

ANNA: No, I come from a well-integrated, typical stable marriage.

DAVE: Then tell me, Anna, tell me about stable and well-integrated marriage.

ANNA (*standing up and remembering. She shudders*): My mother wanted to be a great pianist. Oh she was not without talent. She played at a concert in Brisbane once – that was the high point of her life. That night she met my father. They married. She never opened the piano after I was born. My father never earned as much money as he thought life owed him – for some reason, the second-hand cars had a spite on him. My mother got more and more garrulous. In a word, she was a nag. My father got more and more silent. But he used to confide in me. He used to tell me what his dreams had been when he was a young man. Oh yes, he was a world-changer too, before he married.

DAVE: All young men are world-changers, before they marry.

ANNA: O.K. – It's not my fault . . .

> (*They look at each other.* DAVE *leaps up, switches out the light.* DAVE *stands across from* ANNA, *in a hunched, defeated pose.* ANNA *has her hands on her hips, a scold.*)

ANNA: Yes, Mr MacClure, you said that last month – but how am I going to pay the bill from the store, tell me that?

DAVE (*in Australian*): A man came in today, he said he might buy that Ford.

ANNA: Might buy! Might buy! And I promised Anna a new coat, I promised her, this month, a new coat.

DAVE: Then Anna can do without, it won't hurt her.

ANNA: That's just like you – you always say next month, next month things will be better – and how about the boy, how can we pay his fees, we promised him this year . . .

DAVE: Ah, shut up. (*Shouting*) Shut up. I said. Shut up . . .

(He turns away, hunched up.)

ANNA *(speaking aloud the monologue of her mother's thoughts)*: Yes, that's how I spend my life, pinching and saving – all day, cooking and preserving, and making clothes for the kids, that's all I ever do, I never even get a holiday. And it's for a man who doesn't even know I'm here – well, if he had to do without me, he'd know what I've done for him. He'd value me if he had to do without me – if I left him, he'd know soon enough. There's Mr Jones from the store; he's a soft spot for me, trying to kiss me when there's no one there but us two, yes, I'd just have to lift my finger and Mr Jones would take me away – I didn't lack for men before I married – they came running when I smiled. Ah God in heaven, if I hadn't married this good-for-nothing here, I'd be a great pianist, I'd know all the golden cities of the world – Paris, Rome, London, I'd know the great world, and here I am, stuck in a dump like this, with two ungrateful kids and a no-good husband . . .

DAVE *(speaking aloud* MR MACCLURE'S *thoughts)*: Well, what the hell does she want – I wouldn't be here in this dump at all if it wasn't for her; does she think that's all I'm fit for, selling old cars, to keep food and clothes in the home? Why, if I hadn't married her, I'd be free to go where I liked – she sees me as a convenience to get money to keep her and her kids, that's all she cares about, the kids, she doesn't care for me. Without her I'd be off across the world – the world's a big place, I'd be free to do what I liked – and the women, yes, the women, why, she doesn't regard me, but only last week, Mrs Jones was giving me the glad eye from behind the counter when her old man wasn't looking – yes, she'd better watch out, she'd miss me right enough if I left her . . .

ANNA *(as* ANNA*)*: A typical well-integrated marriage. *(As her* MOTHER*)*: Mr MacClure, are you listening to me?

DAVE *(as* MR MACCLURE*)*: Yes, dear.

ANNA *(going to him, wistful)*: You're not sorry you married me?

341

DAVE: No dear, I'm not sorry I married you.

(*They smile at each other, ironical.*)

ANNA (*as* ANNA): The highest emotion they ever knew was a kind of ironical compassion – the compassion of one prisoner for another . . . (*As her* MOTHER): There's the children, dear. They are both fine kids, both of them.

DAVE: Yes, dear, they're both fine kids. (*Patting her*) There, there dear, it's all right, don't worry, dear.

ANNA (*as* ANNA): That's how it was. And when I was nine years old I looked at that good fine stable marriage and at the marriages of our friends and neighbours and I swore, I swore to the God I already did not believe in, God, I said, God, if I go down in loneliness and misery, if I die alone somewhere in a furnished room in a lonely city that doesn't know me – I'll do that sooner than marry as my father and mother were married. I'll have the truth with the man I'm with or I'll have nothing. (*Shuddering*) Nothing.

DAVE: Hey – Anna!

(*He switches on the lights, fast. Goes to her.*)

DAVE (*gently*): Perhaps the irony was the truth.

ANNA: No, no, no. It was *not*.

DAVE (*laughing at her, but gently*): You're a romantic, Anna Freeman. You're an adolescent.

ANNA: Yes, I'm an adolescent. And that's how I'm going to stay. Anything, anything rather than the man and woman, the jailed and the jailer, living together, talking to themselves, and wondering what happened that made them strangers. I won't, I'll die alone first. And I shall. I shall.

DAVE (*holding her*): Hey, Anna, Anna. (*Gently laughing*) You know what Doctor Melville Cooper-Anstey would say to that?

ANNA: Yes.

DAVE: And what all the welfare workers would say?

ANNA: Yes.

DAVE: And what all the priests would say?

ANNA: Yes.

DAVE: And what the politicians would say?

ANNA: Yes. (*She tears herself from him*) Don't rock the boat.

DAVE (*taking her up*): Don't rock the boat. (*He switches off the lights.*)

(*They look at each other, beginning to laugh. The following sequence, while they throw slogans, or newspaper headlines at each other should be played with enjoyment, on the move, trying to out-cap each other.*)

ANNA: Don't rock the boat – work.

DAVE: Produce goods and children for the State.

ANNA: Marry young.

DAVE: The unit of society is a stable marriage.

ANNA: The unit of a healthy society is a well-integrated family.

DAVE: Earn money.

ANNA: Remember the first and worst sin is poverty.

DAVE: The first and best virtue is to own a comfortable home full of labour-saving devices.

ANNA: If you have too much leisure, there are football matches, the pools and television.

DAVE: If you still have too much leisure be careful not to spend it in ways that might rock the boat.

ANNA: Don't rock the boat – society might have its minor imperfections, but they are nothing very serious.

DAVE: Don't dream of anything better – dreams are by definition neurotic.

ANNA: If you are dissatisfied with society, you are by definition unstable.

DAVE: If your soul doesn't fit into the patterns laid down for you —

ANNA: Kill yourself, but don't rock the boat.

DAVE: Be integrated.

ANNA: Be stable.

DAVE: Be secure.

ANNA: Be integrated or —

DAVE: } Die! Die! Die!
ANNA:

DAVE: The trouble with you, Anna, is that you exaggerate everything.

ANNA: The trouble with you, Dave, is that you have no sense of proportion.

DAVE: Proportion. I have no sense of proportion. I must scale myself down . . . I have spent my whole life on the move . . . I've spent my youth on the move across the continent and back again – from New York to Pittsburgh, from Pittsburgh to Chicago, from Chicago . . . (*by now he is almost dancing his remembering*) . . . across the great plains of the Middle West to Salt Lake City and the Rocky Mountains, and down to the sea again at San Francisco. Then back again, again, again, from West to East, from North to South, from Dakota to Mexico and back again . . . and sometimes, just sometimes, when I've driven twelve hours at a stretch with the road rolling up behind me like a carpet, sometimes I've reached it, sometimes I've reached what I'm needing – my head rests on the Golden Gates, with one hand I touch Phoenix, Arizona, and with the other I hold Minneapolis, and my feet straddle from Maine to the Florida Keys. And under me America rocks, America rocks – like a woman.

ANNA: Or like the waitress from Minnesota.

DAVE: Ah, Jesus!

ANNA: You are maladjusted, Mr Miller!

DAVE: But you aren't, do tell me how you do it!

ANNA: Now when I can't breathe any more I shut my eyes and I walk out into the sun – I stand on a ridge of high country and look out over leagues and leagues of – emptiness. Then I bend down and pick up a handful of red dust, a handful of red dust and I smell it. It smells of sunlight.

DAVE: Of sunlight.

ANNA: I tell you, if I lived in this bloody mildewed little country for seven times seven years, my flesh would be sunlight. From here to here, sunlight.

DAVE: You're neurotic, Anna, you've got to face up to it.

ANNA: But you're all right, you're going to settle in a

split-level house with a stable wife and two children.

DAVE (*pulling* ANNA *to the front of the stage and pointing over and down into the house*): Poke that little nose of yours over your safe white cliffs and look down – see all those strange coloured fish down there – not cod, and halibut and Dover sole and good British herring, but the poisonous coloured fish of Paradise.

ANNA: Cod. Halibut. Dover sole. Good British herring.

DAVE: Ah, Jesus, you've got the soul of a little housewife from Brixton.

ANNA (*leaping up and switching on the lights*): Or from Philadelphia. Well, let me tell you, Dave Miller, any little housewife from Brixton or Philadelphia could tell you what's wrong with you.

DAVE (*mocking*): Tell me, baby.

ANNA: Your America, the America you've sold your soul to – do you know what she is?

DAVE (*mocking*): No, baby, tell me what she is?

ANNA: She's that terrible woman in your comic papers – a great masculine broad-shouldered narrow-hipped black-booted blonde beastess, with a whip in one hand and a revolver in the other. And that's why you're running, she's after you, Dave Miller, as she's after every male American I've ever met. I bet you even see the Statue of Liberty with great black thigh-boots and a pencilled moustache – the frigid tyrant, the frigid goddess.

DAVE (*mocking*): But she's never frigid for me, baby. (*He does his little mocking dance.*)

ANNA: God's gift to women, Dave Miller.

DAVE: That's right, that's right, baby.

ANNA: And have you ever thought what happens to them – the waitress in Minnesota, the farmer's wife in Nebraska, the club-hostess in Detroit? Dave Miller descends for one night, a gift from God, and leaves the next day. 'Boo-hoo, boo-hoo,' she cries, 'stay with me, baby'. 'I can't, baby, my destiny waits' – your destiny being the waitress in the next drive-in café. (*She is now dancing around him*) And why don't you stay, or don't you know? It's because you're scared. Because if you stay, she might turn into the jack-booted whip-handling tyrant.

DAVE: No. I'm not going to take the responsibility for you. That's what you want, like every woman I've ever known. That I should say, I love you baby and . . .

ANNA: I love you, Anna Freeman.

DAVE: I love you, honey.

ANNA: I love you, Anna Freeman.

DAVE: I love you, doll.

ANNA: I love you, Anna Freeman.

DAVE: I love you – but that's the signal for you to curl up and resign your soul to me. You want me to be responsible for you.

ANNA: You'll never be responsible for anyone. (*Flat*) One day you'll learn that when you say I love you baby it means something.

DAVE: Well, everything's running true to form – I haven't been back a couple of hours but the knives are out and the tom-toms beating for the sex-war.

ANNA: It's the only clean war left. It's the only war that won't destroy us all. That's why we are fighting it.

DAVE: Sometimes I think you really hate me, Anna.

ANNA (*mocking*): Really? Sometimes I think I've never hated anyone so much in all my life. A good clean emotion hate is. I hate you.

DAVE: Good, then I hate you.

ANNA: Good, then get out, go away. (*She wheels to the window, looks out. He goes to where his duffle bag is, picks it up, drops it, and in the same circling movement turns to face her as she says*) I hate you because you never let me rest.

DAVE: So love is rest? The cosy corner, the little nook?

ANNA: Sometimes it ought to be.

DAVE: Sometimes it is.

ANNA: Ha! With you! You exhaust me. You take me to every extreme, all the time. I'm never allowed any half-measures.

346

DAVE: You haven't got any.

ANNA: Ah, hell. (*She flings her shoes at him, one after the other. He dodges them, jumps to the bed, crouches on it, patting it.*)

DAVE: Truce, baby, truce . . .

ANNA (*mocking him*): You're going to love me, baby, warm-hearted and sweet? Oh you're a good lay, baby, I'd never say you weren't.

(*The sound of screechings and fighting from the street.* ANNA *is about to slam window down, stops on a look from* DAVE.)

ANNA: Last night the four of them were scratching each other and pulling each other's hair while a group of fly-by-night men stood and watched and laughed their heads off. Nothing funnier, is there, than women fighting?

DAVE: Sure, breaks up the trade union for a bit . . . (*This is black and aggressive – she reacts away from him. He looks at her grimaces*) Hell, Anna.

(*He goes fast to the mirror, studies the black cloth.*)

DAVE: What's the pall for?

ANNA: I don't like my face.

DAVE: Why not?

ANNA: It wears too well.

DAVE: You must be hard-up for complaints against life . . . (*Looking closely at her*) You really are in pieces, aren't you? You mean you went out and bought this specially?

ANNA: That's right.

DAVE: Uh-huh – when?

ANNA: When we quarrelled last time – finally, if you remember?

DAVE: Uh-huh. Why really, come clean?

ANNA: It would seem to suit my situation.

DAVE: Uh-huh . . . (*He suddenly whips off the cloth and drapes it round his shoulders like a kind of jaunty cloak, or cape. Talking into mirror, in angry, mocking self-parody*) Hey there, Dave Miller, is that you, man? (*In a Southern accent*) Yes, Maam, and you have a pretty place around here. Mind if I stay a-while? Yeah, I sure do like your way of doing things . . . (*Accent of the Mid-West*) Hi, babe, and what've you got fixed for tonight? Yes, this is the prettiest place I've seen for many a day . . . (*In English*) Why, hullo, how are you? (*He crashes his fist into the mirror.*)

> (ANNA, *watching him, slowly comes from window as he talks, first crouches on the carpet, then collapses face down—she puts her hands over her ears, then takes them away.*)

DAVE (*into mirror*): Dave Miller? David Abraham Miller? No reply. No one at home. Anna, do you know what I'm scared of? One of these fine days I'll look in the glass, expecting to see a fine earnest ethical young . . . and there'll be nothing there. Then, slowly, a small dark stain will appear on the glass, it will slowly take form and . . . Anna, I want to be a good man. I want to be a good man.

ANNA (*for herself*): I know.

> (*But he has already recovered. He comes to her, pulls her up to sit by him.*)

DAVE: If that God of theirs ever dishes out any medals to us, what'll it be for?

ANNA: No medals for us.

DAVE: Yes, for trying. For going on. For keeping the doors open.

ANNA: Open for *what*?

DAVE: You know. Because if there's anything new in the world anywhere, any new thought, or new way of living, we'll be ready to hear the first whisper of it. When Doctor Melville Cooper-Anstey imagines God, how does he imagine him?

ANNA: As Dr Melville Cooper-Anstey, two sizes larger.

DAVE: But we've got to do better. Anna, look – the walls are down, and anyone or anything can come in. Now imagine off the street comes an entirely new and beautiful phenomenon, a new human being.

ANNA: Jewish boy – you're a good Jewish boy after all waiting for the Messiah.

DAVE: That's what everyone's waiting for, even if they don't know it — something new to be born. Anna, supposing superman walked in now off the street, how would you imagine him?

ANNA: Superwoman.

DAVE: Oh O.K.

ANNA (*in despair*): Me.

DAVE: I know. I know it. Me too. I sit and think and think — because if we don't know what we want to grow into, how can we shape ourselves better? So I concentrate until my brain is sizzling, and who comes in through the door — me!

ANNA: Just once it wasn't me.

DAVE (*excited*): Who?

ANNA: I was sitting here, like this. I was thinking — if we can't breed something better than we are, we've had it, the human race has had it. And then, suddenly . . .

DAVE: What?

ANNA: He walked in, twitching his tail. An enormous glossy padding tiger. The thing was, I wasn't at all surprised. Well, tiger, I said, and who do you belong to?

DAVE (*furious*): Anna, a tiger walks in here, and all you can say is, wild beast, whose label is around your neck?

ANNA: I thought you wanted to *know*.

DAVE: Go on.

ANNA: The tiger came straight towards me. Hullo tiger, I said, have you escaped from the zoo?

DAVE (*mocking*): Of *course* he's escaped from the zoo. He couldn't be a wild tiger, could he?

ANNA (*she kneels, talking to the tiger*): Tiger, tiger, come here. (*She fondles the tiger*) Tiger, tiger — The tiger purred so loud that the sound drowned the noise of the traffic. And then suddenly — (ANNA *starts back, clutching at her arms*) He lashed out, I was covered with blood. Tiger, I said, what's that for . . . he backed away, snarling.

(ANNA *is now on her feet, after the tiger.*)

DAVE (*very excited*): Yeah. That's it. That's it. That's it.

ANNA: He jumped on to my bed and crouched there, lashing his tail. But tiger, I said, I haven't done anything to you, have I?

DAVE (*furious*): Why didn't you offer him a saucer of milk? Kitty, kitty, have a nice saucer of milk?

ANNA (*beside the bed, trying to hold the tiger*): Tiger, don't go away. But he stared and he glared, and then he was off — down he leaped and out into the street, and off he padded with his yellow eyes gleaming into the shadows of Earls Court. Then I heard the keepers shouting after him and wheeling along a great cage . . . (*She comes back opposite* DAVE) That was the best I could do. I tried hard, but that was the best — a tiger. And I'm covered with scars.

DAVE (*gently*): Anna.

> (*They kneel, foreheads touching, hands together. The telephone starts ringing.*)

DAVE: Answer it.

ANNA: No.

DAVE: Is it Tom?

ANNA: Of course it isn't Tom.

DAVE: Then who?

ANNA: Don't you really know?

> (*She goes to answer telephone, it stops ringing. She stands a moment. Then turns to him, fast.*)

ANNA: Love me, Dave. Love me, Dave. Now.

> (DAVE *rolls her on to the carpet. They roll over and over together. Suddenly she breaks free and begins to laugh.*)

DAVE: What's so funny?

ANNA (*kneeling up, mocking*): I'll tell you what's funny, Dave Miller. We sit here, tearing ourselves to bits trying to imagine something beautiful and new — but suppose the future is a nice little American college girl all hygienic and virginal and respectable with a baby in her arms. Suppose the baby is what we're waiting for — a nice, well-fed, well-educated, psycho-analysed superman . . .

DAVE: Anna, please stop it.

ANNA: But imagine. Anything can come in – tigers, unicorns, monsters, the human being so beautiful he will send all of us into the dust-can. But what does come in is a nice, anxious little girl from Philadelphia.

DAVE: Well, Anna?

ANNA: Well, Dave?

(*A fresh burst of fighting from the street.* ANNA *moves to shut the window,* DAVE *holds her.*)

DAVE: I'm surprised I have to tell you that anything you shut out because you're scared of it becomes more dangerous.

ANNA: Yes, but I've lived longer than you, and I'm tired.

DAVE: That's a terrible thing to say.

ANNA: I daresay it is.

END OF ACT II

ACT III

ANNA *and* DAVE *in the same positions as at the end of*
Act II – no time has passed.

ANNA: Yes, I daresay it is.

    (*She goes to the light, switches it on, the room is closed*
in.)

ANNA (*as she switches on the light*): I must be mad. I keep
trying to forget it's all over. But it is.

    (*From the moment* ANNA *says 'It's all over' it is as if*
she has turned a switch inside herself. She is going in-
side herself: she has in fact 'frozen up on him'. This is
from self-protection, and DAVE *knows it. Of course he*
knows by now, or half-knows, and still won't admit to
himself, about JANET. *But he is trying to get through to*
ANNA. *He really can't stand it when she freezes up on*
him. From now until when Mary comes in should be
played fast, wild, angry, mocking: they circle around
each other, they do not touch each other.

    ANNA *goes straight from the light switch to the*
record-player, puts on 'I'm on My Way', goes to the
bottom of her bed, where she kneels, and shuts Dave out
by pretending to work on something.)

DAVE (*shouting across music*): Anna. I could kill you. (*As*
she ignores him) . . . come clean, what have you been really
doing in the last weeks to get yourself into such a state?

ANNA (*shouting*): I've been unhappy, I've been so unhappy I could have died.

DAVE: Ah come on, baby.

ANNA: But I can't say that, can I? To say, You made me
unhappy, is to unfairly curtail your freedom?

DAVE: But why the hell do you have to be unhappy?

ANNA: Oh quite so. But I didn't say it. I've been sitting here, calm as a rock, playing *I'm on My Way*.

DAVE: Why?

ANNA: It would seem I have the soul of a negro singer.

DAVE: Oh Christ. (*He turns off the record-player.*)

ANNA (*too late*): Leave it on.

DAVE: No, I want to talk.

ANNA: All right, talk. (*He bangs his fist against the wall*) Or shall I ask you what you've been doing in the last few weeks to get yourself into such a state?

(*A silence.*)

ANNA: Well, talk. (*Conversational*) Strange, isn't it, how the soul of Western man — what may be referred to, loosely, as the soul of Western man, is expressed by negro folk music and the dark rhythms of the . . . (DAVE *leaps up, he begins banging with his fists against the wall*) I'm thinking of writing a very profound article about the soul of Western man as expressed by . . .

DAVE (*banging with his fists*): Shut up.

ANNA: I'm *talking*. Looked at objectively — yes objectively is certainly the word I'm looking for — what could be more remarkable than the fact that the soul of Western man . . .

DAVE (*turning on her*): You have also, since I saw you last, been engaged to marry Tom Lattimer.

ANNA: Don't tell me you suddenly care?

DAVE: I'm curious.

ANNA (*mocking*): I was in lurve. Like you were.

DAVE: You were going to settle down?

ANNA: That's right, I decided it was time to settle *down*.

DAVE: If you're going to get married you might at least get married on some sort of a level.

ANNA: But Dave, the phrase is, settle *down*. (*She bends over, holds her hand a few inches from the floor*) It is no accident, surely, that the phrase is settle *down*. (DAVE *stands watching her, banging the side of his fist against the wall*) I'm thinking of writing a short, pithy, but nevertheless profoundly profound article on the unconscious attitude to

353

marriage revealed in our culture by the phrase settle *down*.
   (DAVE *lets his fist drop. Leans casually against the wall, watches her ironically*.)

DAVE: Anna, I know you too well.

ANNA: An article summing up — how shall I put it — the contemporary *reality*.

DAVE: I know you too well.

ANNA: But it seems, not well enough . . . We're through, Dave Miller. We're washed up. We're broken off. We're finished.

DAVE (*with simplicity*): But Anna, you love me.

ANNA: It would seem there are more important things than love.

DAVE (*angry*): Lust?

ANNA: Lust? What's that? Why is it I can say anything complicated to you but never anything simple? I can't say — you made me unhappy. I can't say — are you sure you're not making someone else unhappy. So how shall I put it? Well, it has just occurred to me in the last five minutes that when Prometheus was in his cradle it was probably rocked by the well-manicured hand of some stupid little goose whose highest thought was that the thatch on her hut should be better plaited than the thatch on her neighbour's hut. Well? Is that indirect enough? After all, it is the essence of the myth that the miraculous baby should not be recognized. And so we are both playing our parts nicely. You because you're convinced it can't happen to *you*. Me because I can't bear to think about it.

DAVE: Anna, you haven't let that oaf Tom Lattimer make you pregnant.

ANNA: Oh my God. No. I haven't. No dear Dave, I'm not pregnant. But perhaps I should be?

DAVE: O.K. Anna, I'm sorry. I'm sorry I made you unhappy. But — well, here I am, Anna.

ANNA: Yes, here you are. (*In pain*) Dave, you have no right, you have no right . . . you're a very careless person, Dave . . . (*She gets off the bed and goes to the window*)

What's the use of talking of rights and wrongs? Or of right or wrong? O.K., it's a jungle. Anything goes. I should have let myself get pregnant. One catches a man by getting pregnant. People like you and me make life too complicated. Back to reality. (*Looking down*) My God, that poor fool is still down there.

DAVE: Anna, don't freeze up on me.

ANNA: You want to know what I've been doing? Well, I've been standing here at night looking into the street and trying not to think about what you've been doing. I've been standing here. At about eleven at night the law and the order dissolve. The girls stand at their window there, kissing or quarrelling as the case might be, in between customers. The wolves prowl along the street. Gangs of kids rush by, living in some frightened lonely violent world that they think we don't understand — ha! So they think we don't understand what's driving them crazy? Old people living alone go creeping home, alone. The women who live alone, after an hour of talking to strangers in a pub, go home, alone. And sometimes a married couple or lovers — and they can't wait to get inside, behind the walls, they can't wait to lock the doors against this terrible city. And they're right.

DAVE: They're not right.

ANNA: Put your arms around one other human being, and let the rest of the world go hang — the world is terrifying, so shut it out. That's what people are doing everywhere, and perhaps they are right.

DAVE: Anna, say it!

ANNA: All right. You're an egotist, and egotists can never bear the thought of a new generation. That's all. And I'm an egotist and what I call my self-respect is more important to me than anything else. And that's all. There's nothing new in it. There's nothing new anywhere. I shall die of boredom. Sometimes at night I look out into the street and I imagine that somewhere is a quiet room, and in the room is a man or a woman, thinking. And quite soon there will be a small new book — a book of one page perhaps, and on the page one small new thought. And we'll all read it and shout: Yes, yes, that's it.

DAVE: Such as?

ANNA (*mocking*): We must love one another or die, something new like that.

DAVE: Something new like that.

ANNA: But of course it wouldn't be that at all. It would probably turn out to be a new manifesto headed: Six new rules for egotists, or How to eat your cake and have it.

DAVE: Anna, stop beating us up.

ANNA: Ah *hell*.

(DAVE *puts out a hand to her, drops it on her look.*)

DAVE: O.K., Anna, have it your way . . . You're not even interested in what I've been doing since I saw you? You haven't even asked.

ANNA: The subject, I thought, had been touched on.

DAVE: No, honey, I was being serious. Work, I mean work. I've been working. (*Mocking himself*) I've been writing a sociological-type article about Britain.

ANNA: So that is what you've been doing for the last week. *We* were wondering.

DAVE (*acknowledging the 'we'*): O.K. Anna, O.K., O.K.

ANNA: What am I going to be without you? I get so lonely without you.

DAVE: But baby, I'm here. (*At her look*) O.K. Anna. O.K.

ANNA: All right, Dave. But all the same . . . I sometimes think if my skin were taken off I'd be just one enormous bruise. Yes, that's all I am, just a bruise.

DAVE: Uh-huh.

ANNA: However, comforting myself with my usual sociological-type thought, I don't see how there can be such pain everywhere without something new growing out of it.

DAVE: Uh-huh.

ANNA (*fierce*): Yes!

DAVE: All the same, you're tough. At a conservative estimate, a hundred times tougher than I am. Why?

ANNA (*mocking*): Obviously, I'm a woman, everyone knows we are tough.

DAVE: Uh-huh . . . I was thinking, when I was away from you, every time I take a beating it gets harder to stand up afterwards. You take punishment and up you get smiling.

ANNA: Oh quite so. Lucky, isn't it?

DAVE: Tell me, when your husband was killed, did it knock you down?

ANNA: Oh of course not, why should it?

DAVE: O.K. Anna.

ANNA: Everyone knows that when a marriage ends because the husband is killed fighting heroically for his country the marriage is by definition romantic and beautiful. (*At his look*) All right, I don't choose to remember. (*At his look*) O.K., it was a long time ago.

DAVE: Well then, is it because you've got that kid?

ANNA (*irritated*): Is *what* because I've got that kid. That kid, that kid . . . You talk about him as if he were a plant in a pot on the windowsill, or a parcel I've left lying about somewhere, instead of what my life has been about.

DAVE: Why take men seriously when you've got a child?

ANNA (*ironic*): Ho-ho, I see.

DAVE: All right then, tell me truthfully, tell me straight, baby, none of the propaganda now, what does it really mean to you to have that kid?

ANNA: But why should you be interested, you're not going to have children . . .

DAVE: Come on, Anna, you can't have it both ways.

ANNA: No.

DAVE: Why not?

ANNA (*angry*): Because I can never say anything I think, I feel – it always ends up with what you think, you feel. My God, Dave, sometimes I *feel* you like a great black shadow over me I've got to get away from . . . oh all right, all right . . . (*She stands, slowly smiles.*)

DAVE: Don't give me that Mona Lisa stuff, I want to know.

ANNA: Well. He sets me free. Yes, that's it, he sets me free.

DAVE: Why, for God's sake, you spend your time in savage domesticity whenever he's within twenty miles of you.

ANNA: Don't you see? He's *there*. I go into his room when he's asleep to take a good long look at him, because he's too old now to look at when he's awake, that's already an interference. So I look at him. He's *there*.

DAVE: He's there.

ANNA: There he is. He's something new. A kind of ray of light that shoots off into any direction. Or blaze up like a comet or go off like a rocket.

DAVE (*angry*): Oh don't tell me, you mean it gives you a sense of power — you look at him and you think — I made that.

ANNA: No, that's not it. Well, that's what I said would happen. You asked, I told you, and you don't believe me.

(*She turns her back on him, goes to window. A long wolf-whistle from outside. Another.*)

ANNA: Let's ask him up and tell him the facts of life.

DAVE: Not much point if he hasn't got fifty shillings.

ANNA: The State is prosperous. He will have fifty shillings.

DAVE: No, let us preserve romance. Let him dream.

(*Shouting and quarrelling from the street.*)

DAVE (*at window with her*): There's the police.

ANNA: They're picking up the star-struck hero as well.

DAVE: No mixing of the sexes at the police station so he can go on dreaming of his loved one from afar even now.

(*A noise of something falling on the stairs. Voices. Giggling.*)

DAVE: What the hell's that?

ANNA: It's Mary.

DAVE: She's got herself a man? Good for her.

ANNA (*distressed and irritable*): No, but she's going to get herself laid. Well, that's O.K. with you isn't it? Nothing wrong with getting oneself laid, according to you.

DAVE: It might be the beginning of something serious for her.

ANNA: Oh quite so. And when you get yourself laid. (*Conversationally and with malice*) It's odd the way the American male talks of getting himself laid. In the passive. 'I went out and got myself laid' what a picture – the poor helpless creature, pursuing his own pure concerns, while the predatory female creeps up behind him and lays him on his back . . .

DAVE: Don't get at me because you're worried about Mary.

(*He goes over and puts his arm about her. For a moment, she accepts it*) Who is it?

ANNA: Harry. (MARY *and* HARRY *have arrived outside* ANNA'S *door. Can be seen as two shadows. One shadow goes upstairs. One shadow remains*) I hope she doesn't come in.

DAVE: But he shouldn't be here if Helen's in a bad way . . . (*As* ANNA *looks at him*) Hell. (*He goes across to the mirror, where he stands grimacing at himself.*)

(MARY *knocks and comes in. She is rather drunk and aggressive.*)

MARY: You're up late aren't you?

ANNA: Have a good time?

MARY: He's quite amusing, Harry. (*She affects a yawn*) I'm dead. Well, I think I'll pop off to bed. (*Looking suspiciously at* ANNA) You weren't waiting up for me, were you?

ANNA (*looking across at* DAVE): No.

(MARY *sees* DAVE, *who is draping the black cloth across the mirror.*)

MARY: Well, what a stranger. What are you doing? Don't you like the look of yourself?

DAVE: Not very much. Do you?

MARY: I've been talking over old times with Harry.

DAVE: Yes, Anna said.

MARY: I expect you two have been talking over old times too. I must go to bed, I'm dead on my feet. (*There is a noise upstairs. Quickly*) That must be the cat. Have you seen the cat?

ANNA: Yes, I suppose it must.

MARY: I was saying to Anna, only today, I'm getting a proper old maid – if a widow can be an old maid, fussing over a cat, well you'd never believe when you were young what you'll come to.

DAVE: You an old maid – you've got enough spunk for a twenty-year-old.

MARY: Yes, Harry was saying, I wouldn't think you were a day over twenty-five, he said. (*To* DAVE) Did you know my boy was getting married next week?

DAVE: Yes, I heard.

MARY: He's got himself a nice girl. But I can't believe it. It seems only the other day . . . (*There is a bang upstairs. A moment later, a loud miaow outside* ANNA'S *door*) Why, there's my pussy cat. (*Another crash upstairs*) I must go and see . . . (*She scuttles out.* HARRY'S *shadow on the stairs. Putting her head around the door*) Isn't it nice, Harry's decided to pop back for a cup of coffee. (*She shuts the door.*)

    (ANNA *and* DAVE, *in silence, opposite each other on the carpet. Dance music starts, soft, upstairs.*)

ANNA: A good lay, with music.

DAVE: Don't, baby. If I was fool enough to marry I'd be like Harry.

ANNA: Yes.

DAVE: Don't hate him.

ANNA: I can make out Harry's case as well as you. He wanted to be a serious writer, but like a thousand others he's got high standards and no talent. So he works on a newspaper he despises. He goes home to a wife who doesn't respect him. So he has to have the little girls to flatter him and make him feel good. O.K. Dave – but what more do you want? I'll be back on duty by this evening, pouring out sympathy in great wet gobs and I'll go on doing it until he finds another little girl who looks at him with gooey eyes and says: oh Harry, oh Dave, you're so wonderful.

DAVE: It wouldn't do you any harm to indulge in a bit of flattery from time to time.

ANNA: Oh yes it would. I told you, I'm having the truth with a man or nothing. I watch women buttering up their men, anything for a quiet life and despising them while they do it. It makes me sick.

DAVE: Baby, I pray for the day when you flatter me for just ten seconds.

ANNA: Oh go and get it from – Janet.

(MARY *comes in fast, without knocking*.)

MARY (*she is very aggressive*): Anna, I didn't like your manner just now. Sometimes there is something in your way I don't like at all.

(ANNA *turns away*.)

ANNA: Mary, you're a little high.

MARY: I'm not. I'm not tight at all. I've had practically nothing to drink. And you don't even listen. I'm serious and you're not listening. (*Taking hold of Anna*) I'm not going to have it. I'm simply not going to have it.

(HARRY *comes in. He is half drunk*.)

HARRY: Come on, Mary. I thought you were going to make me some coffee. (MARY *bangs ineffectually at* ANNA'S *shoulder with her fist*) Hey, girls, don't brawl at this time of night.

MARY: I'm not brawling. (*To* DAVE) He's smug too, isn't he. Like Anna. (*To* ANNA) And what about you? This afternoon you were still with Tom and now it's Dave.

HARRY: You're a pair of great girls.

(ANNA *looks in appeal at* DAVE.)

DAVE (*coming gently to support* MARY): Hey, Mary, come on now.

MARY (*clinging to him*): I like you, Dave. I always did. When people say to me, that crazy Dave, I always say, I like Dave. I mean, it's only the crazy people who understand life when you get down to it . . .

DAVE: That's right, Mary. (*He supports her*.)

(HARRY *comes and attempts to take* MARY'S *arm*. MARY

shakes him off and confronts ANNA.)

MARY: Well, Anna, that's what I wanted to say and I've said it.

> (HARRY *is leading* MARY *out*.)

MARY: The point is, what I mean is . . .

HARRY: You've made your point, come on.

ANNA: See you in the morning, Mary.

MARY: Well, I've been meaning to say it and I have.

> (HARRY *and* MARY *go out*, HARRY *with a nod and a smile at the other two*.)

DAVE: Anna, she'll have forgotten all about it in the morning.

> (*He goes to her. She clings to him*.)

DAVE: And if she hasn't, you'll have to.

ANNA: Oh hell, hell, hell.

DAVE: Yes, I know, baby, I know.

ANNA: She's going to wish she were dead tomorrow morning.

DAVE: Well, it's not so terrible. You'll be here and you can pick up the pieces. (*He leads her to the bed, and sits by her, his arm around her*) That's better. I like looking after you. Let's have six months' peace and quiet. Let's have a truce – what do you say?

> (*The telephone rings. They are both tense, listening.* HARRY *comes in.*)

HARRY: Don't you answer your telephone, Anna? What's the matter with you two? (*He goes to the telephone to answer it. Sees their faces, stops*) I'm a clod. Of course, it's Tom.

ANNA: It isn't Tom.

HARRY: Of course it is. Poor bastard, he's breaking his heart and here you are dallying with Dave.

ANNA: I know it isn't.

DAVE: Never argue with Anna when she's got one of her fits of intuition.

ANNA: Intuition!

HARRY: Mary's passed clean out. Mary's in a bad way

tonight. Just my luck. I need someone to be nice to me, and all Mary wants is someone to be nice to her.

ANNA: I hope you were.

HARRY: Of course I was.

ANNA: Why don't you go home to Helen?

HARRY (*bluff*): It's four in the morning. Did you two fools know it's four in the morning? I'll tell Helen my troubles tomorrow. Anna, don't tell me you're miserable too. (*Going to her*) Is that silly bastard Dave playing you up? It's a hell of a life. Now I'll tell you what. I'll pick you up for lunch tomorrow, I mean today, and I'll tell you my troubles and you can tell me yours. (*To* DAVE) You've made Anna unhappy, you clod, you idiot.

ANNA: Oh damn it, if you want to play big Daddy why don't you go home and mop up some of Helen's tears?

HARRY (*bluff*): I don't have to worry about Helen, I keep telling you.

ANNA: Harry!

HARRY (*to* DAVE, *shouting it*): Clod. Fool . . . all right, I suppose I've got to go home. But it's not right, Anna. God in his wisdom has ordained that there should be a certain number of understanding women in the world whose task it is to bind up the wounds of warriors like Dave and me. Yes, I'll admit it, it's hard on you but – you're a man's woman, Anna, and that means that when we're in trouble you can't be.

ANNA: Thank you, I did understand my role.

(*The telephone rings.*)

HARRY: He's a persistent bugger isn't he? (*He picks up telephone, shouts into it*) Well, you're not to marry him, Anna. Or anyone. Dave and I won't let you. (*He slams receiver back.*)

ANNA: Go home. Please go home.

HARRY (*for the first time serious*): Anna, you know something? I'm kind Uncle Harry, the world's soft shoulder for about a thousand people. I make marriages, I patch them up. I give good advice. I dish out aid and comfort.

But there's just one person in the world I can't be kind to.

ANNA: Helen's ill.

HARRY: I know she is. I know it. But every time it's the same thing. I go in, full of good intentions – and then something happens. I don't know what gets into me . . . I was looking into the shaving glass this morning, a pretty sight I looked, I was up all last night drinking myself silly because my poppet's getting married. I looked at myself. You silly sod, I said. You're fifty this year, and you're ready to die because of a little girl who . . . you know, Anna, if she wanted me to cut myself into pieces for her I'd do it? And she looked at me yesterday with those pretty little eyes of hers and she said – primly, she said it, though not without kindness – Harry, do you know what's wrong with you? You're at the dangerous age, she said. All men go through it. Oh Christ, Anna, let me take you out and give you a drink tonight. I've got to weep on someone's shoulder. I'd have wept on Mary's, only all she could say was: 'Harry, what's the meaning of life?' She asks me.

ANNA: Anything you like but for God's sake go home now.

HARRY: I'm going. Helen will pretend to be asleep. She never says anything. Well, I suppose she's learned there's not much point in her saying anything, poor bitch.

(*He goes.* DAVE *and* ANNA *look at each other.*)

DAVE: O.K. Anna. Now let's have it.

ANNA (*in cruel parody*): I'm just a little ordinary girl, what's wrong with that? I want to be married, what's wrong with that? I never loved anyone as I loved Dave . . .

DAVE: No, Anna, not like that.

ANNA (*in* JANET'S *voice, wild with anxiety*): When I knew I was pregnant I was so happy. Yes I know how it looks, trapping a man, but he said he loved me, he said he loved me. I'm five months pregnant.

(*She stands waiting.* DAVE *looks at her.*)

ANNA: Well, haven't you got anything to say?

DAVE: Did you expect me to fall down at your feet and

start grovelling? God, Anna, look at you, the mothers of the universe have triumphed, the check's on the table and Dave Miller's got to pay the bill, that's it, isn't it?

(*She says nothing.* Dave *laughs.*)

ANNA: Funny?

DAVE (*with affection*): You're funny, Anna.

ANNA: It's not my baby. I'm sorry it isn't. I wasn't so intelligent.

DAVE: That's right. You've never got the manacles on me, but Janet has. Now I marry Janet and settle down in the insurance business and live happily ever after, is it that? Is that how you see it? If not, this cat and mouse business all evening doesn't make sense.

ANNA: And the baby? Just another little casualty in the sex war? She's a nice respectable middle-class girl, you can't say to her, have an illegitimate baby, it will be an interesting experience for you – you could have said it to me.

DAVE: Very nice, and very respectable.

ANNA: You said you loved her.

DAVE: Extraordinary. You're not at all shocked that she lied to me all along the line?

ANNA: You told her you loved her.

DAVE: I'll admit it's time I learned to define my terms ... you're worried about Janet's respectability? If the marriage certificate is what is important to her I'll give her one. No problems.

ANNA: No problems!

DAVE: I'll fix it. Anna, you know what? You've been using Janet to break off with me because you haven't the guts to do it for yourself? I don't come through for you so you punish me by marrying me off to Janet Stevens?

ANNA: O.K., then why don't you come through for me? Here you are, Dave Miller, lecturing women all the time about how they should live – women should be free, they should be independent, etc, etc. None of these dishonest female ruses. But if that's what you really want what are you doing with Janet Stevens – and all the other Janets?

365

Well? The truth is you can't take us, you can't take me.
I go through every kind of bloody misery trying to be what
you say you want, but . . .

DAVE: O.K., some of the time I can't take you.

ANNA: And what am I supposed to do when you're off
with the Janets?

DAVE (*with confidence*): Well, you can always finally kick
me out.

ANNA: And in a few months' time when you've got tired
of yourself in the role of a father, there'll be a knock on the
door . . . 'Hi, Anna, do you love me? Let's have six months'
peace and quiet, let's have a truce . . .' and so on, and so on,
and so on, and so on . . .

(*The telephone rings.*)

DAVE (*at telephone*): Hi, Janet, Yeah. O.K., baby. O.K.,
I'm on my way. Don't cry, baby. (*He puts down receiver.*)

(*They look at each other.*)

DAVE: Well, baby?

ANNA: Well?

(*He goes out. Now* ANNA *has a few moments of in-
decision, of unco-ordination. She begins to cry, but at
once stops herself. She goes to cupboard, brings out
Scotch and a glass. She nearly fills the glass with Scotch.
With this in her hand she goes to the mirror, carefully
drapes the black cloth over it. Goes to carpet, where she
sits as if she were still sitting opposite Dave. The Scotch
is on the carpet beside her. She has not drunk any yet.*
ANNA *sits holding herself together, because if she cracked
up now, it would be too terrible. She rocks herself a
little, perhaps, picks bit of fluff off her trousers, makes
restless, unco-ordinated movements.* MARY *comes in.*)

MARY: I must have fallen asleep. I don't know what
Harry thought, me falling asleep like that . . . what did you
say? I don't usually . . . Where's Dave?

ANNA: He's gone to get married.

MARY: Oh. Well, he was bound to get married some time,
wasn't he?

(Now she looks closely at ANNA *for the first time.)*

MARY: I must have been pretty drunk. I still am if it comes to that.

(She looks at the glass of Scotch beside Anna, then at the black cloth over the mirror.)

MARY: Hadn't you better get up?

*(*MARY *goes to the mirror, takes off the black cloth and begins to fold it up. She should do this like a housewife folding a tablecloth, very practical.)*

MARY: I suppose some people will never have any more sense than they were born with.

(She lays down the cloth, folded neatly. Now she comes to Anna, takes up the glass of Scotch, and pours it back into the bottle.)

MARY: God only knows how I'm going to get myself to work today, but I suppose I shall.

(She comes and stands over ANNA. ANNA *slowly picks herself off the floor and goes to the window.)*

MARY: That's right. Anna, have you forgotten your boy'll be home in a few days? *(As* ANNA *responds)* That's right. Well, we always say we shouldn't live like this, but we do, don't we, so what's the point . . . *(She is now on her way to the door)* I was talking to my boy this morning. Twenty-four. He knows everything. What I wouldn't give to be back at twenty-four, knowing everything . . .

*(*MARY *goes out. Now* ANNA *slowly goes towards the bed. As she does so, the city comes up around her, and the curtain comes down.)*

Pan Reference Books

Edited by D. C. Browning
EVERYMAN'S ROGET'S
    THESAURUS   65p
'Among reference books *Roget's Thesaurus* stands by itself . . . a treasury upon which writers can draw'
           — TIMES LITERARY SUPPLEMENT

EVERYMAN'S DICTIONARY OF
    LITERARY BIOGRAPHY   75p
'A compilation of enormous value to every writer or student of literature' – J. B. PRIESTLEY

Ronald Ridout & Clifford Witting
THE FACTS OF ENGLISH   50p
An invaluable new edition of an established work of reference that gives the linguistic and literary facts of the English language from adverbs to zeugma.

CHAMBERS ESSENTIAL
    ENGLISH DICTIONARY   60p
A dictionary of the words essential to daily life with clear, precise and informative definitions, giving interesting derivations, illustrative examples of usage, and idiomatic expressions.

Compiled by Robin Hyman
A DICTIONARY OF
    FAMOUS QUOTATIONS   60p
'The collection covers the whole range of English literature'
          — TIMES LITERARY SUPPLEMENT

These and other PAN Books are obtainable from all booksellers and newsagents. If you have any difficulty please send purchase price plus 7p postage to PO Box 11, Falmouth, Cornwall.
While every effort is made to keep prices low, it is sometimes necessary to increase prices at short notice. PAN Books reserve the right to show new retail prices on covers which may differ from those advertised in the text or elsewhere.